The Faith of a Christian

The Faith of a Christian

JOHN AUSTIN BAKER

DARTON·LONGMAN+TODD

First published in 1996 by
Darton, Longman and Todd Ltd
1 Spencer Court
140–142 Wandsworth High Street
London SW18 4JJ

ISBN 0–232–51739–8

A catalogue record for this book is available
from the British Library

Phototypeset by Intype London Ltd
Printed and bound in Great Britain by
Redwood Books, Trowbridge, Wiltshire

To the many friends in whom during my lifetime
I have seen so much of the face of Christ
and especially to my dear wife

Contents

1

The search for truth

The path of those who are from the Church,
circling the whole world, and possessing a firm
tradition from the Apostles, enables us to see that
all have one and the same faith, since all teach
one and the same God and Father, and believe
the same dispensation of the Incarnation of the
Son of God, and know the same gift of the
Spirit . . . and affirm the same salvation of the
whole human person, both soul and body.

Irenaeus, *Against the Heresies*, V, 20, 1

'And I,' says Piers, 'shall apparel me in pilgrim's
wise,
And wend with you I will till we find Truth.'

Langland, *Piers Plowman*, 'The vision of Piers' counsel'

To believe, in the religious sense, is to stake our whole self on
a truth that cannot be proved.

Some make that commitment because the truth in question
seems to them self-evident. Others do so because they are
persuaded by the spiritual authority which they see in their
faith community and in the individuals who have professed this
particular truth down the centuries and who profess it still
today.

But there is a third way. This is to understand such a commitment, if responsibly undertaken, as carrying with it a moral
obligation: to subject 'our' truth to constant scrutiny – not just
once in a lifetime, before initial conversion, but repeatedly, as
knowledge expands, insight deepens, and personality matures.
Proof may be impossible; but we can still look with an honest
eye at the universe around us and at life as we find it to be, use
all the powers of thought we may have, and consult the verdict

of a conscience as informed as we can achieve, before deciding whether on balance we can with integrity declare, or go on declaring, what faith requires. Unless the answer is 'Yes' – or, more important, unless we are at all times open to the possibility that the answer may have to be 'No' – how can we honourably commend that truth as worthy to govern anyone's life, whether our own or that of another?

That is the position from which this book has been written. To me it is axiomatic, non-negotiable. Some may wonder whether it does not condemn one to a permanent state of paralytic doubt, or at least to a quality of faith which is highly tentative and lacking in energy. Indeed it can do; but there is no need that it should. Comprehensive rational certainty in cosmic issues is not attainable. We learn by experience that the understanding which satisfied us at twenty will not do at forty or sixty, and that the formulas in which faith is expressed will always have about them something of the provisional. They point in the direction of truth and away from false or inadequate interpretations of reality; they do not embalm or exhaust the truth.

But, fortunately, faith is not just a kind of intellectual connoisseurship, a critical evaluation of various artworks in a museum of the mind. It is a dedication of thought, heart and will to a vision, a pilgrim journey to explore that vision by living it out. The medieval tag said 'God is known in proportion as he is loved';[1] and faith is like falling in love, a passionate commitment to something or someone of whom we have at first only the most superficial idea.

Yet in one fundamental respect faith is not in the least like falling in love. When we fall in love, we do at least know that the beloved exists. We may well have illusions about him or her through which we have to work, painfully or joyfully, to the reality; but we do know that there is a reality to discover. The religious person, however confident in conviction, cannot know in that sense that faith's ultimate reality is anything more than a figment of the mind. There is always that alternative possibility. So what is the proper response to this fact? Should we say, 'I have committed myself, and no evidence, no argument is ever going to be strong enough to overturn that commitment'? Or should our stance be, 'I have committed myself, and that commitment is total, but if new evidence or new arguments tip the other way the balance of probability on which I made that commitment, then I shall honestly review my beliefs'?

There is a heroic steadfastness about the first of these two approaches which commands admiration. It is also a position which every believer should take up at times of crisis. When tragedy strikes, or extreme temptation or mortal danger, that is no time to attempt a balanced assessment of the reasons for faith. In *Jane Eyre* the heroine, at a time of acute inner and outward pressure to abandon her principles, replies in these words:

> The more solitary, the more friendless, the more unsustained I am, the more I will respect myself. I will keep the law given by God . . . I will hold to the principles received by me when I was sane, and not mad as I am now. Laws and principles are not for the times when there is no temptation; they are for moments when body and soul rise in mutiny against their rigour. Stringent are they; inviolate they shall be.[2]

As with morals, so with faith. On the rack of evil, if courage holds – and who dare be so self-righteous as to condemn where it does not? – not only honour but reason itself counsel us to stand our ground.

But if we hope to take such a stand at a time of trial, then we need all the more in times of tranquillity to make as sure as we can that our faith justifies that devotion. It becomes all the more important to ask searchingly the simple question, 'Is it true?' And that means taking time and pains to be aware of the reasons why it might not be true, and to weigh them honestly.

There is another tension. Every believer is both an individual and a member of some community of faith, and that community is personally significant to them. It will have been the source of at least a great part of the content of their faith and practice. By its fellowship it has matured them, and supported them in their distinctiveness from an indifferent or hostile world. But in return it will seek from them loyalty both to itself as an institution and to its teachings. It claims an authority, based on the inherited wisdom of generations and also on the collective understanding of its adherents now, to guide its members into the fullness of truth and to steer them away from errors of belief or conduct.

The nature and proper role of authority in the Christian Church is a complex issue which it would be premature to discuss at this point. These are matters on which different traditions within Christianity, and different individuals within those traditions, take widely varying views. All we need to note at the moment is that for most seriously committed members the beliefs generally or officially held in their own community of faith will exert a powerful grasp on their allegiance. For some those beliefs may represent the uniquely authentic revelation of the mind and will of God. For others their influence may be a less formally defined thing, springing from affection, gratitude for help in coping with life, a sense of belonging, and a feeling of inner security that the answers to ultimate questions can be entrusted to a more competent tribunal.

The stronger this hold on personal allegiance, the harder it becomes for the believer to test with a genuinely open mind the truth of the community's teachings. Even harder is it to stay within the community and yet disagree openly with official positions. A community of faith which allows too many members to do this too radically soon loses any recognisable identity. Hence a strong community, simply from a sense of self-preservation, will tend to oppress or expel dissentients, or perhaps simply create a climate in which they leave of their own accord. By contrast a weak community may have so little in the way of a coherent and effective world-view to offer that people leave it in search of something more relevant and convincing.

Both these situations are easily descried in the Christian Church today. The first principle can be seen working itself out in the Roman Catholic Church and, in rather different ways, in the Protestant world, where ever since the Reformation the pressure for detailed doctrinal consensus among the members of certain denominations has led to an accelerating process of fragmentation.[3] The second is most clearly seen in a body like the Anglican Communion which, however orthodox its official formularies and whatever its discipline in the past, today sees its distinctive Christian vocation in being a co-operative and consultative federation within which 'a thousand flowers bloom, a thousand thoughts contend'.

When, however, we look beneath the surface into the hearts of individual believers, we may find a rather different pattern. In reality it is doubtful whether any Christian, however devout, actually believes only and always what the community of faith decrees. For one thing, how many Christians actually know and understand with complete accuracy and in full detail what their community *does* decree? For another, there are nearly always some areas in the mind of any member where she or he guards the right to at least a private agnosticism. Both these positions are perfectly compatible with loyalty to the organis-ation and with respect for its teaching authority. But the funda-mental fact is that no two people have exactly the same faith. This is inevitable in the nature of the case. It is, after all, the purest orthodoxy to insist that God is ultimately in himself unknowable, a mystery to which our human words point only by analogy, some more accurately than others. So how could we ever expect that any two human beings, all of whom differ in inherited make-up and cultural formation, should have identical understandings of God? And thank goodness they do not! Is it not immensely to the benefit of any community of faith that its members enjoy (and in theory can share) a wide range of insights into ultimate reality?

In the end the only God any of us can genuinely believe in is the one that speaks to us, makes sense to us, convinces our hearts and commands our obedience. However devoted we are to our Church, however loyal, our devotion and loyalty will have no living content unless they spring from a personal faith in what we, to the utmost of our capacity, conceive to be true. We cannot surrender the final decision on our faith to someone else, saying, 'Whatever it says in the Bible or in the Church Catechism is what I believe.' At the very least, faith, to be authentic, must have its own reasons for accepting such a package. In the *Apologia pro Vita Sua* John Henry Newman provides a classic instance of just such reasons:

> Supposing then it to be the Will of the Creator to interfere in human affairs, and to make provisions for retaining in the world a knowledge of Himself, so definite and distinct as to be proof against the energy of human scepticism, in such a case – I am far from saying that there was no other way – but there is nothing to surprise the mind, if He should think fit to introduce a power into the world, invested with the prerogative of infallibility in religious matters . . . and, when I find that this is the very claim of the Catholic Church, not only do I feel no difficulty in admitting the idea, but there is a fitness in it which recommends it to my mind.[4]

In practice, however, such a block acceptance is no longer characteristic of a majority of Christian believers in western secular cultures. For them personal judgement on how much of a faith-community's teaching to take as one's own has become the norm.[5]

Many Christians within these cultures today are therefore living with a very considerable inner tension. They are convinced that at its core Christianity has hold on a truth which the world needs, which liberates, nourishes and ennobles human life, and which is not to be found fully and clearly anywhere else. They want the world at large to share that truth. But in the traditional content and presentation of the Christian message within their own churches there is much which they cannot with integrity make their own, and which therefore makes them hesitant in commending it to others. It does not correspond to reality as most people experience that. These believers thus find themselves in a sense strangers and pilgrims within their own communities of faith, searching for Truth but not being helped to find it. Nothing would delight them more than that the state of affairs described by Irenaeus in the first of the two quotations at the head of this chapter should apply to the worldwide Church today. But they know that it does not, and their own hearts and minds and consciences tell them that it cannot. So, like Piers Plowman in the second quotation, they have to wend with such as will come with them, until they find Truth.

What are the main concerns which drive them to go on such a pilgrimage, or at least to feel that they ought to make the attempt? First, the universe as we now know it, developing from within by evolution and conflict, consorts uneasily with the idea of a directive, all-controlling God who 'saw everything that he had made, and indeed, it was very good'.[6] Life on earth, and presumably on any other planet in the cosmos where life has evolved, is marked by widespread and often intense suffering for which there appears to be no moral rationale, and any idea that even faithful believers can rely on God to rescue them if they pray to him in their need will not bear inspection.

Then there is the Bible. Not only does it err on matters of historical fact but, far more seriously, it largely propagates the untenable view of a God who intervenes to ensure the just ordering of the world's affairs, while parts of it attribute to this supposedly loving and righteous God commands and actions which in a human being would be denounced as monstrous evils. How, for example, in a world where human beings are so vulnerable to physical and psychological damage and disability, and where healing and strength for body and mind seem so unequally available, are we to suppose that any God worthy of the name would think eternal punishment a just retribution for finite wrongs, however terrible? Or that, if such retribution were just, justice could be equally served by imposing some immeasurable punishment on his own innocent Son in our place? Or, if there is to be exemption from retribution, and a welcome after death into eternal joy and fulfilment for some, why should that be for Christians only? Do Christians have a monopoly of truth and goodness? The very existence of valid questionings such as these proves that they do not. Yet all these ideas are propounded in the Bible. How is such a collection of writings to be read as authoritative? How are Churches which seem to disconnect their powers of moral reasoning when they teach such things simply because they are in the Bible to be heard with respect?

It is understandable that to counter such difficulties Christians should throw into the other pan of the scales an appeal to the beauty and amazing order of the world, and to natural goodness which, as it seems, is found not only in humans but in higher animals. But is the beauty really there in created things, or is it simply a projection onto them of one kind of response which we, to our great good fortune, are able to make? There is, for example, no such thing in the universe as colour. Colour is one way in which we and numbers of other animals usefully perceive our environment. The sea, which is 'beautiful' in one light is hateful in another. Some flowers and trees may strike us as beautiful, but woodland that has run wild may hold far more of ugliness and decay:

> On older trees still than these huge lobes of fungi grew like lungs. Here, as everywhere, the Unfulfilled Intention, which makes life what it is, was as obvious as it could be among the depraved crowds of a city slum. The leaf was deformed, the curve was crippled, the taper was interrupted; the lichen ate the vigour of the stalk, and the ivy slowly strangled to death the promising sapling.[7]

And what of moral goodness? Is the sacrificial behaviour we can see in many species moral, in the sense of freely chosen with knowledge of the consequences, or is it one instinctual pattern, valuable for corporate survival, overriding the individual's equally instinctual urge to save itself? All such questions are directly relevant to religious truth. This is not to say that they make belief impossible. The trouble is that such points are all too often not taken seriously by traditional teaching, if indeed they are acknowledged at all.

For these are not just the objections of those who regard Christianity as superstition, and would gladly see it disappear. They are the distresses of many who hold on in faith to the real God at the heart of the Christian message, but find that message constantly discredited, and their own loyalty made more arduous, by the refusal of the Churches to improve their official statements of belief in the light of such challenges. Jesus once told some opponents that they were 'making void the word of God through your tradition that you have handed on',[8] and this is precisely what has been happening with the theological tradition of the Churches. The reason is simple.

Those responsible in any Christian body for authoritative for-mulations of its teaching are terrified that any substantive change from what has always been said will turn out in time to have been a betrayal of the truth. It is their duty to get it right, and the only way they can feel secure in getting it right is to base everything on the formulas of the past. If you put things the way 'they' put them then, at least you're safe, and you will have the support of all those believers who crave certainty, and who find that craving satisfied by the excitement of dismissing even the most plausible protests of the world. To modify the official teaching in any significant respect could also mean losing quite a proportion of one's membership, for in general it is not the so-called 'liberals' who form breakaway groups but those who wish to tighten the traditional formulas and ways of life.

This paralysis in ways of presenting the Christian faith has an insufficiently recognised but widely debilitating effect on the life of the mainstream Churches. For the people who find their happiness and enthusiasm in believing hobbled by the kind of difficulties we have been considering are not some small clique of over-intellectual sceptics: these worries are shared by thousands upon thousands of loyal worshippers who would never dignify their doubts by thinking of them as 'theology', even though that is precisely what they are. Such people are in fact girding against bad theology, for basic theology is concerned with just these simple-sounding but enormous issues of life and death which occur to every thinking human being. Is there a God? How can God be Love? What is the best way to live? What is going to happen to us all?

Nor is it possible to dismiss this problem as something pecul-iar to over-sophisticated western societies. Over the years I have had the privilege of getting to know a good many Christians in the Sudan. There thousands are being converted to Christianity. Despite war and persecution and famine the Church is growing in response to a very traditional presentation of the Gospel, which comes as spiritual liberation from the fears and fetters of idol worship, as well as providing a standard round which to rally against an oppressive version of Islam. Because of the poverty of the Sudan and its internal crises, educational oppor-

tunities for the African people have in many parts been drastically limited and have sometimes been non-existent. But still
the same fundamental questions are asked: 'Why is God angry
with us? What have we done that he is punishing us?' Such
questions arise directly out of the version of Christianity that
the missionaries first preached; and there is every reason to fear
that unless it is replaced by a more truly Christian presentation
the bubble of Church growth in Africa will, in a generation or
so, collapse as swiftly as it has swollen.

There is another powerful factor which must be mentioned.
The avoidance of central theological issues is related to a malaise
which has affected many major Churches worldwide in the last
fifty years. This presents as an almost wilful insistence on doing
anything but their primary job, namely helping the world to
live its life in the light of the fundamental truth and goodness
revealed by God in Christ. Instead these Churches have been
engaged in reordering their internal affairs: revising canon law,
rewriting their forms of worship, reorganising their structures
and management, devising interminable educational and training programmes, rearranging the interiors of their church build-
ings, and so on and so forth. Perhaps the largest and most
satisfyingly endless of these endeavours has been ecumenism,
negotiating convergence and, in some cases, actual mergers of
Church groupings. All this is done, of course, in the name
of becoming eventually more effective for their true mission.
But the way in which so many Christians latch onto some new
exercise of this kind every time the one in progress is completed
is beginning to arouse suspicions, even in their own hearts, that
maybe all this activity is an unacknowledged escape from facing
the crucial issues and the most urgent tasks.

In the same way by far the greater part of theological activity
in the Churches has concentrated on secondary topics, such as
the nature of ordained ministry, beliefs about the sacraments, the
doctrine of the Church itself, and suchlike. These elements in
the whole doctrinal structure are, at the highest valuation,
concerned only with various means of bringing the central
message of the Gospel to bear on human life, not with that
message itself.

The justification for concentrating on these matters has been that these are the issues on which the Churches are chiefly divided, and therefore the ones that need to be resolved in the interests of shared mission to the world. But the really important differences in belief, the ones already outlined, run not between but through all the larger denominations. They are the common problem which is disabling every Church today. If the diverse Christian traditions are ever to grow together in genuine spiritual unity, then it is this mainland of the faith that they must join in exploring, not the offshore islands. The only hope is to search together for new ways of conveying the heart of faith to people in terms of the universe as they now understand it.

The refusal to put any major investment of thought and energy into this primary project is the chief reason for the depressing fact that, while the Churches refurbish their outlets and devise new sales pitches, the customers increasingly walk past, dismissing the goods on offer as unwanted or unsatisfactory. The biggest weakness in the Decade of Evangelism, in which churches of many traditions have been engaging in the run-up to the millennium, has not been lack of communications skills and techniques, nor even, fundamentally, lack of prayerful enthusiasm. It has been lack of a message. Too many Church members are not sure what to say, whether they believe all of what they are expected to say, or whether anyone else could be expected to believe it either. As for those who have no doubts about what to say, they, alas, have too often merely been repeating words which those outside the Churches, or their parents' and even grandparents' generations, have already heard and found wanting.

These obstacles cannot be overcome by some piecemeal set of 'answers to objections'. There have to be so many of these that the overall effect is simply to deepen the impression that the Christian view of life is weak and needs constant patching to get by. What is wanted is a coherent total presentation of the Christian vision of reality which is true enough to human experience for many of the customary objections not to arise in the first place. But that means being prepared to replace a good many of the time-honoured set pieces with new versions.

Happily there is a growing recognition both of this need and of the fact that meeting it will have to be a collective, ecumenical endeavour. The present work is one of a growing number of attempts to sketch out such an overall vision as a contribution and stimulus to this enterprise. In the course of my own pilgrimage I have come to a place where I can identify with the words of both Irenaeus and Langland with which we began, for in that greatest of all English Christian poems Piers Plowman stands for an orthodoxy of the heart which is not only faithful to the Creed but is also willing to adventure the unsuspected radicalism which the Creed entails. I am passionately convinced that 'the faith once entrusted to the saints'[9] *does* point us to Truth and to the answers to the world's deepest longings – but only if we are ready to follow it through to more radical conclusions than the Churches as institutions have yet been prepared to acknowledge.

2

A science of reality

The truth cannot impose itself except by virtue
of its own truth, as it makes its entrance into the
mind at once quietly and with power.
Dignitatis Humanae (Second Vatican Council, Declaration
on Religious Freedom), sec. 1.

One of the commonest strategies employed by Christian apolo-
gists and preachers in recent times has also been one of the
most wrong-headed and disastrous: the insistence that the language of faith is to be classed with that of poetry, not that of
science.

It is wrong-headed, because it wholly misunderstands and
misrepresents the theological enterprise. Theology – 'thought
about God' – seeks to give a reasoned total account of the
world as seen by faith, and as such is far closer to the approach
of the scientist than to that of the poet. It has been disastrous,
because the concept of poetry is itself ambiguous. It may denote
a use of language by which we are helped to discern with the
heart as well as the mind the reality behind surface facts, that
which gives them their deeper value and meaning. But it can
also be a way of talking about values and meanings which
originate simply from within our own feelings and thoughts,
and which we project onto those facts. If poetry is understood
in that second way, as today it commonly is, then to describe
the language of faith as essentially poetic gives out an entirely
wrong message. It says that religious statements have to do
solely with the values, generated from within ourselves, by
which we choose to guide our lives and the imagery in which
we are moved to express them, not with realities independent

of ourselves which have a nature of their own whether we are
here to think about them or not.

The Bible and 'poetic' truth

Before exploring the kinship between theology and science it
will be helpful to clear away this muddle created by the 'poetic'
approach; and the simplest way to do that will be to look at
some of the biblical material which it has become fashionable
to expound along these lines.

Take as a starting point the classic case of the creation stories
in the first two chapters of Genesis.[1] It is no longer possible to
read these as a factual account of the process by which the
universe and our world within it came to be; and the 'creation-
ists' who argue that it is possible are simply wrong in their
handling of the scientific evidence. We may marvel at the
literary power of the Genesis stories and their imaginative
genius, but we still have to say that that is not how it actually
was. But having said that, we can legitimately go on to note
other things that the stories are saying which are perfectly
compatible with our own different picture of cosmic development: for example, that the sun, moon and stars are not divine
beings,[2] or that *homo sapiens* has endowments which give us
potential control over the destinies of all other life forms on
Earth.[3] Nor is the fundamental thesis of the chapters – that the
universe owes its origin and character to a divine Creator –
affected by the fact that we can no longer believe that God
operated in the way they describe. It is simply that if we wish
to justify such a thesis we now have to do it on the basis of a
different cosmic story.

All this is perfectly straightforward and, one might say, commonsense. It is also in accord with what, so far as we can judge,
the writers and editors who gave the book its present form
thought they were doing. For we have at least one decisive clue
to this intention. In Chapter 5 of Genesis there is a genealogy
purporting to link the first man, Adam, to Noah, whose family,
as they believed, were the only human beings to survive the
global cataclysm of the Flood. Later genealogies[4] similarly set

out to show how the nations of the writers' world, and in particular the people of Israel, were descended from Noah. In this way Adam was, so to speak, 'plugged into' history, that chronicle of humankind of which the readers of Genesis were themselves a part. There is not in Genesis, as there was in other cultures such as the Babylonian, a mythological epic of creation as a sort of separate, timeless preamble to history. The treatment of Adam as a historical character in the same sense that Abraham was regarded as a historical character makes plain that the creation story itself is understood as history.

To say this is not to exclude the dimension of poetry, but we must be careful to keep in mind the distinction we made earlier. Where transcendent realities are to be conveyed, every resource of language is needed. But that does not tell us how the writer or the audience regarded the material. When Homer cast the stories of the Trojan War in immortal verse, he and his hearers undoubtedly thought of them as recalling not only real events and heroes who actually lived but also divine beings who existed and intervened in mortal affairs. Dante and Milton both drew out the spiritual significance of their narratives with incomparable poetic skill; but that the former thought of Hell and the Mount of Purgatory and Heaven as really existing environments, and that the latter regarded the story of the Fall as literally true, can hardly be disputed. Poetic genius endows ideas and stories with greater resonance and deeper layers of meaning; but the fact that poetry is pressed into their service says nothing in itself about the nature of the basic truth they are thought to contain.

The way in which biblical writers envisaged their stories as relating to historical reality varies from instance to instance. Some, for example, have been written to correct an earlier version of events, because someone not just on the basis of extra information but perhaps on purely religious grounds thought, 'It can't have been like that, it must have happened like this.'[5] Others have been created (perhaps out of whole cloth, though one can never be quite sure) in response to a conviction that some ancient prophecy must have been fulfilled.[6] Others again are versions of immemorial legends, sometimes floating from one culture to another, the roots of which

in actual events are lost beyond recall, and which have become
attached to more than one hero-figure.[7] Moreover, indeed, it
is perfectly true that stories of all these kinds and others more
firmly linked to fact are told not just for the record but because
they are thought to reveal some religious truth; and often great
artistry is used to bring this out.

Nevertheless the point about all such material is that the
stories are thought of, justifiably or not, as having actually
happened. Even where we are dealing with conscious fiction,
as in the Book of Tobit in the Apocrypha, which is plainly a
religious romance, the author is imagining things which people
firmly believed could happen: there really were angels and
demons, and God could send the former to protect his faithful
servants from the latter. What you will not find in the Bible is
any writing seemingly about real characters and events but
intended and understood simply as a symbolic account of
human values and ideals.

To use current terminology, the Bible is invincibly 'realist'
in its theology. It talks of beings believed to exist, of events
which, however mysterious, were thought actually to have
happened. 'Faith,' wrote the author of the Letter to Hebrew
Christians, in a sentence of Tacitean untranslatability, 'holds
that what is hoped for has substantive reality, and convinces us
of what cannot be seen'; and a little further on, 'Anyone who
comes to God must believe that he exists'.[8] To press Scripture
into the service of a non-realist theology is an anachronistic
abuse of the text. In so far as woolly talk about 'poetic' truth
has led people to believe that the Bible can legitimately be read
in a non-realist way, then such talk has been party to a spiritual
confidence trick. If the Bible is to be used at all as an authoritative source of religious truth, that must be done on the Bible's
own terms; and the same goes for the whole of classic Christian
tradition. What we are asked to decide is whether on those
terms Scripture and tradition have significant truth to offer.
One cannot salvage them by interpreting them to mean things
their authors never intended, and which they would certainly
have disowned.

The affinity between theology and science

Even to hint at an affinity between theology and science is likely to be seen by some scientists as an insult. To them theology can never be a serious academic subject, and one can very well understand why. 'No one has seen God at any time'.[9] What is to count as evidence for or against his existence? What difference is God supposed to make to life which cannot be explained more simply either in terms of the normal functioning of the material universe or of human psychological states? How are you to set up a controlled experiment to check any hypothesis about God? Philosophically, is not theology a suspiciously slippery subject, where whenever an objection is made to some statement one is always told that words can be used about God only in some oblique sense? It seems that he is never quite what believers appear to the ordinary person to be saying about him: he is, for example, in charge but not responsible, loving but also cruel, good but unfair, a guiding Providence but intervening on no discernible principle, and so on. Analyse any degree course in theology, and you could dismantle it and distribute the bits, some to history, some to ancient languages, some to philosophy, some to literature, some to psychology.

But at least the objectors are really talking about theology – that is, realist theology. *Theo-logy* implies thought about God as an existent entity. Thought about concepts of God is not theology; it is a branch of human studies, of anthropology. Of course theologians do discuss people's ideas of God, but if they are truly theologians they do so in order to assess the adequacy of those ideas as an account of reality. Theology, like science, is about the nature of reality. Even more like science, it is an attempt to give a total account of reality, to explain how all things hang together. That is the first essential affinity between the two subjects: they share a common aim.

This common aim carries with it another shared characteristic. Both disciplines are in principle universally comprehensive in the range of material they study. If science is taken to include, for instance, economics and the social sciences – though not all, admittedly, would agree that it should – it is hard to think of anything which falls outside its scope. Likewise theology, if it is true to its proper nature, must be open to all knowledge. For there can be no information about or understanding of the universe in any of its aspects which is incapable, either by itself or in conjunction with other data, of throwing at least some light on its supposed Author, Sustainer and Perfecter.

This, however, brings up a sensitive issue. It can fairly be said that the use theology has made of non-theological knowledge has too often been merely to press it into the service of particular religious presuppositions. Whether the material in question has been the anecdotes of the medieval bestiaries or contemporary physical accounts of neutrinos, some theologically minded persons have pounced upon it to 'prove' or support some article of religious belief. Equally it could be claimed that some scientists have been too hastily dismissive of pieces of evidence from the religious sphere which do not fit easily into their own world-view. As a reasonable generalisation, religious people have not thought openly or deeply enough about changes which scientific discovery might require them to make in their picture of God, and even believing scientists have been known to keep their faith-insights and their scientific understanding in separate compartments.

Fact and interpretation

Any discipline which is not one of pure thought but seeks to deal with reality outside ourselves will have a complex relationship with that reality. Perhaps in more simple-minded moments we think of this relationship as one of finding out things called 'facts' and then explaining them. The job of the historian, for example, is to discover 'what happened', and then to unravel the ideas, pressures and motivations which brought that about. But the relation between fact and interpretation is never that simple.

Reality is a single whole. We break it down into areas of study or levels of complexity for our convenience, but at some stage we have to work out the complex problem of how those areas and levels are related. That is what makes wide-reaching subjects, such as economics or medicine, psychology or sociology, so difficult. The unified nature of reality also means that we ourselves are part of the reality we study. The relationship between us and it is symbiotic: we are what we are because reality is what it is, and reality is what it is because of what we are. That mutual involvement then limits the ways in which reality can appear to us.

To say this is not to deny that there are such things as raw data. The battle of Waterloo was fought on a particular day, identifiable in one system of human chronology as 18 June 1815. Boiling water (up to a certain height above sea level) scalds unprotected skin. These and millions of others are facts we can know because they have been confirmed by overwhelming testimony. Any sane person will be constrained by such facts in his or her behaviour.

But such pieces of information do not come unpackaged. Even the simplest physical fact, for instance, would be of no use unless we could rely on its being true in all comparable circumstances — in other words, unless we could assume that the universe is regular. Data come to us in a context within which we understand and use them. These interpretative frameworks are what make life viable. Animals inherit the instinctual ability to read certain happenings as signals, to which they respond in ways normally appropriate. Higher animals can enlarge these built-in programmes to a greater or lesser degree by individual learning. At the human level, however, matters are more complex.

Human beings can construct very elaborate interpretative contexts, and ones that sometimes work very badly. The medical theory of humours, for example, because it led to the practice of bleeding patients when that was the last thing that should have been done, must have been responsible for any number of needless deaths. But even very good frameworks of understanding can set up obstacles to progress, precisely because they work so well. It is too easy to assume that therefore they must be right for all data, and so they block our minds to alternative possibilities, as happened with Einstein over quantum theory because of his total reliance on relativity.

How are these frameworks of interpretation arrived at? The

generally accepted view at one time was that raw data were accumulated and then, by the logical process known as induction, regular patterns were observed in the evidence, and explanations formulated to account for these patterns. Such a picture is not wholly false: you cannot arrive at valid explanations except on the basis of evidence, and that evidence must be sufficient in quantity and quality. You need statistics, not just anecdotes. Equally, the accounts you give of reality will never be better than the quality of the information available. The most obvious illustration of this is that until such inventions as the telescope, the microscope and the chronometer a whole range of scientific advances was impossible. Today technological progress, like the broom in the tale of the Sorcerer's Apprentice, threatens to flood us with more information than we have yet devised means to handle.

Just as fundamental, however, as the technical means of arriving at information is the fact that the data you accumulate have meaning only as answers to the questions you have it in you to ask; and these questions may themselves be shaped by the way you habitually look at the world already. Thus a good doctor or psychologist will be aware of the danger of jumping to conclusions about a new case solely on the basis of previous cases which presented similarly, and will be as alert for whatever differentiates this patient from others as for whatever renders them the same. We rightly learn from experience, but we must never be blinkered by it. The same principles apply to the way results are analysed and recorded. New insights into a historical period, for example, may come from asking new questions of information already to hand as well as from searching in new types of source for facts formerly overlooked.

But even when you have your best evidence recorded and analysed, there is no logical drill which will guarantee that you can move from that mass of data to a successful interpretative framework. For this there has to be an act of creation by the mind at a level seemingly below consciousness. As has been said, 'Discovery is seeing what everyone else has seen, and thinking what no one else has thought.' It is this which produces possible new frameworks and, so to speak, tries them on for fit: 'Suppose we look at it this way, will that give us the results we have observed? Will it enable us to predict correctly the outcome of new experiments and new observations?'

In this quest for understanding, our own limitations will always be our greatest hindrance. Most people's minds are neither flexible nor creative enough to generate new ways of seeing and imagining, though this capacity could probably be expanded if the need for it were recognised in education. As it is, a person's cultural formation narrows down the range of thoughts he or she is capable of thinking; and this kind of constraint can be particularly intense within a scholarly community. Precisely because of the high quality of the common intellectual formation they have received, members of such a community can tend to reinforce one another in the same ways of seeing. When any member does break radically away, there may then be strong pressure to exclude the dissident rather than to make the mental leap necessary to test the new ideas. The position taken by some contemporary philosophers of science, that the whole scientific world-view today is simply a cultural construct, is untenable since it is open to the logical objection that their own critique must equally be the product of their culture and is therefore no more to be relied upon than the view they are criticising. It is nevertheless a fact that examples of irrational resistance to accounts of reality perceived as threatening to current orthodoxy have occurred not infrequently even in the supposedly open discipline of science.

The same problems arise, of course, in every discipline, and can be paralleled without difficulty in the history of theology. Indeed they tend to be all the more severe in matters of religious thought, both because belief fulfils deep psychic and emotional needs, and because religious groups, especially those looking back to a founder figure, set such store by loyalty to traditional understandings.

Corrigibility

If, however, theology is to have any claim to be a 'science of reality', then like every other such discipline it must have the quality of corrigibility. If it is not to corrupt and die, its current frameworks of understanding need to be open to constant correction in the light of new evidence or of new ways of looking at existing evidence. Recent reflection on the way such revisions come about in science[10] has lessons for religious thought as well.

A scientist starts, let us say, with a hypothesis, put forward to explain a particular body of evidence. This hypothesis will normally be in line with some larger understanding accepted in that discipline – biology, perhaps, or cosmology – of the way things function, and it will be tested by carefully devised and controlled experiments. If all goes well, then not only is the hypothesis validated but the larger theoretical framework is also strengthened.

From time to time, however, data come to light which resist all attempts to explain them in terms of the prevailing framework. The first response must be to refine the observation process to see whether the new data have been accurately stated. If that is confirmed, then the search is on for a new explanation. Sometimes this can be found in the unsuspected presence of some factor already known; but if not, then one may be on the way to discovering a factor hitherto unknown.

More often than not this newly discovered factor will fit into the existing overall theoretical framework. But if it will not, then that framework begins to come under strain, and has to be modified. The need for modification, however, is a warning signal. All the most successful theories have the beauty of simplicity, and once they have to be complicated by qualifications the chances are that they will eventually have to be superseded. They are not then necessarily thrown on the scrapheap. Newtonian physics is still all you need, for instance, to do most of the jobs that need doing in ordinary life, but it does not cover the behaviour of physical reality in all circumstances or at all levels.

The replacement of a major theoretical framework for understanding reality is, of course, a revolution in human thought. The most familiar example is the change in the standard picture of the universe which took place in the sixteenth century. From the second century CE until then the prevailing conception had been that of the astronomer Ptolemy, which had the Earth at the centre of the cosmos. Copernicus, who died in 1543, replaced that with one which had the Sun at the centre; but his theory was not just a blinding flash of unprepared insight. Astronomers had been aware for a long time of mounting problems with the accepted account, which had to be made more and more complicated to explain them away. The genius of Copernicus was to come up with a new, simpler picture which accommodated these awkward facts. But, of course, his theory was not right either, and after many intermediate changes we are at present thinking in terms of an expanding universe in which wherever you are seems to be the centre.

Theology is, or should be, a discipline subject to exactly the same necessity of revision. What religious believers tend to forget is that, logically speaking, God too is a theoretical framework for understanding reality, and as such has to be justified on the basis of evidence. The existence of God cannot be proved – though the point is often overlooked, theology itself rules out such proof. For by theological definition God cannot be fully described or defined. It is of the essence of the concept of God that the Divine Being can never be completely grasped in human concepts. But only something that can be fully defined can be proved – or disproved – and so, in this life, God will always be a theory about the way things are. Believers may be firmly convinced of the truth of this theory, but if they are they cannot be so on the grounds of pure thought. They have to have reason in experience for accepting it; and if that is so, then, like any other experience-based framework of understanding, the concept of God has to be corrigible. To put it bluntly, religious believers have to be prepared to change their minds about God from time to time.

The Bible and corrigibility

If we look at the way the understanding of God develops in the Bible, we see exactly this process. Different periods have differing pictures of God and of the way he deals with the world, and in particular circumstances each picture seems to work. Early Israel looks back on the days when it was a tribal society ruled by judges, and sees a pattern in the story: when the nation was united in worshipping Yahweh, the God of Israel, then they were strong and defeated their enemies; when they lapsed and joined in the cults of Canaan, other peoples overran them and oppressed them.[11] So they formed what we might call a 'working hypothesis': their national God was not the only god in the universe, but he was strong enough and cared enough to punish them through their enemies when they deserted him, and to give them victory when they were loyal.

In time this became a firm theory. Thus, when they went over to government by kings, though some saw this as apostasy from which no good could come,[12] the assumption of the majority was that the nation would prosper if the king was obedient to the social and religious laws given in Yahweh's name and upheld his worship exclusively, but would be invaded and defeated if he did not.[13] Under the first kings – Saul, David, Solomon and their immediate successors – this theory seemed to give reasonably good results most of the time.

Eventually, however, the pressure of facts began to break it down. Sometimes things went badly when the nation was faithful. The writer of Psalm 44 put it starkly: God used to keep his bargain with them, but now they are like sheep for the slaughter and a laughing-stock among the nations. 'All this,' he goes on, 'has come upon us though we have not forgotten you . . . nor departed from your way . . . It is for your sake that we are being killed all day long'.[14] The final blow was the capture and destruction of Jerusalem by the Babylonians in 586 BCE, followed by mass deportations of the people to Mesopotamia.

The result was a theological revolution, a quest for a more satisfactory account of God's dealings with humankind. Some said flatly that the gods of foreign nations were more effective than theirs,[15] though the majority view was still that the nation had been punished for its sins.[16] But this could no longer stand baldly without qualification. The community, after all, had been morally and religiously mixed, but the good had suffered along with the wicked. A famous story set in an older tradition had speculated that, because God was just, even a very small minority of righteous people in a city would be enough to make him hold his hand or, at the very least, arrange for them to escape the debacle.[17] But in the event this had not happened. Why?

A sudden U-turn of fortune complicated the problem further. The Babylonian empire was overthrown by the Persians, who then allowed deported Jews to return home, and gave assistance in the rebuilding of Jerusalem. Final as it had seemed, the disaster had after all been only a temporary punishment, like others before it. Perhaps it had never been meant to be so catastrophic. Since God had been using human agents, it might always be that they would go further than he had intended, for they, like Israel, were free to obey or disobey.[18] Another interpretation was that in destroying Jerusalem God had purposed that the whole world should understand that he was both holy and omnipotent. He was not dependent on his worshippers, but could and would reject them if they rebelled against him. But, instead of seeing the overthrow of Jerusalem as a demonstration of Yahweh's power and justice, other nations had simply taken it to mean that he was too weak to protect his own. It therefore became necessary for God to rescue his people, and to reinstate them in their own land, as evidence that he was the greatest of all gods.[19]

As regards the indiscriminate destruction of the righteous and the wicked a number of explanations were put forward. One theory was that in the reign of Manasseh, king of Judah from 687 to 642 BCE, evil and apostasy had reached such a pitch that even the reform movement of a later ruler, Josiah, was unable to redress the balance.[20] Sentence had already been passed. Others maintained that there had been no injustice: all who suffered had deserved to suffer.[21] Others again believed that this was for the future: after the nation was restored, a better order would prevail, and God would then ensure that everyone received their just deserts.[22] One more sensitive spirit, however, read the story at a deeper level: the fate of the good who had suffered was in fact an atoning sacrifice for their sinful compatriots. They were the Servant on whom 'the Lord laid the iniquity of us all'.[23]

One fundamental development in the concept of God, mooted long before by some but never fully accepted, now became standard belief. Gods had been thought of as each holding sway in their own lands and over their own peoples.[24] Yahweh might be regarded by his zealous worshippers as stronger than the gods, say, of Syria or Egypt, but the latter were still believed to be real. Mainstream tradition celebrated the liberation of Israel's ancestors from slavery in Egypt as Yahweh's proving his unequalled power by invading a foreign land and snatching his people away in the teeth of Egypt's gods.[25] The return from Babylon was, therefore, understandably seen as a second exodus, like that from Egypt but with a new note. Now the alleged gods of Babylon and other nations are dismissed as 'nothings', no more than the idols of wood and stone, gold and silver, that represented them in their temples.[26] Israel's God was the only being in the whole universe who could rightly be called 'God'.[27] Monotheism had come to stay. An affirmation of faith which other cultures, starting from the perplexing confusion of life and nature, had been unable to attain, Israel had reached by a determination to interpret its own history as a record of the righteous sovereignty of God.

Israel, however, though in possession once more of its holy city, modestly restored, had not regained political independence. It was a province of the Persian empire. If that were, as it seemed to be, Yahweh's will, then the vocation of the community must also change. Its task was to be a theocracy, regulating its internal affairs, daily life and worship by the law of God, handed down and codified by the priests who were its authoritative guardians and interpreters.[28] But though a lengthy period of peace now ensued agonising theological problems still remained, which Israel's thinkers shared with those of other nations. In particular the question of divine justice had now been transferred from the national to the individual level. If God was all-powerful, how were the misfortunes in each person's life to be understood?

Some, relying on the prophetic promise, maintained that God had been as good as his word. The wicked did come to a bad end, even if for a while they enjoyed prosperity and power; and the righteous, though they might suffer for a time, would finally rejoice. We find this view, for example, in the Psalms, either as a general assumption,[29] or in forms of confession and of thanksgiving for forgiveness to be used liturgically by sufferers, whether seeking relief from sickness and other afflictions or praising God for relief received.[30] For the innocent who suffer through the malice of enemies who persecute or falsely accuse them there are liturgical protestations of innocence, to be used as prayers for redress through God's intervention.[31]

One of the world's great spiritual writings, the Book of Job, develops a classic Near Eastern literary form to give voice to a number of different accounts of suffering: the simple view that if a person is afflicted, then however righteous they may seem to have been, somewhere there is a hidden guilt which God has found out;[32] the idea that at least some suffering is educative;[33] and the radical approach that humankind is only one small ingredient in the creation anyway and so cannot rationally suppose that everything is run for its own benefit and is to be understood on that basis.[34] The narrative framework of the material in its present version, however, adds a new dimension: in a world where the righteous were always protected and only the wicked suffered, truly moral goodness would be impossible.[35]

A further response, though an untestable one, emerged in the second century BCE, when the Jewish homeland had come under Greek rule, and Judaism had to endure attack both from external persecution and from assimilation to pagan culture within. At this time many loyal Jews were martyred. Among some believers this stimulated faith that a righteous God would bring into being at some future date a re-created world in which, at a final judgement, the resurrected dead would receive either reward or punishment.[36] In hellenistic Judaism a comparable belief was expressed in terms of the immortality of the soul.[37]

In 70 CE, after four years of rebellion in Palestine, Jerusalem was taken and sacked once more, this time by the Romans, and the Temple was razed to the ground. The anguished question mark which this placed over Jewish faith is poignantly reflected in a meditation of searing honesty, the work included in the Apocrypha as 2 Esdras. In so far as any 'answer' is propounded (though the value of the work does not depend on that), it is that for the soul to grow into the stature needed for the greater life beyond this one it has to pass through suffering here.[38]

The point of this survey, however, is not to examine the questions of suffering and divine justice, which will occupy us in a later chapter, but to illustrate the simple but crucial truth that in the Scriptures common to Judaism and Christianity the concept of God is not unchanging. It is constantly subject to modification in the light of experience – indeed, how could it not be, when one main thread running through those Scriptures is that God reveals himself through history? For Christians the arrival of dramatic new evidence in the life, death and resurrection of Jesus resulted in a radical redesign of their understanding of both God and the world.[39] In other words, during all those centuries corrigibility was something built into faith. Those who would not accept new understandings – such as the Sadducees who rejected belief in a life after death,[40] or those Christians who could not see that God might not require Gentiles to keep the Jewish Law – eventually died out. A faith that is not corrigible has neither vitality nor viability.

The Church and corrigibility

Within organised Christianity, however, there has built up over the centuries a deep-seated resistance to the very idea of corrigibility. At bottom the reason is belief in Jesus as God's final and definitive word to humanity. In the earliest days this finality had a very literal meaning: the end of this world-order was approaching, and through Jesus God had disclosed the only way to survive that cataclysm, and gain eternal life in the new creation. As this expectation receded, the historical finality was replaced by a doctrinal one. What more could God have to offer, now that he had revealed himself not just in words but in a person? Nor was that personal life concerned only with teaching. God had become human to carry out a particular task, a sacrifice to expiate the sins of the whole world for all time. Faith in that sacrifice was the passport to eternal life; and that being so there clearly was nothing more that God needed to do or that humanity needed to know. Loyalty to the inheritance of faith, understood as a body of basic truths authoritatively expressed, secured salvation. It is significant that Christianity is the only world religion which has developed what are called 'creeds', concise statements of essential beliefs to which every member is in theory required to subscribe. In such a context to call in question even a single detail of the way in which such core beliefs have been defined could imply that earlier generations of Christians had been in error, and thus cast doubt on the certainty of salvation.

Given these developments, corrigibility was clearly never going to be a prominent characteristic of Christian faith. In practice, it is true, individual believers have modified their pictures of God in the light of changes in human thought and culture, one notable example being the widespread rejection of doctrines of eternal punishment. This, of course, appears to go against teaching attributed in the gospels to Jesus himself,[41] and therefore raises the question of corrigibility in an acute form. Not surprisingly, movements within the Churches aimed at returning to some pure original or scriptural revelation have tended to make belief in eternal punishment for those who die outside faith in Christ one of the crucial tests of authentic Christianity.[42]

The most serious consequence of this whole process has been that official institutional Christianity has found itself more than half paralysed in the realm of theological thought. How can it go against the reported words of the Founder? How dare it depart from the sacred revelation in Scripture? Where would be the guarantee of its authority if it did? Even the Roman Catholic communion, which lays great stress on the teaching authority which God has vested in the Church, can contemplate new teaching only if it can be shown to be implicit in what has been said already, or at least to be wholly compatible with it. Such attitudes (and they are found in every denomination) force theologians to search for complicated ways of using biblical or doctrinal formula which will give them some space for the honest amendment of past errors while remaining faithful to the tradition – what we might call 'trip around the bay' rather than 'launch out into the deep' religion.[43]

The Churches need to understand that there can never in any field of thought be an authority which will guarantee that what one says is true. Truth has to commend itself by its fit with reality as we increase our knowledge of that. This is the basis of science, and it is the only possible basis for theology. The Bible records a mighty growth in human spiritual understanding precisely because the people involved in that process were not afraid to change their minds. The only journey the Bible authenticates is the pilgrim journey of Piers Plowman.[44]

One irony of this paralysis of fear in official Christian thought has been that Christians have in many respects failed to explore the new and revolutionary insights implicit in the beliefs they do officially hold. A better match with reality by no means requires Christians to abandon all the core beliefs they have inherited. On the contrary, at the time when these beliefs were formulated, and even for long after that, unavoidable limitations of thought or knowledge have sometimes kept the Church from a full grasp of all that they had to offer. As a result the Church has then attributed final authority to what is no more than a partial insight into the truth it has received. Only as our mental grasp on the universe enlarges and our moral perceptions deepen with new human experience do we begin to see more clearly the wisdom these beliefs bring to our existence.

Language and ultimate reality

This raises another issue over which theology and science face very similar questions: the relation between the terms that make sense to our minds and whatever is the case 'out there'. That there are puzzles of this sort in the findings of science is well known. When we try to move from experimental data to describe the reality that produces them, we can find ourselves forced into statements that on the face of it are logically incompatible. One case often quoted is that of the nature of light, which under one aspect has to be spoken of in terms of waves, but under another as a stream of particles. Since the observations themselves have been confirmed many times over, we have to conclude that the nature of the reality which gives rise to our observations is in part opaque to us. Can we say anything more than that 'it is a state of affairs which results in such and such phenomena'?

The classical view that our words and concepts describe the reality 'behind' our observations is now held only by a minority. At the other extreme some philosophers of science have wanted to argue that we can know nothing of reality in itself. Our formulations reflect only our own minds. Is it not strange, for example, that mathematicians can invent for their own purely mathematical purposes what are known as 'composite numbers', and then scientists start observing phenomena which can be understood only in terms of such numbers? Is it that, as the beings we are, we ask only questions generated by the sort of minds we have, and answer them only in the sort of terms we are capable of creating?

The majority of scientists at present would probably agree that the truth lies somewhere between these two extremes. The scientific procedure of prediction and verification means that in the light of the information we have we reason that this or that ought to be the case. We then look for experimental confirmation of this conjecture, and sometimes we find it, while at other times our predictions turn out to be wrong. This suggests that, however inadequate our accounts of reality may be, they do to some extent reflect an independently existing state of affairs. If our predictions were always wrong, reality would be a total mystery; if they were always right, we might suspect that we were in truth simply spinning a dream, and finding only patterns projected from inside ourselves. The fact that the whole exercise 'works', not least in its technical applications, is best explained by assuming that we are thinking thoughts which relate meaningfully to the way things actually are.

All in all, then, the standpoint sometimes known as 'critical realism', which holds that our concepts can in some sort express the nature of reality even if they do not literally describe it, and that as we know more we can improve these concepts, is the one that does best justice to the facts. Such issues tend to arise most often, not unnaturally, when dealing with the outer edges of scientific investigation. In particle physics, for example, it may be impossible for various reasons either to look at what we are studying or to describe fully what we find when we do look. Such reasons include the fact that in certain circumstances any observations we make appear to alter what it is we are observing, or that observation of one aspect of the object precludes observation of another at the same time, as in the famous Heisenberg 'uncertainty principle' with regard to the position and momentum of an electron. This latter instance neatly illustrates the kind of problem that has to be faced in talking of such realities. Heisenberg's own view has been expounded as follows:

> Instead of assuming that an electron has a precise position and velocity that are unknown to us, we should conclude that it is not the sort of entity that always has such properties. Observing consists in extracting from the existing probability distribution one of the many *possibilities* it contains. The influence of the observer . . . does not consist in disturbing a previously precise though unknown value, but in forcing one of the many potentialities to be actualised.[45]

Clearly, if language is to be used at all in such contexts, it has to say things to which there is no obvious parallel or analogy in our day-by-day experience. Even if we understand the words, therefore, we still have difficulties, perhaps inherently insuperable difficulties, in imagining what the reality is like to which they refer. No one has seen an electron at any time. All we can say is that some reality, on some such lines, must exist to do justice to the phenomena we observe; and the possibility always remains open that one day someone will come up with a better, if still indirect, account.

Theology is not exactly comparable to the physical sciences, and nothing is to be gained by pretending that it is. But because, in its own way, it is striving to present a total account of reality, it does confront issues of a similar kind. The ultimate reality with which theology is concerned, namely God, is also one that no one has seen at any time. If we believe in its existence, we do so on the basis of evidence in our own or other people's experience which seems to point to such a reality behind it.

Here too we are working on the outer edges of thought. When we come to describe such a reality, we find that, like Sweeney Agonistes, 'I've gotta use words when I talk to you',[46] and the words as words may have meaning one can understand. But no one can imagine the reality to which they refer, because the world of sense from which we draw our images does not behave like that. Hence theology, again like frontier science, has to use analogies, and also negatives, marking out certain limits by saying that the reality in question is not to be thought of in this way or that. At the same time, as in science, some concepts do better justice to the evidence than others, and therefore deserve to be regarded as better accounts of the reality behind it. But on what sort of evidence does theology draw, and how are we to assess it?

The nature of theological evidence

In principle no kind of knowledge is irrelevant to theology. If we believe in a God who has dealings with the universe, then anything that happens may need to be inspected for clues to those dealings.

What we cannot do is set up controlled experiments to verify our accounts of God, for the reason that God, in religions such as Christianity, Judaism or Islam, is thought of as possessing not only the attribute of free will but also complete knowledge of every situation and perfect insight into every human soul. It would therefore be quite useless to compare, for example, a group of x people in a particular predicament, who pray to God for help, with a control group of equal number in the same predicament who do not pray, and seeing which group comes off best. For even if God did know perfectly every detail of each individual situation, and intervened to bring about the best possible outcome for each one who prayed but not for those who did not, we could never tell because we do not know those details or those possibilities.[47]

Interestingly enough, however, biblical religion did have its own counterpart to the process of scientific verification. A major element in ancient Jewish religion, and to a lesser extent in early Christianity, was prophecy. Prophecy, at least in its greatest exponents, was concerned as much with ethical and spiritual teaching as with prediction. But prediction was always an essential ingredient, because the prophets backed up their demand for the righteousness God required by declaring vividly what would happen if the nation did or did not meet those demands. A true prophet was both someone whose teaching confirmed the divine law, and also someone whose predictions as to how God would act came to pass.[48] Because God did not act out of character, failure to predict correctly the course of events, thought of as controlled by God, discredited the prophet's understanding of the divine nature.

Today prophecy in this ancient sense does not feature largely in the life of the mainstream Churches, and not all Christians any longer think of God as manipulating the course of history. But many individual believers do still see the hand of God in their personal lives. They may look back over the years and discern a special providence at work even in adversity and failure, guiding them to a good beyond all they could ever have envisaged for themselves. Or divine intervention may be seen in individual events: help, for instance, arrives when urgently needed, because someone felt compelled to come round or to telephone, or a piece of charitable work is saved by a large donation out of the blue. Prayer may have been made for such help or it may not. The incidents are not evidence in the sense of inexplicable happenings, hinting at divine origin. But to faith they appear as important support for a God-centred vision of the world.

Much the same may be said of experiences in the spiritual life, and not only those linked with the practice of worship, prayer and meditation. Thousands of accounts from people of every kind, by no means only the consciously religious, have been collected and compared, and certain features constantly recur. These may be described broadly in such terms as heightened awareness of the world around, often irradiated with a light that has no physical source, a sense of union or communion with all things, the conviction of a spiritual presence or power within or behind external reality, strong feelings of inner joy or serenity, being taken out of or beyond oneself, and so on.[49] Experiences of this kind can be paralleled from many cultures, and seem to be in some sense natural to humanity. To the religious believer the capacity for such experiences, though not in itself proof of a spiritual dimension to reality, certainly fits very happily with its existence.

Of particular significance, however, for Christianity in its classic form have been those events which cannot be accommodated within the current understanding of the universe and its operations and which are therefore termed 'miracles'. The nature and place of the miraculous (or indeed of any divine intervention in the world) is something that can be handled only within a more general picture of the kind of God one believes in; and an attempt will be made, therefore, to give an account of it in the final chapter.[50] Here all that need be borne in mind is that the miraculous is central to Christianity to a degree unique among world faiths, because without belief in the foundation miracle of Jesus' resurrection Christianity would never have existed.

Yet when all these specific types of evidence have been considered, it still remains that the factual bedrock for any theological account of reality must be the general nature of the universe and the character of life on this planet. If God is to be believed in not just as a symbolic organising principle in the human mind but as an existent reality – and one, moreover, that has a coherent moral character and makes a difference to what happens – then what is said about him must be compatible, first and foremost, with our scientific, historical and psychological knowledge of ourselves and of the cosmos we inhabit. Only so can theology be in any sense a 'science of reality'. Let us, then, conclude this chapter with a brief survey, necessarily broad-brush in its treatment, of the most significant features of the cosmic environment from which we have emerged and in which we have to live.

What kind of universe?

The first and most obvious fact about the universe[51] which distinguishes our knowledge of it from that available to our forebears is its *immensity.* Take the farthest point in space which our instruments have so far been able to detect, and imagine that we are setting out to go there in a starship, cruising at the speed of light. Now think of that journey in terms of crossing the Atlantic. After a hundred years we would have travelled the equivalent of 40 metres from the beach. In such a cosmos, with its hundred million galaxies, it is wildly improbable that humankind is the only or even the most advanced example of a rational, moral and spiritual type of being. If planets are the most suitable setting for the emergence of life, our own star, the Sun, is far from being either the oldest or the youngest, so that other planetary systems are constantly coming and going. Planets are extremely difficult bodies to detect, but recent scanning has located one elsewhere in our own galaxy.

The most significant characteristic of our cosmic home, however, is not its size but that it is *an evolving system.* It is not static, maintaining itself in the condition in which it has always been. It has a history, and a history of a particular kind, a story of an inner potential, unfolding not only in new forms but also in increasingly elaborate ones. This feature appears early on, in the process by which from the primary constituents of hydrogen and helium all the elements known to us eventually emerge. It appears in the formation of various types of star, of galaxies, planets, black holes and all the other furniture of space; in the creation of amino acids, the bridge to life with all its biochemical variety; in the evolution of complex adaptive systems, of which on this planet we are the most advanced example. Of all these developments it can be said that the seed of which they are the diverse flowering was, in some sense, there from the beginning.

A warning note, however, is in place here. We need to distinguish between the fact of evolution and the mechanisms of evolution. All living creatures are related, because DNA is common to them all. But there are unanswered questions about how the immensely complex developments we can trace came about, and how they can have done so within the timescale of the Earth's history. We know that Darwin's own ideas of the mechanisms have had to be supplemented, and also that the unfolding story is not a steady progression but a series of steps and plateaus. Nor do we have remains or fossils from many of what must have been critical junctures to help us. Moreover, while the process as we at present understand it can account for the emergence of new species,[52] the way more radical changes came about is still obscure. The reconstruction of the story cannot be said yet to have excluded all need for nudges or injections from outside, whether divine or other, though equally it does not yet positively demand them. There is more to be learned, a great deal more.

The third basic feature of the cosmic system is that it works by an interplay of three factors. The first of these is *regularity or order*. The components of the universe behave in statistically regular and predictable ways, and this regularity is the essential matrix for everything else. Without order there could be no stable environments, and without these nothing would ever evolve, for it would not endure long enough. Likewise, rational creatures would never have come to be, for only in a regular environment can one form frameworks of understanding, learn from experience, predict the future, and direct one's actions accordingly.

The second of the three factors is *random or unpredictable potential*. It was once believed that if you could make a complete inventory of the way everything was at the start you could in theory work out how it was bound to develop. But though order and regularity are the norm they are not the rule. Not only is the nature of physical reality such that it is impossible to arrive at a truly complete account of even any one thing, there is also this ingredient of unpredictable potentiality. Whether in the history of photons or particles or genetic material, there are undetectable options. We cannot know which option will be taken, which potentiality realised, until after the event. Hence most notably there arise spontaneous mutations in living creatures, in addition to those brought about by external factors such as radiation.

The third factor is *chance*. Chance is something different from either regularity or randomness, and is compatible with both. Chance may be described as the coincidence of two or more elements in cosmic history which then affect each other's fate. Thus the asteroid and the planet behave each in its ordinary way; but if, as a result, they happen to collide the effect on the history of each is decisive, as may have been the case on Earth when the dinosaurs and most of their contemporary life forms were extinguished. The dog and the baby rabbit function each in accordance with its nature; but if the dog kills the rabbit, the rabbit will not grow up to breed, and its particular contribution to the genetic pool will, for good or ill, be lost. What is known as 'chaos theory' (a strange name for a view so fundamentally deterministic) offers more complex examples. Given the necessary series of coincidences, the effect of some tiny event may be abnormally magnified so as to produce a result that would ordinarily never come about, and so cannot be foreseen.

The universe, then, operates by the interaction of order, random potential and chance. Of these, order is primary. Random possibilities, if actualised, behave in an orderly way, as do the causes and effects of chance events. But it is the combination of these three characteristics, each in its proper proportion and place, which explains why there is such a thing as cosmic history, and why that history is one of evolution.

When we look at the results of this evolutionary character of the cosmos, we discover a fourth essential truth about the way we have to understand it; namely that any account, to be adequate, has to consider reality not just analytically but *holistically*. This applies even at the most primary levels of physics. It appears, for example, from quantum theory that those basic building blocks, the quarks, cannot exist in isolation: they have to combine with other quarks to form a proton or other particle. Or again, though it is perfectly meaningful to talk about an electron as an individual entity of a particular kind, an electron bound into an atom ceases to be such an individual entity: the atom has to be studied as a whole with its own distinctive characteristics. At the same time these characteristics are in part determined by the fact that no two electrons bound into an atom can be in identical states as regards, let us say, energy level or momentum. Though they have ceased to have identifiable individual existence, they yet all contribute different ingredients to the total state of the atom.

Such phenomena as these are but the most elementary instances of a principle which is worked out with greater and greater complexity as we move up the ladder of being. This principle asserts that no entity can be understood simply in terms of its constituent parts and their particular qualities. Once the parts are combined into a new entity, that entity will display qualities of its own which are not to be found in the ingredients considered by themselves. The total system operates at a new level.

So it is that when complex chemical constituents are combined in ways that give rise to living matter this new phenomenon which we call 'life' cannot be adequately described in terms of the inorganic ingredients which make it possible. On the same principle we cannot give a sufficient account of the activity we know as 'thought' simply in terms of the electrical and chemical activity in the brain. It is true that thought is never found without such activity linked with it, but the system has to be considered as a whole. The physical activity in the brain affects the nature of the thought, just as the electron affects that of the atom; but the reality which is there to be understood is a single entity within which the physical elements are incorporated into something that in itself exists on a new level. That is why it was perfectly logical, if imaginatively highly adventurous, for Teilhard de Chardin to argue that with the emergence of mind the cosmos as a whole had now to be viewed differently.[53] The more one stresses the essential unity of all reality, the more one is obliged to regard the evolution of new levels of reality as affecting the way we need to understand the entire system.

Once we reach the more developed forms of life, we discover a further extension of this principle. In the higher animals and in humankind the individual cannot be understood in isolation but only as *being-in-relationship*. What I am is not the product simply of all that there is inside me which goes to make up the entity known as 'me', even viewed holistically. I am what I am because of an ongoing history of relationships with other beings: family, society, the environment. There is no adequate account of such beings as ourselves which does not include the larger total system of which we are a part.

It is important not to lose sight of a fifth feature of the cosmos, which would seem to be inseparable from its evolutionary character, and that is its *imperfection*. The word is used here not with any moral connotation, but simply to refer to the many ways in which especially the higher developments in nature fail to work, or fail to work reliably. Genetic coding, for example, malfunctions in a significant proportion of cases, resulting in plant or animal offspring which are non-viable or in some way defective or abnormally vulnerable.

Humankind in particular carries a heavy hereditary burden. Human beings are so complex that the scope for dysfunction of one sort or another is greatly increased. We inherit from the evolutionary process not only many strengths and precious attributes but also residual characteristics of our ancestors which are inimical to us if we are to realise our distinctively human potential. Like the atom, we are ourselves not merely a bolting together of independent parts. But even as a new system, operating at a higher level, we recapitulate within ourselves elements which were adapted to a less complex context, and which are in some ways not suited to the situations created by our new powers. Thus responses which may have had practical survival value in other species, or in the early history of our own, are not necessarily appropriate in a global village of six billion people where accelerating technological progress threatens to exhaust resources and destroy the ecosphere and enables us, if we will, to annihilate all life many times over.

Human beings, moreover, are psychologically vulnerable and unstable. Our intelligence, working co-operatively, creates a world full of greater challenges than many people are able to meet; and society finds itself with growing numbers who have no clear contributory role and in whom any sense of self-worth is callously destroyed. The long period of dependence in infancy and childhood, increased by civilisation, gives rise to emotional demands on parents, children and society which are beyond the capacity of anyone to meet completely and of some to meet at all, with all the disabling and distorting consequences for personal life with which we are familiar. Genetic factors and social, family and environmental pressures may mean that some can cope with existence only by adopting minority lifestyles or non-normal behaviour which others may at the very least find it hard to tolerate. Some can survive only by denying reality and retreating into a psychotic world of illusion; and indeed all of us find it necessary in some degree to inhabit an inner world more endurable to our specific temperament than the real one. All such problems strain the frameworks of morality and ethics which society and, in particular, religions formulate to hold themselves together.

The sixth and final characteristic of the universe which needs to be considered is its *contingency* – that is, that its existence is neither self-explanatory nor self-evidently necessary. It may well be, as some scientists have suggested, that in order to be viable any universe would have to be in essentials of the same type as the one we have. Some have even tried to set out the mathematics to show that this is so. But that still does not explain why there should be an actual physical cosmos embodying these equations. Even though the older classical understandings of causation may no longer be adequate, it still remains true that events are found only in connection with other events and realities in relation to other realities. But to what reality is the cosmos as a whole related?

The point may be illustrated from current scientific accounts of the origin of the universe. Cosmologists can, with computer models, go back, albeit still with many unknowns, to a moment 10^{-43} of a second after the inauguration of space-time (commonly called the 'Big Bang'). But of Point Zero we can say nothing, for there the concepts of physics no longer apply. It is what is called a 'singularity' – in other words, something unlike anything else we know. But the very reasoning which impels the scientist to say that there cannot be nothing, that there must be an unknown something, is the same reasoning which impels the theologian to say that there must be 'what everyone calls God'.[54]

In using that phrase St Thomas Aquinas was choosing his words with care. He has sometimes been misrepresented[55] as trying to prove the existence of the God in whom Christians believe. But he was not one to make such an elementary logical blunder. All he was saying is that the nature of the universe as we know it demands that there be some ultimate reality to bring it into existence; and since one attribute of the Being generally referred to, not just by Christians, as 'God' is to be that reality, then so far as that attribute is concerned and no farther 'God' must exist. So far as the argument from contingency goes, it does not take the theologian any further than the scientist. Both stop at a singularity, but one of them calls it 'God'.

Of recent years, however, attempts have been made on the basis of the scientific picture of the cosmic starting point to put more theological content into that singularity. When the universe began with the exploding of a point of infinite density and infinitesimal magnitude, then the tolerances permissible within that event, if it were to have the results it has had, were quite incredibly small. If, for example, the initial velocity of expansion had varied by one part in 10^{17}, we are told, the whole affair would have ended relatively quickly, either in the collapse of the cosmos under its own weight or in its drifting off into some vast dissipation producing nothing of interest, certainly not organic life or ourselves. Or again, if the surplus of particles of matter over those of antimatter had been more or less than the one in a billion which seems to have obtained at the beginning, the cosmos as we know it would have been impossible. Why should there have been precisely this tiny imbalance? The same kind of question can be asked about a number of other factors. The odds against all of them having the values necessary for the development of the universe have been compared to those of escaping a collision while driving a car blindfolded through the rush hour.

Is there some super-law, some 'Theory of Everything' as it has been named, which would show us why all these things had to be the way they were? Or was there an immense range of possibilities, in which case the odds against the particular outcome we have got were indeed astronomic? Or, as some have speculated, has there been an incalculable series of universes, each producing the next by collapsing to a point of infinite density after a greater or lesser period of expansion, so that our universe was, so to speak, bound to come up sometime?[56] Or, following yet another conjecture, is every possible variation in fact realised, so that there is actually an infinite number of contemporaneous universes, in only one of which can, say, you or I exist? Such a scenario is by its own rules impossible to test even indirectly, and is therefore intrinsically unscientific. It also seems to offend against the principle of 'Occam's Razor',[57] that one should never posit more realities than are absolutely unavoidable.

From the standpoint of religious belief there are two comments to be made. If we assume that the present universe is the only one there has been, and that the variables at the start need not have had the values they did, then certainly that is comfortably compatible with the idea of creation by an intelligent and purposive being. It is not irrational on that basis to believe in a Creator of that kind. But there is no logical route by which one can *prove* from the odds against the precise conditions necessary for the universe we have that those conditions were the result of intelligent, purposive action. However astonishing the coincidences, we cannot rule out the possibility that things simply happened that way. The religious believer has to be content with the thought that, on this point at least, there is no conflict for faith between head and heart.

The other comment is this. If we opt for the theory of a super-law or for the idea of a process whereby the cosmic dice are rolled again and again until, just this once, our numbers happened to come up, we still cannot evade the question of contingency. Why should even a super-law ever have been embodied in material fact? However long the series of oscillating universes, why should it ever have started? One's picture of God will vary with the story one chooses, but the logical requirement of some necessary source for existent being will not go away.

The more we probe the mysteries of the universe, penetrating the fundamental secrets of matter and energy, of space and time, where paradoxes become normal and what prosaically is impossible has to be taken for granted; the more we follow the prolific magic of evolution or explore the complexities of our own brains; so much the more will the sensitive imagination be filled with exalted amazement and reverent humility. What must the source of such wonders be? Yet at the same time anyone seriously concerned with religious belief cannot but be aware of huge question marks raised by this journey into truth. The evidence on which faith has to decide is so ambiguous. If in some ways the cosmos does seem to demand a God, what can that God really be like? It is the claim of Christianity, however, to have one new piece of evidence which at least begins to make sense of the whole. That is the story and person of the man called Jesus, whom even his early followers described as the one who was 'before all things, and in him all things hold together'.[58]

3

The mystery of Jesus

Strong Son of God, immortal Love,
  Whom we, that have not seen thy face,
  By faith, and faith alone, embrace,
Believing where we cannot prove . . .

Thou seemest human and divine,
  The highest, holiest manhood, thou:
  Our wills are ours, we know not how;
Our wills are ours, to make them thine.
                    Tennyson, *In Memoriam*, 'Introduction'

If we would come to any true understanding of Jesus, we must first be rid of a common misconception. Jesus was not 'the Founder of Christianity'.

Jesus was a Jew. His faith was the Judaism of his day, radically reshaped in accordance with his own spiritual vision, but still Judaism;[1] and there is no evidence that he planned to supersede it with another system of belief. What Jesus taught was in many respects very different from the faith which even the rest of the New Testament proclaims, and certainly from developed Church Christianity.

The reason for this is perfectly straightforward. The first Christians never claimed to be handing on a religion taught by Jesus. They were preaching a belief about Jesus and his central place in God's purpose. They did indeed draw some distinctive elements of their worship, practice and ethical conduct from memories of Jesus and his teaching. But if anyone, in their minds, was the 'founder' of their particular 'Way',[2] it was not Jesus but God the Holy Spirit. For it was by the inner light given to them, as they believed, by God himself that they had come to see Jesus as God's appointed Saviour, first of the Jews and then, through the Jews, of the whole world.

Paradoxically it was this which led them, sometimes astonishingly quickly, to adopt positions – on, for example, the religious status of Gentiles – which diverged from Jesus' own. The Holy Spirit did, they believed, create in them what St Paul calls 'the mind of Christ',[3] ensuring that new developments would be in keeping with what Jesus would have taught or done in the new circumstances. But they felt under no compulsion to justify what they were doing by ascribing it to the specific guidance of Jesus during his lifetime, in the way that the whole of the Jewish Law in the Old Testament was said to have been given by God through Moses. It is significant that the occasions on which Paul cites the authority of Jesus for some ruling are very few, while other New Testament writers do so not at all.[4]

The first Christians, therefore, did not feel under pressure to make Jesus and the Church converge in every particular. That the gospel writers used a good deal of freedom – elaborating and enlarging, writing in what they thought he must have meant, fitting material into places where it seemed to suit, cutting or toning down problem details – is clear from comparative study of the gospels. In John's gospel, indeed, the details are used to build up a very different portrait with its own distinctive theological understanding. But the primary object was always to tell people about Jesus, to pass on the traditions, and not to subordinate everything to the interests of edification or Church authority.

We cannot construct a reliable in-depth biography of Jesus the man. Our information is far too limited, nor does it answer the questions we want to ask; and one person's assessment of which details are authentic will always differ in some degree from another's. But there is a key issue which the New Testament has already identified for us; and if we approach the gospels for light on that, much material will authenticate itself, because it helps to explain why things turned out as they did: namely, that Jesus came to be simultaneously the one invested with 'all authority in heaven and in earth' and also the source of creative spiritual freedom for his followers.[5]

The resurrection of Jesus

We start from the one fact about Jesus which is indisputable: his disciples claimed that he 'rose from the dead', or rather (since this was their more frequent way of expressing it) that 'he was raised' – that is, that God had raised him.[6] That no one could rise from the dead unless God made that happen seemed to them self-evident. So far as humankind has been able to discover, there is no path through death which a person may tread to come out into new and greater life. If that were to happen, we would have to posit some factor operating in ways quite different from those we observe anywhere else. For the contemporaries of Jesus, the only candidate – and for the modern believer still the most obvious one – for such a role was God. The resurrection of Jesus meant that God had put his mark on this man uniquely out of all the men and women who had ever lived.

The New Testament registers no claim by anyone to have seen the actual resurrection. Anything that could occur in historical reality would have to be a consequence of the resurrection, not the resurrection itself; and this is all that the Easter stories in the New Testament purport to relate. But they also insist that the experiences of which they tell were such that the factual resurrection of Jesus was the only origin which could explain them. If that belief was mistaken, then these experiences have no greater claim to be a clue to God's values and purposes than any other account of human spiritual intuitions. But if it was not, then God has put his tick in the 'Jesus' box beside the multiple-choice question of the universe.

This assertion is particularly unwelcome at a time when our western culture is seeking to reduce inter-faith rivalries. The point is grasped clearly enough in Judaism, even more brutally indeed since the Holocaust:

> If the heart of the Jewish-Christian conflict is the issue of Christology, its inner heart is the affirmation/disaffirmation of the Resurrection of Jesus Christ . . . The Resurrection comprises the centre of the Christian 'theology of replacement', wherein the old and false Israel is reputedly superseded by the new and true Israel. A no-less powerful

and more concrete factor is the dogma that the event of the resurrection is not a mere human idea or human spiritual experience but is exclusively a deed of God . . . The insistence that the Resurrection is God's deed constitutes the foundation of Christian triumphalism and supersessionism.[7]

Islam too finds it necessary to reject the idea of a factual Resurrection of Jesus, though it resolves the issue in a different way by denying Jesus' death on the cross, and so the need for any such miracle.[8] A triumphalist view of Christianity does not necessarily follow from a factual understanding of Jesus' resurrection, as will be argued in Chapter 4. But the problem cannot be solved by pretending away the factual character of the original Christian claim.

For one thing the New Testament will not allow it. Paul sets out the assumption behind the traditions clearly enough, when he writes to the Corinthians:

> If there is no resurrection of the dead, then Christ has not been raised; and if Christ has not been raised, then our proclamation has been in vain and your faith has been in vain. We are even found to be misrepresenting God, because we testified of God that he raised Christ – whom he did not raise if it is true that the dead are not raised.[9]

The same assumptions lie behind three reports of Paul's words in Acts. In the first, when he has been arraigned before the supreme Jewish council, he calls out: 'I am on trial concerning the hope of the resurrection of the dead.' The second comes when, defending himself at Caesarea before Herod Agrippa II, he asks: 'Why is it thought incredible by any of you that God raises the dead?' The third occurs in a rather different context, Paul's missionary work in Athens. Brought to a gathering of citizens on Areopagus to explain his preaching of 'Jesus and Resurrection', his address has to break off when he affirms that the true God has 'fixed a day on which he will have the world judged in righteousness by a man whom he has appointed, and of this he has given assurance to all by raising him from the dead'.[10] The reaction of some, we are told, as soon as Paul mentioned the resurrection of the dead, was derision, though others were prepared to pursue the matter.[11] Given normal hellenistic hopes for life after death, which were essentially of escape from the body, this response clearly indicates that an objective resurrection event was both intended and understood. The issue is not affected if Luke has here supplied Paul with a model speech suited to the occasion. What Christian preachers meant by the resurrection is the same either way.

In all these instances the resurrection of Jesus is regarded as the realisation of something hoped for by many Jews for themselves. This is further confirmed by what Paul goes on to write to the Corinthians immediately after the passage quoted above: 'But in fact Christ has been raised from the dead, the first fruits of those who have died'.[12] What is related of Jesus is what all God's faithful servants can look for in their own case. The stories were therefore taken and meant to be taken as factual and historical.

All this means that we cannot escape the need to make up our own minds what we believe on this question of fact; and the reader will find the evidence and arguments summarised in Appendix A.

Conclusive proof is, of course, not possible either way. For this reason it is often said, even by preachers on Easter Day, that picking over the story of the first Easter is a barren exercise. What we need to do is to accept by faith the conviction of the first disciples that beyond the Cross Jesus was 'alive for evermore',[13] and on that basis open our hearts and lives to his loving sovereignty. Then we shall know by our own experience that he is alive and real today.

Certainly what matters most is not that we should simply believe with our minds a statement about something that happened long ago. That was never the purpose of making the statement in the first place. It was meant to change people's lives, and that is still its central objective. But we cannot use that as a way of evading the issue.

To see why this is so we have only to ask one simple question. If the tradition had contained no stories offered in evidence, but merely the bald assertion by the apostles that they knew Jesus was alive again, would anyone have taken that seriously?

It is, to say the least, very unlikely. Why should anyone, then or now, interpret their own spiritual experience in terms of a still living Jesus unless they had reason, either from their own knowledge or from someone else's reliable report, to believe him still alive? Moreover it is not just the basic message of the stories that is significant. The *kind* of experience they describe is also important, as the 'witnesses to the resurrection'[14] always understood.

This raises another crucial issue. We cannot stop at saying 'Yes, I believe' or 'No, I don't believe'. We have to have a meaningful idea of what it is to which we are saying 'Yes' or 'No'. The stories claim to describe certain experiences, interpreted as encounters with Jesus risen from the dead. If that interpretation was correct, then we can be sure that observation, memory and language were all being strained to the limit of their capacity and beyond. It is also a well-established feature of the way people give evidence that first time round they struggle to find words to express the images retained in the mind, but that next time they fall back on their memory of what they originally said. At both stages a process of 'making sense' of our testimony, of 'tidying it up', and even of 'improving' it, is liable to take over. There is every reason to believe that this happened in the case of the disciples' Easter recollections and of the passing of these recollections into tradition. That does not justify us in saying that nothing happened, that it was all made up. But it does mean that we need to ask what we ourselves think was happening, what sort of events the disciples might have been experiencing which would give rise to the record we have inherited.[15] At this point it will be convenient to summarise the answer to that question arrived at in the Appendix.

The experience of the first disciples convinced them that God had not simply revived Jesus, to continue life as it had been before, much as Jesus himself is related to have done for Jairus' daughter or the widow's son at Nain or his own friend, Lazarus.[16] God had given Jesus a new kind of life, one true to Jesus himself, in which he could still engage with his companions on earth in a human way, but one also which transcended the normal limitations of our existence. It was as if he could choose to be present at any time or place in whatever mode would best suit God's purposes in that situation. So Mary Magdalene saw him first as a gardener, Cleopas and his friend as a traveller, the fishermen by the lakeside as a loitering stranger, Paul on the Damascus road as a radiant being from another world.[17] But before each encounter was over those involved knew with absolute certainty who he was, and that their own lives had been healed, and fired with a new spirit.[18]

These are not what the ancient world as well as ourselves knew as 'ghost stories'. They are not the way Jewish writers who believed in a future resurrection had ever imagined it. They are attempts to convey unique and mysterious, but at the same time solid, sensory and utterly real, experiences which left them with only one possible conclusion: their Jesus, who had been dead and buried, was not only alive but possessed now of a life which perfectly embodied who and what he was. In the years during which they had known him that Jesus had been partly hidden, glimpsed at moments, guessed at from puzzling clues, then lost to sight. Now they knew that it was in a life characteristic of the divine order that he was truly at home. That was his native air, and death could never touch him again.

On the diamond point of that testimony rests all that the Christian Church has been drawn to believe and proclaim about Jesus. What kind of a man was he? That is not just a modern question. If you go to a complete stranger, and say, 'God has raised X from the dead', the two natural responses, then as well as now, are: 'How do you know?' and 'Tell us more about X.' On the first question something has already been said. What about the second?

The gospels as evidence for the life of Jesus: (1) the miracles

During his mortal life Jesus had been the subject of sharp controversy and conflicting judgements. The reason why the religious hierarchy felt driven to condemn him to death was that they saw him as a self-confessed perverse teacher, leading the people astray in ways that were dangerous both to the spiritual life and the political survival of the nation.[19] The claim that Jesus had been raised from the dead was an outright defiance of that condemnation, for it shouted aloud that God's verdict had been very different.[20]

Small wonder, then, if authoritative efforts were made within Judaism to suppress the preaching of Jesus' resurrection.[21] What seemed to be at stake was nothing less than the soul of Israel's faith. The disciples' claim could not possibly be true. God would not have done such a thing, least of all for someone whose method of execution had placed him under the curse of God's own Law.[22] But since bald assertion and counter-assertion were manifestly going to get nowhere, Jesus' followers were forced to marshal other supporting evidence; and this they did by appealing to Jesus' miracles.

In Acts 2 Peter is presented as speaking to the crowd of 'Jesus the Nazorean, a man attested to you by God with deeds of power, wonders, and signs that God did through him among you, as you yourselves know'. In Caesarea, in Cornelius' house, Peter again relates 'how God anointed Jesus of Nazareth with the Holy Spirit and with power; how he went about doing good and healing all who were oppressed by the devil, for God was with him. We are witnesses to all that he did'.[23] How are we to assess this claim?

The gospels are unanimous that Jesus did perform 'wonders' and 'works of power', and that these were a major factor in his fame and influence.[24] In considering this aspect of his mission it is better to stay with the New Testament terminology of 'signs' and 'wonders' and 'works of power' than to use the modern and philosophically loaded term 'miracles'. To talk of miracles raises issues such as the regularity of the material universe, and whether this can ever be overridden by spiritual means, questions which formed no part of the Gospel background. Some of Jesus' works of power, if correctly reported, would seem to be of this kind; others, such as certain of the healings, might be understood in psychosomatic terms. The New Testament did not differentiate in this way. What its writers meant by a 'sign' or a 'work of power' was something which God did through the person concerned,[25] and which therefore revealed truth, first and foremost about God's own purposes and character, and secondly about that person's own standing with God.[26] It was nothing to do with any power inherent in the person who performed the work, but solely a matter of God's choice of one for this service and witness. This implies, certainly, that the works so done were of a kind beyond the capacity of human beings unaided; but it does not require them to be such as we would label intrinsically 'impossible'. Some of the healings, for example, are cures which we now know how to achieve by medical means, but which at that time no doctor could have accomplished.[27]

We shall return to the question of miracles in the final chapter, but a brief word is relevant here. It is important to understand that miracles are not about 'doing the impossible'. 'The impossible' means 'that which cannot be done'; and if something really cannot be done, then even God cannot do it. But there may be many things which we think impossible but which in reality are not. Some of these may be things which we cannot do now, but which, when the fundamental principles of life and the cosmos are more fully understood, we shall be able to do one day. Others may be things we shall never manage on our own but which are possible to our Creator for reasons we may never understand.

To say this is not to sign an open cheque for credulity. There are, for example, certain things about which we already know enough to declare them intrinsically impossible: for example, the resuscitation of a dead person after certain biochemical changes have taken place in the body. Beyond that point there would have to be an act of new creation, the feeding in of a hitherto unrealised possibility. We would therefore be justified in saying that Jairus' daughter and the widow's son at Nain were not in fact clinically dead; and in the former case Jesus' words as reported can be understood as insisting on this fact himself.[28] The case of Lazarus is more extreme, since the story claims that his former life was resumed after his body had reached an advanced stage of corruption; but this would surely have called for a resurrection, comparable to that of Jesus, not for the resuscitation actually described.

The basic layer of tradition in the gospels about Jesus' miracles takes a more sober view. For the most part it concerns acts of spiritual healing. That sufferers with various illnesses and disabilities both of body and mind, sometimes very severe ones, have been and still are cured after spiritual ministrations of one kind or another is a fact so well attested that only a determined bigotry can refuse to acknowledge it. Whether such ministry arises from natural powers of which as yet we know little, or whether in some instances God is distinctively at work through the healer, the fact remains that such cures do happen. There is therefore no reason to assume that Jesus cannot have performed them, or to doubt the general reliability of the gospels on this point. It is worth noting that Jesus makes no exclusive or exceptional claim for himself on the basis of his healings: others were given the same power.[29] Interesting too is his repeated insistence that the critical factor was the faith of the sufferers,[30] the other side of that coin being the comment that in his own home town he could heal only a few, because his fellow-citizens could not believe that God would work through someone they knew so well.[31]

There is a realism about all this which enhances its credibility. The fact that the gospels, like Jesus himself and the other people of whom they tell, saw many illnesses as the work of evil spirits, and thus both practised and understood spiritual healing as a form of exorcism, is no reason to doubt that cures were really effected. In so far as the belief of the sufferers was a vital element in the process, that belief needed to take the form accepted in their own faith and culture. The conviction behind this particular form, namely that disease is an evil, need surely present no more problems for faith now than it did then. As to the question whether psychic forces external to the sufferers and exercising a malign effect upon them do exist, all one can say is this: such cases are a tiny handful compared with the numbers that some religious enthusiasts would have us believe occur. But there are well-documented instances, on which medical and religious experts have collaborated, which seem to testify to the existence of such realities, though their nature is unquestionably obscure. This, of course, does not affect the fact that most of the illnesses attributed in the gospels to such malevolent interference ought to be assigned to other causes, and that even fatal harm can be done by taking the first-century Church as a guide in diagnosis.

A few of the works of power narrated in the gospels, however, raise rather different problems. These are the ones that it was once customary to label 'nature miracles', because they involved manipulation of the external world, for example in the stilling of the storm[32] or Jesus' walking on the water.[33] Such a distinction is not particularly logical. Works of healing bring about changes in the physical material of the human body and are not really explained by talking about 'the power of mind over matter'. If this power exists and can be exercised on matter within our bodies, why not on matter outside them?

A cautionary note, however, may perhaps be inferred from a tradition related by both Matthew and Luke. John the Baptist, during his final imprisonment by Herod Antipas, sent two of his followers to Jesus to ask him whether he were in fact the God-sent deliverer for whom Israel was looking. In reply Jesus draws attention to two aspects of his work: his healings and the preaching of his message of hope for the poor.[34] There is no mention of any other kind of wonder.

What are the nature miracles involved? They are in fact relatively few in number. Three are private to the disciples, and two are open and public. In the first group come the two already mentioned: the stilling of the storm and the walking on the water, the element of the marvellous in the latter being heightened in different ways by both Matthew and John. In addition there is the folklore-type story of the paying of the Temple tax with a coin found in a fish's mouth.[35]

Of the two public signs the major one is that known as 'the feeding of the multitude' or 'of the five thousand'. All four gospels record it in basically the same terms.[36] John adds circumstantial details of his own, which seem to have no point except to stress the concrete historical reality of the event.[37] It is also John who relates that it was this sign which convinced the crowds that Jesus was the 'Coming One', the longed-for Deliverer, and which stirred them into a revolutionary frenzy in which they were about to proclaim him king.[38] One motif behind all the accounts is probably that Jesus is as great as

Moses, for whom God fed Israel in the desert,[39] or Elijah and Elisha, both of whom are said to have multiplied food.[40] The superabundance of the provision, carefully noted in all versions, is implied in Mark to be revelatory.[41]

The second such incident, the water which was made wine at the wedding feast in Cana, comes in John's gospel alone.[42] Again, a revelatory excess in the scale of the sign is suggested,[43] disclosing Jesus' glory – that is, his hidden relationship with God – and evoking answering faith in his disciples.[44]

Similar stories have been credited to Christian saints down to modern times[45] and also to holy figures in other faiths.[46] Nevertheless there are significant questions raised by these particular gospel traditions, though they are hard to define because they concern elusive matters, such as what feels morally and spiritually fitting – and that criterion may be no more than a grand name for one's own narrowness of soul! Why were the five thousand fed? Was it simply an act of practical compassion in an emergency, made necessary by the way so many had stayed with Jesus to hear his teaching? That is the way Mark presents a strange repeat version of the incident, in which Matthew follows him,[47] though in the primary story there seems no need for such a dramatic intervention.[48] And did no other occasion ever arise when feeding the hungry would have been a necessary good work? Yet, if relief of need was not the motive, what was? That cannot anyway have been the reason for the turning of water into wine at Cana, where a kindly gesture to save a young bridegroom, perhaps a family friend,[49] from social embarrassment is about as far as it can have gone.

There is almost a jokiness in some of the stories. Why scare the disciples out of their wits[50] by walking past their boat on the Sea of Galilee in the middle of the night, when the poor devils were having hard enough work of it as it was? In all the versions of the feeding of the multitude, too, there is an undercurrent of something very like teasing in the way Jesus begins by puzzling his disciples, and a similar tone occurs in the story of the fish and the coin. The feel is reminiscent of tales from other sources about divine visitants in disguise, as though Jesus knew he could perform these wonders any time if he wanted to, but used the power only occasionally as a gesture of kindness or simply for a bit of fun.

It is plainly true that the gospels were written in the light of Easter for a community which not only believed in Jesus' resurrection but was busy drawing radical conclusions about him from that belief. Every disciple heard and told the story of Jesus' life with hindsight. It is hardly surprising if this led to the intrusion of that note of 'divinity in disguise', or to the elaboration of various incidents. But the fact that the gospels present certain events as pointing to the later convictions of the Church about Jesus – as for example that he was the eternal Word or Wisdom of God – does not mean that these were either the conclusions drawn by the disciples at the time or the message that Jesus himself meant to convey. After the stilling of the storm the disciples ask, 'Who then is this, that even the wind and the sea obey him?' – a question that clearly is meant to suggest but one answer.[51] But if the event did happen as described, was it meant to awaken such faith? Jesus has been calmly sleeping while the disciples panic, and his words need imply no more than that they lacked faith in God their father. The actual wonder is performed simply to calm their fears.

How then did Jesus himself see the place of works of power within his own mission? One tradition tells how the orthodox religious leaders challenged Jesus to authenticate himself by showing them a 'sign from heaven' – that is, some wonder which, being unmistakably divine in origin, would invest Jesus with an authority no one could fail to acknowledge.[52] Jesus rebuffs them roundly. Only 'an evil and adulterous generation' – that is, a people which had turned from God and from the covenant, the relationship of mutual trust which he had insti- tuted – would make such a demand. This stance on Jesus' part is precisely the one foreshadowed in the policy-defining story of his temptations in the desert after his baptism,[53] where Jesus is portrayed as having renounced the use of wonders as a way of winning adherents to his cause. His escape from the crowds after the feeding of the multitude is in line with this. A similar conviction lies behind the formula in which Jesus is said to order those he has healed to tell no one about their cure, a practice remembered as so characteristic that it is attributed to him even in contexts when it is obvious that the cure could not have been concealed.[54]

The gospel according to John touches on this issue at a number of points. It makes frequent use of the word 'sign' for works of power. In the evangelist's own comments or in Jesus' mouth this normally carries the implication that the work is done not only for its own sake but to signify some truth beyond itself; but when used by others it may mean no more than a 'wonder'.[55] This ironically underlines the blindness of the people and of Jesus' critics, who do not really see the sign, because they fail to perceive its meaning.[56] In John, as in the other gospels, doubters ask for a sign to convince them,[57] and their demand remains unsatisfied.

In this gospel, however, Jesus also talks explicitly about the 'works' which he does. These are 'the Father's works',[58] which Jesus performs through the power given by the Father in order to do the Father's will.[59] To anyone who has spiritual eyes to see, therefore, they witness that it is the Father who has sent Jesus.[60] One theme in the gospel is that in his confrontations with his opponents Jesus is, as it were, 'on trial';[61] and it is in this context that he appeals to his works, and to the Father made known through his works, as witnesses in his defence, justifying his teaching and his claims.[62] John's dramatic irony is again in evidence when the man born blind, whose sight Jesus restores, is excommunicated for putting forward just this argument in support of Jesus.[63]

The overall picture, therefore, is not a simple one. Before coming to any conclusion we shall need to look at two other aspects: Jesus' teaching, and his understanding of himself and his role. But an interim judgement might go something like this. A sober critical assessment will not delete all 'works of power' from the record. They are too deeply embedded in the recollection of Jesus – the healings in particular, but also the feeding of the five thousand. Such works of power could not but be part of the evidence about Jesus; and all who found themselves challenged to make a response to Jesus had to evaluate those works. Jesus could have prevented this only by refusing to perform any works of power, but that would have been, as he knew, to deny the compassionate and liberating nature of the kingdom of God which he proclaimed.

In other words, Jesus could not escape doing works which were also 'signs', but that does not mean that he was doing them primarily as signs. They both could and should evoke faith; but they were not done in order to evoke faith, and in fact would succeed in doing so only in those who first received his moral and spiritual message. Nor should we decide too hastily what, in Jesus' own mind, did constitute right faith in himself. Something on these lines is certainly the predominant impression given by all the gospels from their differing stand-points; and it is this which leads one to believe that the so-called 'nature miracles', at any rate as presented, reflect irrecoverable incidents which played only a marginal role, and even a poten-tially misleading one.

The gospels as evidence for the life of Jesus: (2) the teaching

For Judaism, works of power, even if substantiated, could never by themselves be reason enough to accept someone as an emiss-ary of God.[64] The key criterion was always right teaching and practice. The grounds which Jesus' opponents put forward for discounting his signs, or even for ascribing them to evil forces, were, as all the gospels make clear, to do with fundamental disagreements about the terms of our human relationship with God.

This, and not some personal jealousy or political self-interest, was the deepest reason why his critics said that he was casting out demons by Beelzebul, the prince of demons.[65] If Jesus was right in what he taught, then it could be believed that God was at work through him. But he was not right, he was 'leading the people astray',[66] and so his powers must come from the realm of darkness. It was that judgement which Jesus character-ised as 'sin' or 'blasphemy' against the Holy Spirit,[67] because it ascribed God's work to the devil; and the reason why it could never be forgiven was simply that if your moral sense is so twisted that you see good as evil, you can never grasp what it is that needs forgiveness, and therefore calls for repentance.

What was it that made Jesus in the eyes of many deeply religious people so dangerous? Why was it that a man whom his followers were to venerate as the cornerstone of a new spiritual temple was to others nothing more than a stone unfit for use?[68]

One clear certainty about Jesus is that the 'kingdom' or 'sovereignty' of God was a key reality for him, as it had been for John the Baptist before him. Jesus' reverence for John was immense, as we can tell not only from words of Jesus recorded in the tradition and from the fact that he went to John for baptism,[69] but also from the embarrassment these things seem to have caused Jesus' followers.[70] For Jesus, John was in a unique category, a man between two worlds, that of Israel's past and that of the coming kingdom.[71] He was greater than any of Israel's heroes,[72] even Moses, even Abraham, because to him it had been given to foresee and proclaim the fulfilment of God's sovereignty on earth. But precisely because that sovereignty, when consummated, would turn upside-down all existing earthly canons of status and importance, 'the least in the king-dom of heaven is greater than he'.[73] The gospel writers perhaps saw that as putting John in his place, but it is nothing of the kind. It is not really about John at all but about the kingdom – an extreme way of stating the paradoxical radicalism of God's values as contrasted with those of our defective human order. It is in line with other sayings about the 'greatest' and the 'least', the 'last' and the 'first', or about God's giving the highest place to little children:[74] The community of the disciples is to reflect this kingdom quality by paying highest honour to those who perform the most menial tasks.[75]

When Jesus began his public career, he took John's campaign slogan as his own: 'Repent, for the kingdom of heaven has come near!'[76] How did Jesus envisage this divine kingship? John's idea of it seems to have gone little further than a vision of judgement[77] – punishment for the wicked, joy for the right-eous – which cannot have amounted to more than the initial stage of God's exercise of his sovereignty. Of Jesus' thoughts we are told more; but what we are given is in some ways intriguingly unexpected and also tantalisingly fragmentary, like a strange and distant landscape viewed through gaps in swirling mist.

At times Jesus talks as if wondering out loud: 'With what can we compare the kingdom of God, or what parable will we use for it?'[78] The kingdom, when we think what it is to become in the end, starts from beginnings that are absurdly, impossibly small.[79] It changes everything with which it comes in contact, but does so secretly, silently, invisibly.[80] It is to do with values, choices, with giving your life for what really matters.[81] The innocent heart recognises it for what it is, as do those whom life has left with no great opinion of themselves;[82] but the ones who in worldly or spiritually conventional terms are successful and powerful are blinded by other loves, and disabled from entering.[83] The coming of the kingdom is thus unavoidably a process of judgement: when God is sovereign, those whose priorities are not his cannot be at home in his country, but those who do share them find life there an unending festival.[84]

If we ask how, where or when this kingdom is to be inaugurated, the answer is in part that it is already present in the lives of the simple- and single-hearted – the poor, the meek, the merciful, the peacemakers.[85] The signs of its coming are everywhere, but because the signs are not what we expect or desire we fail to discern them for what they are.[86] If we need to ask the question, we shall never find the answer.[87] But when the kingdom is at last openly and completely established it will need no announcement.[88]

All this is in tune with what Jesus has to say about God's methods in a parable which the first three gospels all regard as of key significance, though it is not explicitly about the kingdom. In the story of the sower[89] Jesus pictures God working not by manipulating events but by letting creation respond in its own spontaneous ways to his initiative. In imagery startlingly in keeping with what we now understand of the role of randomness and chance in the cosmos,[90] the sower simply blankets the land with the seed of God's future, and some survives and flourishes, while some does not. The analogy came from standard Galilean farming practice, but the implication for religion was revolutionary. Just as, to a large extent, God lets the cosmos make itself within the parameters he has set or continuingly develops, so he lets the kingdom make itself. He simply introduces into the world a new creative element to which each soul cannot avoid responding in its own way.

The message of the sower story is exemplified in practice in Jesus' own use of parables. Parables (literally, 'comparisons') were a traditional teaching method in Israel, one device of those whose profession it was to train up potential leaders of society. But those comparisons were not meant to be obscure; that would have frustrated their object. By enjoying their aptness the hearer was supposed to make their message his or her own. By contrast the gospels record that many people, even those closest to Jesus, found his parables perplexing.[91] How was this to be understood?

The answer offered by Matthew, Mark and Luke is disconcerting. Jesus is said to have prefaced an explanation of the use of parables by quoting God's command to Isaiah to make the people stupid and spiritually deaf, so that they would not repent and be saved.[92] Jesus then goes on to interpret the parables as if they were allegorical stories of the kind found in later prophecy and apocalyptic writing, which have to be decoded before they reveal their meaning.[93] This, however, is hard to square with other evidence. On the rare occasions when Jesus does use the allegory form it is in such a simple and transparent manner that those at whom the story is aimed find it only too painfully clear.[94] In general, we are told, the crowds were gripped by his teachings,[95] nor would it have been in keeping with the underlying beat of urgent mission running through the narrative[96] for Jesus to have set out to mystify people.

Nevertheless there is this theme of bafflement and misunderstanding. It was no doubt partly inevitable that parables about the kingdom should perplex, because the kingdom itself is a mystery. But there is also a more fundamental answer. To many people spiritual truth, however clearly or simply expressed, is opaque. If their mindset is such that they cannot even begin to think in the teacher's terms, the penny will not drop. Indeed, it is possible for the hearers to neutralise in this way what is being said, even while enjoying the performance. For most of us Jesus' words, whatever conventional respect we pay them, still today go against the grain of our souls, so that we 'indeed listen, but never understand, and . . . indeed look, but never perceive'.[97] In this sense the parables are themselves a process of judgement.

One way to gain insight into the spirit of Jesus' teaching is to compare it with that available in the Palestinian Judaism of his day. As to ultimate objectives he and other teachers would have had no quarrel. The Pharisees in particular were concerned to enable all kinds of people, the ignorant as well as the educated, to live in accordance with the will of God.[98] Their method of achieving this was to provide authoritative direction on what to do in various situations, deriving this from the primary deliverances of the biblical Law, and from the developments of these handed down from teachers to disciples through the generations. They were in fact carrying on what all acknowledge as the business of ethics: reconciling principles where they appear to clash, identifying priorities, expanding past wisdom to meet new circumstances.

Jesus is said to have criticised some of their judgements on the ground that the developments had ended up by contradicting clear basic commands in the original Scripture;[99] and that is an objection that the rabbis of the time would have accepted. But Jesus is also shown going behind the Law, and enunciating new moral guidelines rather different in character. It is important not to exaggerate the divergence between Jesus and other Jewish teachers of his time. The rabbis were not simply concerned with what might be called the small print. They pondered just as much on the unifying root principles of the Law, the creative motivation behind it; and love for God and for neighbour were already recognised as the great commandments, as the gospels themselves testify.[100] Though Jesus is credited with a form of the Golden Rule which runs, 'In everything do to others as you would have them do to you',[101] while the version preferred by Rabbi Hillel is, 'That which you hate do not do to another', both see this as the heart of the Law and the Prophets. It is also mistaken and unfair to describe Jesus' form as 'positive' and Hillel's as 'negative'. Both are positive, and each has its particular value as an aid in the choice of loving conduct toward one's neighbour. Nevertheless there is a difference of thrust in Jesus' teaching, which may perhaps be summed up as follows.

The task of the teacher, as the rabbis saw it, was to think through the ethical and religious situations that might arise in life so that the ordinary person who wanted to keep God's Law, but who was not experienced or expert enough to know in all cases what this entailed, might be enabled to do so. This guidance would also help such a person to overcome the 'evil impulse', which God had allowed in human nature so that men and women could grow in authentic moral virtue. What Jesus was trying to do was to equip people with a new vision of God and neighbour, to foster new inner attitudes, so that they could make decisions pleasing to God for themselves. His practical instances, therefore, were more in the way of examples of the kind of conduct a right spirit would produce rather than the systematic application of a codified tradition.

In working out his approach Jesus seems to have been much influenced by the Old Testament Wisdom writers. His teaching displays something of a penchant for proverb-type sayings,[102] and in one case he is remembered as quoting their worldly-wise counsel directly.[103] But his indebtedness to that tradition went deeper. Just as their own reflection on life and the world about them led the sages on occasion to moral insights as high as anything in the Law or the Prophets,[104] so Jesus' own reading of God's values as discernible in the ordering of the world led him to some radical absolutes. His teaching on marriage and divorce is one example;[105] but by far the most fundamental is that about love for enemies.[106] Because God has made a world in which the indispensable blessings of rain and sun fall on the good and bad alike, so human beings are to make no distinctions on moral grounds, but are to love and pray for those who hate and injure them as much as for those who do them good. Only so can we be authentic children of our Father in heaven.

In the Palestinian environment the natural temptation was to see these commands as constituting a new legal system to replace the old. This is the way they are presented in Matthew's gospel, where the so-called 'Sermon on the Mount' sets out a selection of Jesus' teachings in a setting seemingly intended to echo the giving of the Old Testament Law on Mount Sinai. Matthew also appears to treat all Jesus' injunctions as though in kind they were the same as the teachings of the rabbis, but simply pitched at a higher moral or spiritual standard. His gospel is notoriously hostile to contemporary Judaism,[107] commending the Christian way as the perfection at which Judaism aimed but which it failed to reach: 'unless your righteousness exceeds that of the scribes and Pharisees, you will never enter the kingdom of heaven'.[108] At the same time Matthew gives us a Jesus who stresses the authority of rabbinic teaching,[109] and the permanent validity of the Old Testament Law[110] – possibly an indication of the kind of church order which Matthew wanted to see in the Christian community. That is not to say that these utterances are not based on words of Jesus. Jesus appealed to Scripture, and recognised its authority. But if and when he said that the righteousness of the kingdom would exceed that of the teachers of his day, it is more than unlikely that he was thinking of his own moral injunctions as legal requirements in the same sense as those of the rabbis.

Another clue to the nature of Jesus' commands is perhaps to be found in those cases where he seems to go to irrational extremes. How, for instance, are we to take such words as, 'if your right hand causes you to sin, cut it off and throw it away'?[111] In its form it is a command of a standard legal type, but to treat it as such would be the ethics of the madhouse. What, in any case, can it possibly mean? A hand or foot or eye are not things that of themselves can cause anyone to sin. As Jesus himself said, the source of sin is in the heart,[112] and it will still be there, even if the senses that supply it with material are removed. The only interpretation of such sayings coherent with Jesus' other recorded teaching is that they are not literal commands, systematic or otherwise, but a jarring and dramatic way of getting people to heed the fact that total dedication to good is worth the harshest sacrifice. The absurd extremism of the injunction is not part of some nightmare legal synthesis, but chosen because resistance to that principle is itself so extreme and so deeply rooted within us.

Perhaps, however, the decisive pointer to the core of Jesus' moral teaching is that he never made a right relationship with God or neighbour dependent on moral success. His foundation demand is for penitence for our own failures and forgiveness for those of others. 'God will forgive you, if you will forgive those who wrong you,' is his theme.[113] The one who goes home from the Temple accepted by God is not the Pharisee listing his obediences but the tax collector acknowledging his faults.[114] At the heart of the pattern prayer taught to Jesus' disciples is the plea for forgiveness for ourselves in the same way as we have forgiven others. It is inconceivable that Jesus would have made all depend on this, unless he had been convinced that most of us would make a mess of things most of the time.

For all the seemingly impossible absolutes with which Jesus confronts us, therefore, the air we breathe in his ethical landscape is one of realism. As we reflected earlier,[115] humans are psychologically and morally precarious and fractured beings. The chances of being able to learn all the ethical directives necessary for a good life, or to apply them correctly if learned, are toweringly against us. In such a world the basic prerequisite for peace and security is the willingness to forgive and be forgiven. This alone can also provide the space needed for growth in virtue; and Jesus is uniquely perceptive in having made it the foundation of individual moral wellbeing and of collective ethical life.

As with everything else, this grew out of Jesus' being a Jew, and out of the wisdom of the Jewish faith about our human relations with God and with one another. A substantial part of the Jewish Law is concerned with ways in which we can approach God for forgiveness. Atoning sacrifice, accompanied by confession and penitence and, where possible, reparation for wrongdoing, was central to the devotions of Judaism. Nor was this understood as some pious action by which human sinners could, as it were, make up for what they had done. It was a gift from God in the form of an act of obedience which he had promised to recognise, so as to put reconciliation within the reach of everyone.[116] In addition to these ritual means of access to God's mercy Judaism also recognised the efficacy of penitential prayer on its own, when the Temple sacrifices were not available.[117] Jesus develops this tradition in two ways: first, by making penitential prayer within a personal relationship with God the norm; and secondly, by insisting on our forgiving others as the precondition of forgiveness from God.

The corollary of all this is that moral teaching cannot be presented in terms of detailed regulations. Once accept that people are morally frail and will always fall short and get things wrong, then precise prescriptions for what is to be done in this case or that are not going to meet their deepest need. That approach merely guarantees that everyone, save for a minority of ethical athletes, is going to live either in a permanent poison cloud of guilt, failure and self-despair or in growing indifference to the whole moral enterprise. In the society to which Jesus belonged all three types were represented: the professionally righteous; those who felt themselves rightly despised; and those to whose daily situation the ever more complex rectitude of the religious establishment had little relevance. It was to the two latter groups that Jesus appealed most strongly, giving to each a chance to respect themselves as moral and spiritual persons, loved by God.

In one place it is said of Jesus that such people responded to him because they felt that, unlike most religious teachers, he spoke with authority.[118] What might have been meant by that? The rabbis had an authority which was not merely individual, deriving from their education and office, but also collective and traditional: they represented the accumulated conscience of the nation. But by its very nature their teaching grounded its authority on precedent, on appeal to other teachers in the past, either by demonstrating consensus or by logical development. There is no evidence that Jesus had or sought that kind of authority, even though some may have addressed him as 'Rabbi' – a title, incidentally, which on one occasion he is represented as rejecting.[119] To judge from the record, the authority people saw in him probably derived from three sources: he talked about life as it was for them; he focused on moral essentials; and he did not feel it necessary to justify what he said by referring to acknowledged experts of the past – indeed, he was prepared to set himself up against them.[120] The only support he did cite was Scripture, interpreted by his own incisive brand of commonsense.[121] In addition he was plainly something of a spellbinder as a speaker.[122] He could tell stories, make jokes[123] and put arguments which anyone could follow,[124] and was a poet into the bargain.[125]

Jesus could be very clear cut about the kind of conduct God looks for. He was not an 'anything-goes-so-long-as-you-mean-well' type. But he insisted that the only way of growing into such conduct was first to seek purity of heart and motive,[126] on the principle that sound fruit comes only from a healthy tree.[127]

The incident which frames the story of the Good Samaritan is illuminating here.[128] The lawyer raises the question, what kind of life will get me into heaven? When Jesus asks him in return what the Law has to say, he specifies the two great commandments, love toward God and neighbour. Jesus then says, 'You have given the right answer; do this, and you will live.' But do what? What does it mean in practice? The lawyer seizes on one obvious difficulty to start with: how do you define 'neighbour'? In response Jesus tells the famous story which, as has often been pointed out, refuses to answer the question, 'Who is the neighbour I am to love?' The neighbour is the one who loves; and by implication no one is disqualified from receiving that love. The lawyer takes the point, and is sent away with the command, 'Go and do likewise.' But obedience to that command obviously does not lie in the details of first aid, transport and accommodation, though these were right in that particular incident. It is simply 'showing mercy',[129] an attitude which will produce appropriate action in each situation. What such action ought to be cannot be decided in advance. There will be many things it cannot be, but apart from these the field is open.

Jesus' approach is a radical corrective to a temptation which perhaps especially assailed his devout contemporaries, but which afflicts all conscientious human beings, religious or not, in every generation. If our prime concern is to avoid reproach (or sin) and, like the lawyer, to 'justify ourselves', then without some authoritative ruling as to what is right in each new set of circumstances we shall be tormented by perpetual anxiety. Jesus' answer is 'Stop worrying! Simply do as love and compassion dictate.' He takes for granted that like the Good Samaritan we shall also show practical commonsense. Proper love and compassion will always assess the likely consequences of what they do for the one they are trying to help. But, that much granted, we are simply to do our best, without discriminating as to whether the other person is worthy or unworthy, friend or foe.

This story also highlights another key feature in Jesus' teaching. What he commends is intended for universal application. He talks about the way people are to behave to one another as people. This applies whether those concerned are Jews or Samaritans, rulers or their subjects,[130] religious professionals or lay people. Hospitality is to be shown not just to those who can return it but to anyone who can enjoy it.[131] Love is not simply for members of your own group or those who have proved themselves your friends, but for torturers and persecutors and all who do you harm.[132] The whole cast and thrust of his teaching was inclusive. His own practice was to embrace the outcast;[133] his sternest condemnations were for those who by behaviour or regulation kept others out.[134] The lost, as he sees it, are those who exclude themselves.[135]

This universalising principle, however, is not, in Jesus' teaching, a way of discovering moral laws. He was not an Immanuel Kant before his time, arguing that whatever imperative could be universally applied would be morally binding. He took certain key attitudes, values, principles, either direct from Scripture or developed out of Scripture by his own observation and reflection, and insisted that these were to be applied in all relationships, and not qualified according to circumstances.

In all this there is a sword that divides. Almost all would agree that there are principles which, if everyone put them into practice, would make the world a better place. But from that common ground run two diverging lines of thought. The first, upheld by the great majority, argues that, because there are always those who will not act on these principles, life cannot be regulated by such notions. 'Do as you would be done by' must yield to 'Be done by as you did'; and so the ideas in question are never put to the test.

The other line insists that those who grasp how essential these principles are to any hope of a good life for the whole world must shape their own lives by them, however small a minority they may be. If they do not, they are betraying not only their own integrity but also all those fellow creatures, human and other, who need the principles in question to prevail. On this view the full potential for good in any situation can never be realised by stepping outside what is good. It is not a question of whether 'the end justifies the means' but of grasping that in some degree flawed means always result in a flawed end. The one who is single-heartedly good will not, therefore, wait for everyone else to see things in the right way. Unless those who can see the good are prepared to practise it, alone if necessary, it will never gain even a toehold in the world's life.

This latter path was the one Jesus steadfastly set his face to follow, and he called on his closest associates to do the same. He was under no illusions as to the cost. It meant 'taking up the cross' or, in modern terms, carrying the post to which we are to be tied in front of a firing squad, or a rope for our own gallows.[136] Luke expands the image to make it in some degree the disciple's daily experience.[137] To live by the spirit of God, to live the life of the kingdom with Jesus as our mentor, is to go open-eyed into a life of repeated suffering; but not to embrace that suffering is to reject the possibility of true fullness of life altogether.[138] With such a message no wonder that Jesus was certain that committed followers would never be more than a few.[139] His vision of how to be human – truthful,[140] non-violent,[141] non-acquisitive,[142] totally sharing and caring[143] – has always inspired some adherents, never many, and certainly never all who profess to be Christians. By the majority in every century, focused only too understandably on security and quality of life for themselves and those closest to them, it has been discounted for its imprudence and impracticality. The thought that if humankind were universally to adopt it security and true quality of life could be assured for all, does not impress them. The wisdom of this world is clear that this is not going to happen. But what if Jesus' vision were 'the foolishness of God'?[144]

It was this sense that human life in Israel was facing the wrong way, prepossessed with the wrong things, and that this could lead only to disaster in this world and exclusion from the next, which gave Jesus' mission its sense of extreme urgency.

He and his friends are young men in a life-or-death hurry. Mark tries to catch this in the opening sections of his gospel by the repeated use of a simple stylistic device: 'at once' Jesus did this, 'at once' they did that.[145] When they go out on mission journeys, there is no time to stay and win round those who will not respond to the message; they must move on,[146] reach as many as possible. Much of the harshness and starkness of the gospel utterances needs to be understood in this context. Some of the bitterest suffering in serving the cause of the kingdom came from the refusal of neighbours and friends, members like them of God's chosen people, to try to understand.[147] It was not just the Galilean towns[148] but Jerusalem itself which, on its day of days, failed to discern the things that belonged to its peace, and left Jesus nothing more to give but tears.[149]

The gospels as evidence for the life of Jesus: (3) his spirituality

Inexorably now, we are drawn to the pivotal feature of the account of Jesus in the gospels, acknowledged as such even by those whose assessments of him differ widely in other respects, that his whole life was dominated and directed by the relationship with God which he believed to be his. What can be said about that? In one way it is absurd even to try to talk about someone's inner spiritual life when the traditions about him contain so little that even purports to be his personal testimony on the subject. But we can at least look at what has been recorded of Jesus' own beliefs about God and of his own teaching and practice in the area of prayer and worship.

The obvious point at which to start is Jesus' use of the term *abba*.[150] One of the few Aramaic words preserved in the New Testament, it is there rendered by the Greek for 'father', and this has remained the standard translation in other languages. It must surely be one of the most authentic memories of Jesus,[151] evidenced by its use almost as a mantra by the Greek-speaking Church. For St Paul, one proof of our being brothers and sisters of Jesus by adoption was that, when moved in worship by the

Holy Spirit, Greek Christians would cry out *abba*, just as Jesus had done.[152] It was also the word handed down in the tradition to express the intimacy of Jesus' wrestling with God in Gethsemane, the power of the plea that had to be refused.[153]

Some oversimplification surrounds *abba* in much popular preaching today. It cannot be equated simply with a child's use of 'Daddy'. Though the word certainly was used by children, so it was used also by grown-up sons and daughters. It has to be understood in terms of the culture, where intimacy and affection were combined with reverence and respect toward the father as head of the household. It could also be used as a noun, as in the delightful story of Hanan, the Galilean holy man. During a drought he was mobbed by children crying '*abba, abba*, give us rain!' In reply he prayed, 'Lord of the universe, render a service to those who cannot distinguish between the *abba* who gives rain and the *abba* who does not'.[154] We glimpse here a world of faith near to the time of Jesus, where *abba* could be used of any venerable human father-figure and also of God himself, though in the story the holy man does not actually address God as *abba* in his prayer.

It may not be pressing things too far to draw from this trait of Jesus' relationship with God two significant inferences. First, the combination of the reverence we would expect with the intimate affection we might not have expected; and secondly, the sense of being one of a family. Even if, on Jesus' lips, the word does express a sense of special closeness to God, he was also ready to teach his friends to use it too. Not only in the two versions of the Lord's Prayer but more widely Jesus is said to have encouraged them to approach God with this disposition and this language.[155] This was the right relationship for all human beings to God; and he himself was one among many potential brothers and sisters.

This inference is supported by a saying of Jesus in Matthew's gospel which now appears as the middle member of a threesome of injunctions about titles not to be used in the community of disciples: 'And call no one your father on earth, for you have one Father – the one in heaven'.[156] This connects with other sayings, in which Jesus stresses the need for his cadre of close followers to break the ordinary ties of human family. But it also calls for the earthly family relationship to be replaced by a family centred on God: 'Whoever does the will of God is my brother and sister and mother'.[157] There must have been a spirituality undergirding such demands; and Jesus' relationship with the Father in prayer will not have been a solo mysticism. He was always conscious of those, women and men, who had left all to follow him in the cause of the kingdom.[158]

This teaching, however, needs to be seen within a wider context. One fact about Judaism which those whose spirituality is shaped by the concepts of 'church' and 'religion' too easily forget is that it is concerned with every department of human life. There is nothing which falls outside God's ordering; every-thing is an opportunity to show him love and faithfulness by obedience to his will. In principle Judaism does not have any-thing corresponding to a church in the sense of an organisation, distinct from the community as a whole, which provides the means to fulfil the religious aspect of one's life. Today, sadly, the synagogue may come to fulfil this role, where secularism has eaten into the community; but ideally and scripturally the whole people of Israel constitutes the religious congregation. To be a Jew is also to worship and serve the God who is 'King of the Universe'. Love for God, in response to God's faithful commitment of love toward his whole people, is meant to be the overarching dimension of every Jew's existence.[159]

This basic orientation Jesus shared with every other Jew of his day. His mission was to all Israel, to every school of thought, every social category.[160] The essentials for a right relationship with God were accessible to every person within the scope of everyday life. Jesus did not enlarge his mission strategy to preach to non-Jews – partly, it seems, because the time might be too short even to reach all those Jews living in Israel[161] – but there are also traces in the tradition, treasured by the later Gentile Church, that like other Jews of his day he did not limit God's kingdom to Israel alone.[162]

The centrality for Jesus of this theme of the kingdom of God places him on the spectrum of Judaism within the band characterised by prophetic inspiration and concern about God's final consummation of history – what technically would be called the 'charismatic-prophetic' and the 'eschatological-apocalyptic' emphases. Mark's comment that after Jesus' baptism by John the Spirit of God 'immediately drove him out into the wilderness'[163] is but one of a number of traditions classing Jesus with those who experience direct and powerful guidance from God, amounting at times almost to a sense of an external and irresistible compulsion. The story in Luke of his staying behind as a boy in the Temple,[164] whether factually true or only aptly invented, is one example. In John there is mention of a sudden, unexpected change of course on Jesus' part when he tells his brothers that he is not going to Jerusalem and then decides to go, almost as if he had just received new instructions.[165]

These three elements – a relationship of reverential intimacy with God, open to all; a concern with ordinary human life; and a commitment to and expectation of the coming of the kingdom – converge in 'the Lord's Prayer'.[166] Recorded in somewhat differing forms in Matthew and Luke, it is presented as a model or pattern for all praying, in one to the crowds, in the other to the circle of disciples.[167] The two versions almost certainly come to us from a common original in which Jesus' words had already been translated into Greek,[168] but both render back successfully into the Aramaic he used.

Whichever form is the earlier, the basic contents of both are something like this:

> *abba,*
> may your holiness be confessed,[169]
> your kingdom come.
> Give us today
> our food for the coming day;
> and release us from our debts,
> as we release our debtors.[170]
> Do not put us to the test,
> [but rescue us from evil.][171]

The axis of the whole prayer is the kingdom. The first half is a reiterated appeal for the kingdom to come. The petition for God's name to be hallowed or sanctified, when understood against its Old Testament background, asks that the nations shall acknowledge God's holiness because they will have seen it manifested and vindicated in events – in other words, that God's kingdom shall come and God's will be done.

The second half of the prayer is set firmly in that context. The first request, for the means of life for the next twenty-four hours, has two meanings, one obvious and one hidden. The obvious one is that, if we truly long for the coming of the kingdom, we shall live a day at a time, and will not pray for our needs to be met further ahead than that. To do so would be to encroach upon God's freedom to act as he knows best, an attitude incompatible with genuine devotion to his sovereignty. The hidden sense may well be that 'the coming day' is the day of the kingdom's dawning, and the food that of those who sit down to feast in God's new world – and may that come today! The second request is for forgiveness of sins, so as to be able to stand before God when the kingdom arrives, together with the recognition that we have no right to ask that forgiveness for ourselves if we refuse it to others. The third is a plea that the coming of the kingdom, accompanied by the final cosmic battle between good and evil, may not so crucify us that our faith fails, and we fall into the power of anti-God. All of these, however, are also clearly prayers everyone can make and needs to make every very ordinary day of their lives: food for today, forgiveness for our sins, and protection for our feeble faith.

Such a prayer has little to do with a portfolio of insurance policies, a double garage and a well-stocked freezer. It also has little to do with the maintenance of 'Christian civilisation' or the religion of social revolution. It is a prayer of the poor and powerless, including the authentically humble who know themselves to be poor[172] and fundamentally dependent on God for everything. No wonder that, when used in church or in private by those of us who are comfortably situated and, in human terms, secure, it can feel hollow and empty! We are not in a place, material or spiritual, where the prayer can come to life. But those who are in such a place find it of all prayers one most worth praying; and those who discover it to be so need in no sense be Christians, for there is not a specifically Christian word in it from beginning to end.

If this was the priority for prayer which Jesus gave his followers, then it will also have set the character of his own. But the pattern prayer cannot have been for him, any more than it can be for anyone, the whole content of dialogue with God or of searching for God's will or of communion with his holy love. In Jesus we have someone who regularly attended synagogue,[173] and thus regularly heard the Scriptures. He was literate,[174] and able to recite a passage from the scroll.[175] He went up to Jerusalem for the great festivals;[176] and his driving out of the Temple those who sold animals and birds for ritual slaughter[177] does not imply a rejection of sacrificial worship, such as we find among the Essenes, but only of the profiteering associated with it. The story of the Last Supper shows us Jesus presiding either at a Passover or at a fellowship meal of the kind familiar in rabbinic circles, and leading the prayers and thanksgivings.

One feature of Jesus' spirituality creates special difficulties for many of us today, and that is petition. The tradition contains some very strong statements of his on this subject. To ask is to receive, to seek is to find, to knock is to have the door opened.[178] Faith, if sufficiently strong, can do anything;[179] if two or three disciples agree on a request to God, it will be granted.[180] John has Jesus put the same point, if in rather different language: the Father will do anything that is asked in Jesus' name.[181]

It is true that these absolute assertions are in places qualified. The stories, for example, about knocking up your neighbour in the middle of the night, or about the widow and the unjust judge, may originally have meant that God may not respond at once either, and that you have to keep on at him – as Luke, indeed, at one point makes explicit.[182] In John's gospel, prayer 'in Jesus' name' presumably means only such prayers as Jesus himself might make or approve, or, as in one passage, prayer offered by those who keep Jesus' command to love one another.[183] But such minor qualifications do nothing to meet the real difficulty, namely that those who ask in faith do not always receive; and if that is so, was Jesus' spirituality built on an illusion?

A first step toward an answer is perhaps to be found in St John. Here Jesus comes across as someone who approaches God in prayer with enormous confidence: 'Father, I thank you for having heard me. I knew that you always hear me . . .'[184] But this is not a matter of Jesus' being sure that God will always do whatever he, Jesus, happens to want. Instead it is rooted in an intimacy with God which enables Jesus to think about any situation as God thinks. This obedient harmony with God's will is conveyed in sayings such as, 'the Son can do nothing on his own, but only what he sees the Father doing: for whatever the Father does, the Son does likewise,' or, 'The Father and I are one'.[185]

If what Jesus meant by petitionary prayer was this kind of sensitive co-operation with God, then this throws a new light on the story of the Garden of Gethsemane. For the first time we hear on Jesus' lips the words, 'yet, not what I want, but what you want'.[186] Perhaps the true interpretation is that Jesus really is unsure what the Father wants and therefore what he ought to be asking. His cry to be spared the appalling end that lies ahead is an anguished plea to be shown for certain which road he is meant to take. Once he has that answer, he can steady himself to set out along it.[187]

But this episode has to be seen in its place between two others. The first is the Last Supper where, from all accounts we have of it, Jesus was in no doubt that he must die on the morrow and that it was God's will that he should.[188] In Gethsemane, with arrest imminent and his friends asleep, that brave acceptance is shaken. Did it really have to be this way? Could not God devise another solution just as effective? His recovered resolution holds on through the hours of rejection, humiliation, injustice, interrogation and torture. But then – the second episode – the spiritual darkness returns blacker, more crushing than ever. What he had thought he understood, had indeed commended to others as the way of obedience, now has no meaning, no purpose at all: 'My God, my God, why have you forsaken me?'[189]

What Jesus taught about prayer is true and important, and a word will be said in Chapter 6 on applying it in our own lives. But it was not the whole story. His own experience had to complete that with a deeper lesson. In the struggle with evil there may come a time when we have no idea what purpose can be served by what is happening or how. Cry out as we may, there comes no answer. All we can do is endure in the faith that if we have trusted God and he seems to have abandoned us there must be a reason. 'My God, my God, why . . .' is the ultimate prayer.

The gospels as evidence for the life of Jesus: (4) his personal character

Christianity has always maintained that in Jesus we have some-one who, though authentically human, was sinless. How, on the evidence in the gospels, do we assess Jesus as a moral exemplar?

For the first disciples, as we noted earlier, the issue did not arise. God had raised Jesus from the dead and thus finally ratified his naming of Jesus as the beloved Son in whom he was well pleased[190] – and who would dare dispute God's verdict? Our own day tends to see the matter the other way round. As people have found the story of the Resurrection more remote and problematic, so they have turned to the record of Jesus' life to see whether that justifies the claims made for him as, for example, the revelation of God's character in human terms.

The outcome has been that since the Renaissance, and increasingly over the past hundred years, Jesus has been sub-jected to criticism on ethical grounds. Some extreme opponents have attacked him as the source of many features in our western culture which they regard as moral or psychological ills. Some-times a loathing of institutional Christianity, unhappily rooted perhaps in the critic's personal experience, or a condemnation of Christian history has been extended to cover Jesus himself as the one allegedly responsible. Mostly, however, because the Christian claim has been not just that Jesus was good but that he was perfect, critics have been content to accept him as a morally outstanding figure and teacher and to dispute only that he can be regarded as free from all faults and failings. This, for reasons which will become clear, is a much more elusive ques-tion on which to reach a verdict simply on the details of the tradition.

There are, however, three major difficulties in reaching a decision on this matter. The first is a built-in problem in the nature of the evidence itself. All study of the gospels has to reckon with the spin given to the material – even if in all good faith – by the gospel writers and, presumably, by the oral tradition before them. It is fair to assume that there will at least have been features in the historical Jesus which provided the starting points for the salient elements in the gospel portraits; but one cannot put unlimited weight on details of what Jesus is described as having said or done. If this applies to the positive ingredients in the story, it must also be valid for the negative ones, those, for instance, that cause us moral unease.

The difficulty is well illustrated by the issue of Jesus' denunciations of certain aspects of Judaism. As presented in John and Matthew particularly, these have been condemned as both intemperate and unfair. That Jesus did attack features of the religious life of his nation is something that cannot plausibly be written out of the script; and if he made such attacks, then everything else we know about him suggests that they will have been pungent and powerful. But did he say the actual words attributed to him in John or Matthew? Or have they been heightened by the perceptions and prejudices of Matthew and John themselves?

Both writers, it is clear, are deeply hostile to Judaism. The very use of the term 'the Jews' in John's gospel is unjust and an incitement to hatred. This tone may be linked with steadily worsening relations between John's congregations and the local synagogues. But more fundamentally John's whole retrospective understanding of what Jesus was claiming for himself, to which we shall shortly return,[191] has in his eyes made the refusal of many of his fellow Jews to believe in Jesus the ultimate rejection of light in favour of darkness.[192] Given this conviction on John's part, how are we to assess such passages as the following:

> [Jesus] said to them, 'You are from below, I am from above; you are of this world, I am not of this world. I told you that you would die in your sins, for you will die in your sins unless you believe that I am he.' They said to him,

'Who are you?' Jesus said to them, 'Why do I speak to you at all? . . .'[193]

Unquestionably John believed that these words – which strike many readers today, Christian as well as non-Christian, as arrogant, self-righteous and insulting – expressed the spiritual reality within the historical events. We can also accept that in the memories he was dictating to his disciples he was distilling the essence of actual exchanges. But the style he ascribes to Jesus throughout is so different from that reflected in the other gospels that it must be unsafe to base any judgment on his precise phrasing; and when we also bear in mind the attitude to Judaism from which he starts, caution must be redoubled.

As regards Matthew, we have already noted some sources of antagonism toward the parent faith.[194] When, therefore, Matthew alone, to take one example, attributes to the Jewish people at Jesus' arraignment before Pilate that terrible cry, 'His blood be on us and on our children!'[195] – words which have been used as the justification for more cruelty, and from Christians, than any other single nation has had to suffer in the history of the world – few scholars today would wager their reputations on the historical accuracy of that story. But if so, why should the passages in which Matthew puts attacks on Judaism into Jesus' mouth be taken as a precise record, when they are plainly inflated by comparison with Mark and Luke? The problem is that there is simply no way to decide. If the Jesus of the gospels is at various points presented as unfair to his opponents, this may nevertheless be unfair to Jesus. But the nature of the material, in this matter as in others, makes it impossible to be sure.

A second difficulty is created by our own culture. Liberal opinion in the west, both secular and in the Church, has become sensitive to the harm done by intemperate language, whether in one-to-one relationships, in politics or the workplace, in relations between races, religions and the sexes, or in home or community life. Legal sanctions are put in place to protect what we now see as rights in this area. This is becoming the conventional ideal, if not always the practice; and it has great merits. But one effect is that the more it is accepted, even if only as an ideal, the more damage actual verbal violence is likely to do. This is only one possible convention among many in managing human relationships, and it also has real limitations. It can lead to the hypocritical and unhealthy bottling up of criticism and grievance, disable people for independent thought and righteous anger, and abet a climate in which there are few generally accepted standards.

The contrast with biblical culture could hardly be more marked. What is perhaps truly significant about Jesus is that in comparison with the ancient prophets or even with religious writings closer to his own day he was relatively mild and restrained. The overall impression left by the gospels is that in controversy he preferred reasoned argument or questions that would make people think and awaken their consciences.[196] Moreover the tepid temperature of much religious commitment in our culture ill qualifies us to judge those who, like Jesus, rate the claims of God as absolute. Many, even then, must have hated him for taking away their sons and husbands and womenfolk for his work,[197] and for setting the demands of the kingdom above the pieties, so sacred to every Jew, of family life.[198] But does that mean he was wrong to do so, that God did not want that challenge to be thrown down?

Much is made by some of the one act of physical violence recorded of him, when he overturned the tables of the money changers in the Jerusalem Temple, and the counters from which birds were sold for sacrifice, and denounced the dealers for making what should have been a house of prayer into a bandits' den.[199] But there was real ground for protest: worshippers had to offer sacrifice, yet they were compelled first to change ordinary currency into Temple coinage at a disadvantageous rate, and then to use that official coinage to buy their animals from the Temple sellers. It was not at all the same thing as vending coffee in the cathedral cloisters, or postcards in the nave, at normal prices to people who don't have to buy if they don't want to. This was a racket, and the more offensive for being in a holy place. As for the actual form of the protest, it was no more drastic than that of the anti-nuclear protesters who cut perimeter fencing or bang a dent in an aircraft with nuclear strike capability; and, whatever the strictly legal status of those actions,

God forbid that we should brand those who perform them as sinners in his sight!

The third difficulty stems from the narrative style of the gospels themselves. Dependent as they largely are on stylised and simplified pieces of oral tradition, they offer very little by way of psychological observation. We are rarely given any clue as to the personal dynamics of each encounter. Thus, on the basis of the written text, Jesus' remarks to the woman of Syro-Phoenicia who asked him to cure her daughter[200] could be condemned as racist and religious bigotry. But the story can as easily be read as one of Jesus wryly sharing with her a dilemma he found agonising, and getting a shrewd and humorous answer for which he was genuinely grateful. How can anyone tell? A tone of voice or a twinkle in the eye have no place in the record.

A story may be quite reliable enough to give us the thrust of what was said and an outline of what was done, and yet give us little idea of what it would have been like to be there. One example is an incident which causes problems for quite a number of readers today, that of the Gadarene swine.[201] The story tells of a man who was possessed by a whole regiment of evil spirits. When Jesus began to exorcise them, they pleaded to be allowed to take over a herd of pigs feeding nearby, since otherwise they would have to return to the pit of hell, where properly they were not due till the day of judgement.[202] Jesus granted their request, whereupon the spirits left the man and entered the pigs. But not even so did they escape the pit, because the maddened herd stampeded into the Sea of Galilee and drowned, so that the demons were homeless after all.

To a modern sensibility this could all read as though Jesus could not have cared less about drowning two thousand pigs, not to mention the economic disaster to their owners – who, of course, were only Gentiles anyway! But have we any idea from this story what really happened? If, as is not uncommon in both gospel and modern exorcisms, the possessed person began shouting and protesting violently as the struggle between Jesus and the parasitic psychic entity intensified, that might have been enough to panic the pigs with the sad result described.

The rest might then be simply the attempt in the tradition to explain the event.

As regards Jesus and animals in general, some who are keenly concerned for animal welfare today find the gospels sadly lacking. The callous cruelty which daily inflicts pain, deprivation and distress on hundreds of millions of sentient creatures worldwide, chiefly in the food industry but also in other areas, has moved many (among whom I am proud to be included) to put our treatment of animals high on the ethical agenda. To these evils the Churches have historically contributed by their official teaching, and they still appear largely indifferent. Christians have therefore turned to Jesus for support on this issue, but find that the gospels have little to offer. The main reason for this is undoubtedly that the problem as we know it today did not exist. The Jews, as references in the gospels illustrate,[203] were in general humane in their treatment of animals, whose urgent needs overrode even the obligation to keep the Sabbath. Abstinence from meat, however, was a mark only of certain sects in Judaism and early Christianity,[204] and there is no good evidence that Jesus himself took this position. His stand in principle and practice against violence and cruelty in any form, however, does most certainly place him alongside the modern animal welfare movement as a whole.

Similar questions can be raised, in relation both to Jesus and to the New Testament in general, with regard to issues such as slavery and gender equality. Jesus refers frequently to slaves,[205] but nowhere has anything to say about slavery as an institution. In our society that would be an indisputable moral defect. But how is it to be rated in the ancient world, in Israel where slavery was more akin to bonded labour, and where there were rules for the automatic freeing of slaves at fixed intervals if the slaves themselves wished it? Was not Jesus anyway teaching and demonstrating an attitude to all human relations which, if lived out between owner and slave, would make the slave's technical position less significant in practice, as we see from Paul's letter to Philemon?[206]

The questions with regard to the status of women are more complex. In a society in which the wife could not divorce her husband but could very easily be divorced by him – and that, at least in the opinion of the laxer school of thought at the time, on utterly trivial grounds – Jesus' strict teaching against divorce was heavily loaded in favour of the woman. For as things were the divorced wife too often found herself socially degraded, kept on sufferance in her father's household or, if that resource was not available, reduced to cohabiting or prostitution.[207] Women seem to have recognised in Jesus someone who understood them and treated them with respect even when they were outcasts.[208] He went against rabbinic convention by conversing with them in the street[209] and, if they sought it, was willing for them to join the men in listening to his teaching.[210] Women, married and unmarried, travelled with his party on their mission journeys and not only looked after them but supported them financially.[211] If he did not send them out to preach and heal, that was because to have done so would have been a futile exercise in that society, ineffectual and misunderstood so far as the work was concerned, and dangerous for the women themselves. Nor did he include a woman or women among his closest disciples, again for obvious reasons. But Jesus' fundamental attitude to women was distinctive enough within his contemporary situation to send a message which today, after many centuries, is at last being rightly interpreted.

If we apply the simplest test, namely to rate Jesus' score against a checklist of actions generally agreed to be wrong, we have to say that nothing can be proved against him. No dishonesty, no sexual immorality, no murder, no corrupt practice. He was signally free from coveting his neighbour's goods. He paid his taxes and advised others to do the same.[212] When his followers seemed likely to breach the civil peace, he deflated the pressure.[213] He refused to resist those in authority.[214] So far as the Jewish Law is concerned, while there are instances of his disregarding for good reason those supplementary regulations designed to keep people at a safe distance from inadvertent breaches of the Law itself,[215] no one seems to have been able to hold actual Law-breaking against him. Even later on, when Jewish attitudes toward Christians had hardened and reference to Jesus was becoming almost taboo, the only charge laid is that he was a sorcerer – no doubt a dark view of his reputation as a miracle-worker.

In the light of all this it is only fair to ask what more could be expected of anyone. Ethically no one can do more than spell out basic principles, and act on them so far as the conditions of their time allow. If sometimes it seems that more is being asked of Jesus, that is because even the critics are assuming that if he was, as Christians claim, God incarnate, then somehow he ought to have anticipated all possible moral needs for all time – or at least taught what we today think ought to be done! But this is wholly to misunderstand what the doctrine of Incarnation is about. It is not about God demonstrating a timeless, ideal, individual existence, which would be an utter impossibility. It speaks of choosing a particular community and culture at a particular period in history, and living out the will of God for humankind in that environment and on those terms. It is taking history seriously, and so instructing us to do the same for our own historical situation.

Nevertheless the limitations of a particular age do not exempt us or anyone else from all moral criticism. The point comes up sharply when we look at Jesus' teaching about divine judgement and the fate of the wicked after death. In the light of his own teaching might we not have expected something other than what we find in the tradition?

Once again we have to take a critical look at the material, if we are to form a balanced judgement. One passage in particular, that known as the parable of the sheep and the goats, calls for attention, because it is the only one where 'everlasting' punishment is unmistakably decreed.[216]

Christians are not the only people who warm to this parable for its vivid and powerful commendation of practical charity as the quality in human life which we should most cherish, and which is dearest to the heart of God. But when it is quoted in this sense it is always taken as teaching universal charity toward any human being in need. Yet is this what is meant? The actual words are: 'Truly I tell you, just as you did it to one of the least of these my brothers, you did it to me'.[217] What is the reference of the phrase, 'my brothers'? It occurs only in the gospels, where it is defined in ethical terms: 'Whoever does the will of God is my brother and sister and mother'.[218] If we apply this to the parable, Salvation depends on doing good to those of holy life, an attitude alien to Jesus' own practice of friendship toward sinners. Other features also suggest that this passage, as we have it, cannot come from Jesus.[219]

Significantly, the fate of the wicked is a special preoccupation of Matthew, who of all the gospel writers gives by far the most attention to this topic. He puts into the mouth of Jesus many more references to hellfire than any of the others: in Mark and Luke it comes in only one passage each, in John not at all. Matthew alone speaks of 'everlasting' fire,[220] just as he alone has the image of sinners thrown into 'outer darkness, where there will be weeping and gnashing of teeth'.[221] John has neither fire nor darkness imagery, but has Jesus speak only of being 'lost' or 'destroyed'.[222] The balance of the evidence overall is that Jesus did indeed believe that souls could be cut off from God after death, and lose the joy of the kingdom, and that he warned his hearers of that danger with unambiguous severity. But the majority witness is that he did not teach eternal punishment.

By now two things should be clear. The first is that it is not possible to decide the issue of Jesus' moral perfection on the basis of the Gospel texts, not least because the record covers only a tiny percentage of his life, about most of which we know nothing at all.

Our survey, however, has not been fruitless. For the second fact to have emerged is that the material we do have significantly fails to provide any clear case where Jesus was morally at fault.

A further point needs to be made. Theologically, sin is defined as purposeful disobedience to the known will of God. Any verdict on Jesus' sinlessness in the strict sense of that term might appear out of the question, since no one can claim to know what the will of God was in each circumstance of Jesus' life. To rest one's case on such an argument would, however, be unfair in the extreme; and it has therefore been the purpose of this section to look at certain words and actions of Jesus that might seem to raise moral issues, and to assess them as best we can. So far as sin in the theological sense is concerned, two facts are decisive: first, that there is more than enough evidence in the tradition to show that to do the Father's will was the overriding purpose, hour by hour, of Jesus' whole existence;

and secondly, that in the Resurrection God surely declared that that purpose had been fulfilled.

But if this is so, how do we explain a rather different answer to our question which was there on the page all the time? Mark, Matthew and Luke all record the story[223] of the rich man who came to him and said, 'Good Teacher, what must I do to inherit eternal life?' And Jesus replies, 'Why do you call me good? No one is good but God alone.' Jesus, it would seem, did not claim perfection; why should we presume to claim it for him?[224]

The straightforward reply is that the more truly good any person is, the less they will think themselves good. This springs directly from the human condition. Even if their conscience is clear of any breach of the moral code, that will not entitle them in their own eyes to claim to be good, because they of all people will be aware of how much deeper a thing goodness is than just keeping the rules, however excellent.[225] Had Jesus accepted the rich man's sincerely meant homage, that would indeed have given us grounds to doubt his goodness.

The gospels as evidence for the life of Jesus: (5) his belief about himself

The story of the rich man brings us to another key issue. What did Jesus believe about himself and his mission?

In G. K. Chesterton's *The Everlasting Man* there is a passage which strikingly distils the full drama of the traditional idea on this subject. It ends with the following words:

> There is more of the wisdom that is one with surprise in any simple person, full of the sensitiveness of simplicity, who should expect the grass to wither and the birds to drop dead out of the air, when a strolling carpenter's apprentice said calmly and almost carelessly, like one look-ing over his shoulder: 'Before Abraham was, I am'.[226]

On this view Jesus not only *was* God, the Second Person of the Blessed and Undivided Trinity, he *knew* that he was God.

The reasons for rejecting this account of Jesus' self-awareness will be set out in the opening pages of the next chapter. Here we are concerned with what the gospels have to say which might bear on the subject. The Chesterton quotation is no bad starting point, because it appeals to one of the few reported sayings of Jesus which unequivocally supports the classic Christian view. John puts the absolute 'I AM' into Jesus' mouth on several occasions,[227] but nowhere is it more plainly meant to convey the 'I AM' of the divine name in the Old Testament than here.

First then, what clues do the gospels offer? So far as Matthew, Mark and Luke are concerned, there is no evidence at all to suggest that Jesus was conscious of being God. There are plenty of instances pointing to his sense of special intimacy with God as his Father, and of having been sent by him,[228] just as there are words in which God proclaims Jesus as his uniquely beloved Son.[229] If we read these through Christian doctrinal spectacles, then they can certainly be given that interpretation. But in no way do they demand it, any more than similar phrases in the Psalms (on which they are modelled)[230] imply that the Israelite kings were divine, or thought themselves to be so.

It is in St John's gospel alone that the issue arises, and even here indisputable examples are few. When Jesus says, 'I and the Father are one',[231] this may seem unequivocal, but what follows explains it in a less decisive sense: Jesus is the 'son of God' whom the Father has consecrated and sent into the world; his works show that the Father is 'in him', and he 'in the Father'. This falls short of a claim to be oneself divine, as do the words of Jesus in his prayer at the Last Supper: 'So now, Father, glorify me in your own presence with the glory that I had in your presence before the world existed'.[232] We are habituated to the orthodox interpretation of such words, and forget that they need imply no more for example, than an awareness of pre-existence, not deity, and were at times taken to mean that by non-orthodox theologians. Even the response to Philip's request 'Show us the Father', is ambiguous.[233] 'Whoever has seen me has seen the Father' seems categorical enough; but it cannot be a statement of identity, because Jesus' whole spirituality, in John as in the other gospels, is built round his relationship with the Father precisely as 'Father'. Hence once again Jesus explains what he has said with the formula, 'I am in the Father and the Father is in me.'

Except then for the 'Before Abraham was' saying, on which Chesterton acutely seized, there are no recorded words of Jesus which unequivocally confirm the traditional view that he was aware of himself as God. Moreover the fact that this saying and the few others that come closest to it occur only in St John's gospel itself creates a problem. John has his own distinctive view of Jesus' origin and being, as we shall shortly see. When, therefore, we find in John alone words of Jesus which could be taken to support this view, we need to read them against the background of John's whole method as a gospel writer. John was not indifferent to historical fact. The story he tells is recognisably the same story as that in the other three gospels, and where they disagree it is by no means certain that John is always the one who is wrong. But at the same time he has his own parallel agenda.

John is concerned to bring out the hidden truth which he saw as implicit in the words of the tradition. Minute analysis identifies in John hundreds of fragments reflecting the same material found in the other three gospels. But they have been rearranged, like the pieces of a tessellated pavement, and incorporated into an overall design of a markedly different character. One feature of the design, for instance, is the way Jesus makes religious statements about himself in the 'I am' form: 'I am the bread of life', 'I am the light of the world', 'I am the door', 'I am the good shepherd', 'I am the resurrection and the life', 'I am the way and the truth and the life', 'I am the true vine.' Such formulas have a background in hellenistic religion of the period, and are best understood as created to communicate the mystery of Christ. It is because they are so successful in doing this that they have become so precious to Christian believers down the centuries. But comparison with the other gospels affords overwhelming evidence that they are spiritual truths, not historical record.

If we accept, then, that Jesus was not conscious of being God, what clues do the gospels give us as to his understanding of himself and his mission? Are there, for example, particular titles or roles which he claimed for himself?

This has been the route normally explored by New Testament scholars. Thus at one time it was commonly held that Jesus had seen his vocation in the figure of the 'Suffering Servant' as portrayed in Isaiah 40–55. It may well be that certain verses from these prophecies helped to form Jesus' own spirituality. But there is nothing in Jesus' words as reported in the gospels to suggest that he was conscious of Isaiah's 'Servant' as a role model, nor indeed is there evidence anywhere that anyone at that time had read such a figure either into or out of the prophet's text. The 'Suffering Servant' is very much a product of a later way of reading the Bible. Two titles, however, have rightly called for attention as significant in the gospel record: the first is 'the Son of Man', the second, 'Messiah'.

The academic literature on the title *Son of Man* is immense and has seen the rise and fall of many theories. Fortunately there is by now agreement on certain basic conclusions. As a title the phrase is found only in the gospels and once in Acts.[234] At one time it was widely believed that the title was in use in the Judaism of Jesus' time to refer to a heavenly being who would come at the end of the world to administer God's judgement. The origins of this figure were traced to the book of Daniel, where 'one like a son of man' is received by God in heavenly audience, and given eternal sovereignty over all the nations.[235] Supporting evidence was seen in non-scriptural Jewish writings.

This whole edifice has now collapsed, and the true story is reconstructed roughly as follows. In the Aramaic that Jesus spoke, 'son of man' or 'the son of man' were phrases used to refer either to oneself or to oneself as a member of a category of people or to human beings in general. When the Church moved out to the Gentiles, and Jesus' sayings were translated into Greek, this idiom was rendered literally, and seemed to refer to a definite individual, meriting capital letters (as we would say) – that is, 'the Son of Man'. That the identification of Jesus with the figure in Daniel was being made in the Christian community is clear from the description of him in Revelation as 'one like a son of man'.[236] In the gospel tradition 'the son of man' was then taken to mean Daniel's coming judge, and sayings were adapted or elaborated on this basis. In short, Jesus never spoke of himself as the 'Son of Man'; he had never heard of it. It was a later Christian invention.[237]

The same cannot be said of the title *Messiah*, 'Anointed One'. The kings of ancient Israel were 'the anointed of Yahweh'. In the time of Jesus there were various expectations of one who should come to deliver the nation from foreign oppression and to set up God's ideal kingdom. 'Messiah' or 'the Messiah' was one title by which this saviour figure was commonly known. Did Jesus believe that he was called to be this promised Messiah?

That the gospel writers see Jesus as the Messiah is plain enough.[238] Moreover the fact that the epithet *christos*, 'anointed', the Greek translation of 'Messiah',[239] has throughout the New Testament become virtually an extra personal name alongside 'Jesus' suggests that considerable time has elapsed since it carried its original sense, and that therefore the proclamation of Jesus as Messiah by his followers was part of the Church's earliest preaching.

The crucial relevant incident in the gospel tradition is said to have occurred near Caesarea Philippi. Jesus asks his disciples what popular opinion is saying about him: who do people think he is? After hearing various speculations he asks them what they think, and Peter replies, 'You are the Messiah'.[240] The words that follow are significant. Usually they are rendered on the lines of 'he sternly ordered them not to tell anyone about him'. But the ordinary sense of the word used for what Jesus did is 'rebuke, reprove': 'he rebuked them so that they should talk to no one about him.' The difference in emphasis is slight, but it raises a doubt. Was Jesus saying, 'Yes, I am the Messiah, but don't tell anyone', or, 'Don't talk like that about me to anyone', meaning, 'I am not the Messiah'. Interestingly, Luke's version of the story, if anything, supports this second interpretation: 'He rebuked them, and ordered them not to say this to anyone.'

This reading of the passage might be further supported by the fact that Jesus goes on at once to 'teach them that the son of man' (that is, simply himself, not the supernatural judge from heaven) 'must undergo great suffering, and be rejected . . . and be killed'.[241] Again, this used to be read as Jesus' radical reappraisal of the Messiah's vocation, but it could equally well have been his attempt to get them to understand why he was not the Messiah. The violence of his rebuff to Peter – 'Get behind me, Satan!' – when Peter tried to stop him talking like that would certainly make sense if that had been his aim.

It was, of course, not the way Matthew and John understood him. In Matthew Peter is blessed, assured that God himself has revealed this to him, told that he is the rock on which Jesus will build his victorious Church, and given the power to grant or withhold admission to the kingdom.[242] The reference to the Church, found on Jesus' lips only here and in one other passage in Matthew (itself suspect for other reasons[243]) and never in the other gospels, does however make the authenticity of these verses highly doubtful.

In John, Andrew believes in Jesus as Messiah immediately after he has had his very first meeting with him,[244] and later in the gospel Martha professes the same faith.[245] Yet these incidents are almost secondary, for in this gospel alone Jesus personally declares himself to be the coming Messiah – but to a woman, and a Samaritan at that.[246] John makes clear that no one else was present at the meeting; and when the woman tells her fellow townsfolk about it, she does not say that Jesus has claimed to be the Messiah, but simply hazards that he may be on the basis of his clairvoyance about her private life.[247] Whatever the germs of historical fact in this story, it is hard not to see its present form as having an agenda from John's own later life: where the 'Jews' are unbelieving, the Samaritans whom they hate and despise are quick to find faith.[248]

The other major relevant episode is Jesus' trial before the High Priest. In Matthew, Mark and Luke Jesus is challenged to say whether or not he is 'the Messiah' (Luke) or 'the Messiah, the Son of God' (Matthew) or 'of the Blessed' (Mark). In Mark Jesus replies 'I am'; in Matthew the equivalent semitic idiom, 'You have said so'. But in Luke he refuses to give a direct answer: 'If I tell you, you will not believe; and if I question you, you will not answer'.[249]

There are differing versions of what Jesus said next. Matthew and Mark combine quotations from Psalm 110 ('you will see the Son of Man "seated at the right hand of power" ', i.e. of God) and from Daniel 7 ('and "coming with the clouds of heaven" '). This strongly recalls the early Church practice of seeking out Old Testament quotations foreshadowing faith in Jesus, and combining them to form 'testimonies'. The 'Son of Man' figure is also, as we have seen, a Church invention.

But is the allegation that Jesus claimed to be Messiah any better founded? That is indeed the basis for his condemnation for blasphemy in Matthew and Mark.[250] But Luke's variations are suggestive. He drops the Daniel quotation altogether, and has the Council rephrase their question in the form, 'Are you then *the Son of God*?' It is to this that Jesus replies affirmatively, 'You say that I am'.[251] This makes it all the more significant when we turn to John's gospel and find that nowhere in his story of Jesus' trials is Messiahship mentioned.[252] On the contrary John has the Jewish leaders say to Pilate, 'We have a law, and according to that law he ought to die, because he has claimed to be *the Son of God*'.[253]

The accounts of Jesus's 'trials' or interrogations are certainly shaped in some degree by the demands of Christian propaganda; the Jews reject their Messiah even when he declares himself. But behind them it is possible to detect how the divergent accounts of Matthew and Mark on the one hand, and Luke and John on the other, might have arisen. Jesus could not in conscience give an unequivocal 'Yes' to the question, 'Are you the Messiah?' But equally he could say nothing but 'Yes' to the question, 'Are you the Son of God?' To the Council and to Matthew and Mark 'Son of God', as an honorific of the ancient kings of Israel and thus applicable to the future messianic ruler, was equivalent to 'Messiah'; so Jesus must have meant 'Yes' to that as well. Luke and John, using (even if for theological reasons) a more precise oral tradition, avoid equating the two.

Outside the Caesarea Philippi passages and the accounts of the trial there is little to support the view that Jesus thought of himself as the Messiah. In each of the first three gospels there is a story of Jesus scoring off the scribes by 'proving' from Scripture that the Messiah is not to be descended from King David,[254] an incident that suggests a certain personal detachment from the question, and sits uncomfortably alongside Matthew's and Luke's genealogies claiming that Jesus was of David's line.[255] John's gospel tells of popular arguments about whether Jesus could really be the Messiah, when none of the supposed marks of the Messiah were true of him.[256]

To sum up: whatever the Church came to believe, the evidence that Jesus thought he was the Messiah and claimed to be such is neither extensive nor of particularly good quality. But investigating it does bring out one feature which has not been given as much attention as it deserves. From what has been said earlier it will be remembered that the central axis of Jesus' spirituality was his sense of an intimate relationship with God, characterised specifically by his use of the word, *abba*. After pondering the matter for many years, it does seem to me that this is the one concept which we can be sure was decisive for Jesus' understanding of himself. As 'a son of man' or 'this son of man' he spoke of no more than his identity as a fellow human being. But when calling God *abba*, and claiming from experience the right to encourage others to do the same, he was speaking out of a personal relationship which carried with it a controlling vocation, unique to himself and to that time and place, unique in its urgency for his whole nation and even for some outside it.[257] So far as this situation could be expressed in words, to think of God as *abba* demanded that he understand himself as God's 'son'; and this inevitably, since 'Son of God' was a messianic title, raised not just for others but for him the question, 'Am I then the Messiah?'

I would dare to suggest that for Jesus this was an unresolved issue, and that this explains his odd, even angry response to Peter in the earliest and best gospel tradition, and his refusal to allow his disciples to talk about this to others. All that he knew he could be sure about was the relationship of father to son, son to father; and that, as he became more and more aware, brought with it a vocation to rejection, suffering and death which it was hard to reconcile with the traditional picture of the Messiah.

The interpretation of Jesus in the New Testament Church

For the earliest Church, however, exulting in the Resurrection, Jesus' status, mission and role were no longer a mystery in the sense of an enigma, to be handled with caution and reticence. He was a mystery in the technical religious sense of the time, namely a secret which had been hidden in the heart of God from before the beginning, and had now been made known to and through God's chosen people.[258]

The first and most obvious revelation was that Jesus was the Messiah that Israel had expected but failed to recognise: 'Therefore let the house of Israel know with certainty that God has made him both Lord and Messiah, this Jesus whom you crucified'.[259] Of the figure of the heavenly 'Son of Man' no more need be said than to note that linked with it is belief in Jesus as the one who would return at the end of time to judge the world on God's behalf.

What in the light of later developments are most significant, however, are the remarkable efforts to link Jesus with God, not just as God's human agent or servant but at the level of his nature and being. They are remarkable because so un-expected in a religious movement which not only sprang out of Judaism but was for a whole generation still enmeshed with it. Judaism stood out from the surrounding faiths by its ardent and uncompromising monotheism: there is one God only, and God is one. It stressed also the immeasur-able gulf between God and every creature. God in himself can be compared to nothing else, and is beyond human understanding.

The chasm to be crossed between that position and the more advanced New Testament statements about Jesus seems inexplicably wide. The solution most often proposed, especially by opponents of Christianity, has been to blame St Paul. He is supposed to have taken a simple Jewish faith, in which Jesus was a prophet or teacher, and by his Christ-mysticism transformed it into a cult with a divine saviour-hero, typical of several in the Mediterranean world of that time. But this account will not stand up. Not only is St Paul insistent on his loyalty to the faith of his forebears and his own Jewish identity,[260] but his authentic writings, whether in content or style or ways of thought, are essentially Judaistic.[261] More decisive still, the only passage in the authentic letters of Paul which presents Jesus as divine in nature is now agreed to be a quotation from an earlier Christian hymn.[262] Finally, of the other three key statements in the New Testament on this matter none is from Paul's own hand.[263] But if not from Paul, then whence?

To understand how such a development might arise within a Jewish religious culture we need to recognise an important note in the spirituality of Judaism in the last centuries before the Christian era. As noted above, a distinguishing mark of Judaism was its uncompromising monotheism and its insistence on the incomparable power and holiness of God and his unsearchable wisdom: 'For as the heavens are higher than the earth, so are my ways higher than your ways and my thoughts than your thoughts'.[264] But in harness with this overwhelming sense of awe and unworthiness in the presence of God was an equally strong consciousness of need for God. How could limited and sinful human beings ever live as God intended without God's own inward help: 'Who has learned your counsel, unless you have given wisdom and sent your holy spirit from on high?' Or again: 'Create in me a clean heart, O God, and put a new and right spirit within me.'[265]

During this period, therefore, believers came to develop a number of older ideas in new ways, to express their awareness of contact with God and of the help they needed and received from him. The concepts of God's spirit, for example, or of the angels that were his messengers had been part of Jewish religion for centuries, but now they began to take on a more general daily role in the spirituality of the devout.[266] The Law was seen not as an impersonal code of regulations but as God's chosen means of imparting fullness of life.[267]

Of special importance for our present concern is the figure of the divine Wisdom. This came to be thought of, in certain circles at least, as not just an abstract attribute of God but in personal terms. The imagery is of a woman, an associate of

God in the creation itself, joyfully concerned for humankind and ready to inspire and guide any soul that will love her faithfully.[268] But, though presented as more than simply an aspect of God's own being, this figure never quite achieves independent reality. This ambiguity is not due solely to the power of Jewish monotheism; it also reflects the logic of the particular religious crisis. The human soul is trapped by a dilemma: it cannot be in direct touch with God and live,[269] yet nothing less than that direct intimacy with God can meet its need. Hence the Wisdom that comes to dwell in the soul must be divine, yet it cannot be God in person.[270]

The influence of this Wisdom concept on early Christian thinking about the mystery of Jesus has been increasingly recognised in recent years. It goes far to provide an explanation for one amazing leap of faith. From being the Man of Nazareth who was crucified and then raised from the dead Jesus was, in one generation, hailed as the Father's agent in creating the universe and in the continuing work of holding it in existence: 'for in him all things in heaven and on earth were created, things visible and invisible . . . all things have been created through him and for him. He himself is before all things, and in him all things hold together'.[271] It is significant, therefore, that in the opening section of the Letter to the Hebrews, where Jesus has the same cosmic role in the creation, imagery is applied to him which is very close to that used about divine Wisdom in the book known as the Wisdom of Solomon.[272]

A more general affinity to Wisdom thinking is to be found in the early Christian hymn quoted by St Paul in his Letter to the Philippians. Here Jesus is described as one who was by nature divine but 'emptied himself' to share the human condition, even including death.[273] Though there is here no direct borrowing from Wisdom texts, the spiritual function performed is in essence the same: the gulf between humanity and God is bridged; the divine comes to meet human need in a form humankind can bear. The Godward end of the bridge is categorically affirmed again in the Letter to the Colossians – 'for in him the whole fullness of deity dwells bodily'[274] – in a passage which goes on to spell out how Jesus rescued sinful humanity by identifying with it.[275]

The clearest and most emphatic of all these statements is the prologue to St John's gospel.[276] Here is revealed the heavenly background to the earthly story which is to follow. John speaks not of God's Wisdom but of his 'Word', which is both the *logos* of Greek philosophy, embracing reason and communication in one concept, and also the creative, active divine Word of the Old Testament.[277] This Word, like Wisdom, is 'with God in the beginning', and through it 'all things come into being'. The Word comes into the world bringing the true light, the light that constitutes the rational soul in every human person. Even so, most of humankind, even God's people Israel, cannot recognise him. The only ones who receive the fullness of life that all need are those who discern the divine glory in the 'flesh', the human reality which the Word has 'become'. That human reality is Jesus, from whose 'fullness' of divinity all may receive the grace and truth they need. The God whom no one has ever seen or can see is made known by the Son, who alone can of right call God 'Father', but who opens up to every soul the chance to become in truth a child of God.

That this essential agreement should have emerged from several very different circles within the scattered Christian fellowship so soon[278] after the end of Jesus' earthly life is quite astonishing. We have noted one factor in the religious situation which may have helped them to interpret him in this way. But that needed material to work on, and there was nothing in his life to demand that interpretation. His story was an authentically human story, and in some ways an insignificant story. He did not move along the axis of world power. His nation was small and largely despised. His closest colleagues were young working men from a second-rate provincial backwater. Though to some he died a martyr, to others he was at best a foolish activist, at worst a blasphemous and dangerous demagogue. So we come back to the point where this long chapter began: the Resurrection. It is that and that alone which, by singling out Jesus with the finger of God puts the question to which the New Testament sketches out the first draft of the eventual astonishing answer. In the next chapter we must see where the Church went with that answer, and where tragically it failed to go.[279]

4

The buried talent

Herein is the greatest of God's gifts, that all may
call God their Father, and Christ their Brother.
St Leo the Great

One like the Good Samaritan
and somewhat like Piers Plowman
Came barefoot, bootless
without spur or spear . . .
'This Jesus of his nobility
for love hath undertaken
Not to be known as perfect God
but in Piers Plowman's arms to joust'
Langland, Piers Plowman, 'The harrowing of hell'

One truth about God is unique to Christianity, and of unique
importance to the world. Yet it is a truth which has never been
fully grasped nor lived and proclaimed as it deserves.

That truth is the doctrine of the Incarnation, the formal
theological definition of the way in which the various New
Testament insights into the mystery of Jesus, described at the
close of the previous chapter, were to be reconciled and understood. That there should have been difficulty in agreeing with
precision on the heart of imagery so rich and diverse is hardly
to be wondered at. Once pre-eminent authority had been
granted to the writings which came to make up the canon of
Christian Scripture, the implications of these now sacred formulas were bound to be read differently by different schools of
thought. Nor does the history of the disputes do credit to the
charity of those concerned, whatever it may say about their
intellect. Treachery, persecution and violence abounded, and
in the end the victory of the ultimate orthodoxy was secured

as much by the political backing its adherents were able to attract as by its own persuasive force. Nevertheless, in spite of all, the answer eventually arrived at was (or so it will be argued here) the right one.

What was that answer? It is not one that can be expressed simply as a statement about Jesus in isolation. It requires a special concept of God as its setting, the doctrine of the Trinity. That doctrine and the one concerning Jesus developed in mutual dependence. Without question, however, this development was Jesus-driven: that is, it was the conviction that certain things had to be said about Jesus, yet within the terms of the biblical monotheistic faith, which generated the model of God as truly one yet existing in three distinguishable persons, in each of whom nevertheless the fullness of God is wholly present. More will be said about this doctrine in the final chapter. For the moment let it suffice to keep it in mind as the philosophical background to what has been the classic Christian belief about Jesus.

What is the content of this belief? Basically, that the subject of the historical experiences of Jesus of Nazareth, from conception to death and beyond, was the Second Person of God the Holy Trinity, the one whom, in the light of Jesus' relationship with God as *abba*, 'Father', we refer to as the 'Son'. In the words of the Nicene Creed[1] (literally translated) the Son, who is 'God from God, light from light, true God from true God . . . was made flesh from holy Spirit and Mary the virgin and became enhumaned' or 'entered into human existence'. The eternal Son enters not just into a body but into a complete human nature with all the spiritual, mental and emotional characteristics that go with that.

The formularies of the universal Church[2] go to some lengths to stress that the personal identity of Jesus is that of the divine Son. Jesus is a single unified person, just as we are, not a human and a divine person inside the same skin. Nor is he a unique hybrid being, nor is either his humanity or his divinity suppressed by being absorbed into the other, nor is a new person created at his conception. There is only one person involved, the Second Person of the Trinity. It was that person and no other who walked in Galilee.

But he did so as an authentic human being. In more everyday terms we can express this by saying, for example, that 'God became one of us', or 'God shared our human life', or 'in Jesus God experienced what it was to be truly human'. The claim is not merely that Jesus was an ordinary human being who in his life showed us fully and faithfully what God is like, a man wholly inspired and controlled by God's own character. He was God in person, living an ordinary human life as it should be lived. It is in this that the distinctiveness of the Christian belief resides, when it is compared with ideas of divine incarnation found in other faiths. Not only does this Incarnation refer to an identifiable human being, known to have lived at a particular time and in a particular place, but also the Christian belief does not envisage the spirit of God taking over a human being as the medium of its presence, say, or the deity merely showing itself in human guise.

The very fact that not dissimilar ideas are around, however, suggests that brief definitions, however careful, are not enough. If it is to be unambiguously clear what is meant, they need to be fleshed out by examples in answer to certain questions.

For instance, when we say things like, 'God shared our human experience', what kind of situation do we have in mind? The point can be simply illustrated by reference to F. Anstey's humorous Victorian novel, *Vice Versa*. For those whose pleasures in reading matter are less dated let it be said that the plot concerns a small boy who is enabled to change places with his father. Bultitude *père* finds himself physically a replica of his son, and is packed off to endure all the horrors of life at the son's ghastly boarding school, while Bultitude *fils* looks just like Dad, and goes off to the City and the club. Is that kind of transformation our mental picture of God incarnate? Does the doctrine mean that God, like the elder Bultitude, descends to a lowlier form of life but is conscious all the time of being from a different world, and endowed with very different powers and feelings from all those around him? If so, then God may have shared our situation, but he certainly did not share our experiences, any more than Mr Bultitude, though precisely in his son's usual circumstances, shared his. Experience depends not just on what happens to us but on what sort of person or being we are.

Thinking in terms of mainstream Christian belief about the Incarnation, there are two possible views about Jesus' personal experience. The first is that he could have endured all the events of human life but felt them, understood them and responded to them from the standpoint of God. One immediate objection to such a view might argue that it would be impossible for immortal God to endure human death, but that is not necessarily a difficulty. It is so only if we make particular assumptions about what happens when we die, but of course we do not actually know what does happen. If, for example, there is some spiritual aspect of a human being which still lives after bodily death, then there is no reason why immortal God, if living as a human personality, should not have essentially the same experience as ourselves when the physical body dies.

The real trouble with such a view is that on those terms God's experience while living would be quite different from ours. Someone conscious of being God would approach death, for instance, with the knowledge that it was only a temporary passing experience and with an awareness of what waited beyond it. That is one thing we cannot do. *We* do not know for certain, even if we have a religious faith in resurrection or immortality, whether or not death is final, or what, if it is not, lies beyond. If Jesus were conscious of being divine, then he certainly could not, in the words of the Letter to the Hebrews, 'taste death for everyone'.[3]

But the alternative view also has its difficulties. To be someone is to be a particular someone, with particular endowments. If God the Son were not aware of his own essential being, in what sense would he as himself be experiencing anything? This objection has considerable force and raises a fundamental issue for all belief in God: in what sense, if any, are we right to talk as glibly as we do about God as 'personal'? The word in its modern usage certainly has little in common with technical theological talk about the 'Persons' of the Trinity. This is a matter which will have to wait until we have considered some other topics; but we shall return to it in the final chapter, when we ask what we can hope to say about God as God.

Yet from another angle it may be possible to say something useful, even at this stage, about what it might mean for God to shed awareness of his divine identity, but still to continue to 'be himself' in some genuine sense. All one can do is offer an analogy; but that is, after all, one classic way of trying to throw light on the nature and workings of God.

Let us imagine a human person in some such situation as the following. As a result of an accident he is partially paralysed, and his mental faculties are somewhat impaired. He still has his senses – sight, hearing, smell, touch and taste – but speech and motor activities such as writing are difficult. In addition he has suffered total amnesia. All this has happened to him in a foreign country, where the flora and fauna and scenery are unfamiliar, the culture is radically different from his own, and the language is completely unknown to him. He has no access to nor means of communication with anyone who knew him before. Something on these lines would be about as drastic a change as it is possible to imagine within the terms of one human life, short of events that would actually destroy the personality, such as major psychotic illness. If the person concerned managed to survive at all in conditions of such psychological deprivation, the way he did so would still be determined in part by the kind of person he had been before, his essential self. The new life would be lived by him, not by someone else.

The point of such an analogy is not to suggest that for God a human existence would be one of such dire cruelty as this illustration implies. Its purpose is simply to help us imagine a little more clearly what would be needed for any being to live as itself in a form of life radically more restricted than its own. In essence what is required is that there must be scope for the same kind of relationship to other beings as had held good before the change. Thus, if there had been something we would call understanding (that is to say, rational and sympathetic insight into the nature and interrelationships of things), or something akin to value (the ability to think in terms of good and evil, of beneficial and harmful, and to desire and pursue the one rather than the other), or something of what we mean by love, then the new life too must offer scope for understanding, value and love. Otherwise the being concerned could not in any meaningful sense continue to be itself. A man or woman could not, so far as we can tell, be himself or herself as an ant.

In the case of God, therefore, if he is, as has been believed, a moral being, then he could not be himself as a creature incapable of reflecting on good and evil. If he is wise, he could not be himself as a creature incapable of interpreting experience in terms of thought. If he is loving, he could not be himself in a form of life incapable of attaching value to other beings for their own sake, or of caring about their welfare, or of allowing them freedom to be themselves. What is more, logic will require that as he enters the new form of life the transferable qualities must be the ones that are essential to the distinctive divine selfhood, the attributes that define his character.

There are here some interesting implications for the picture of God. If God can become authentically incarnate as a human being, then such aspects of the divine as power over the cosmos or infallible knowledge of all creation and its history are not essential to the definition of his character. They may be facts, but they are not the heart of what it means for God to 'be himself'. The divine Son can still be the Son with no memory of his former glory[4] – indeed, to be truly human he must not remember it. Neither that nor many other realities need to be in his consciousness for him to be able to engage in what is still a genuinely divine relationship with other beings. Belief in the doctrine of the Incarnation demands that we invest that doctrine with ultimate control over our picture of God's moral personality. Jesus is 'the image of the invisible God', and it is in his face that we see 'the light of the knowledge of the glory of God'.[5]

Why accept this interpretation of Jesus rather than some other?

The ultimate reason for accepting the classic doctrine of Christianity concerning Jesus is that, if we are to have faith in God at all, then this is the only version of God on offer which is morally believable or even tolerable. The justification for saying this is the same as that which led Christians from the convergent and approximate insights of the New Testament to the absolute declarations of the Creeds; and that is the crucifixion.

The Christian message is about someone who is God's uniquely accredited agent of truth and love, holiness and deliverance in the world – and he ends up on a cross. It is hard to think how God could have made his point more plainly. Jesus even cries out before he dies, 'My God, my God, why have you abandoned me?' For he was indeed on his own. God had not nailed him there, and God was not going to come to take him down. Jesus had gone to the cross, which he could have escaped, because he, he himself, believed that this was what serving God demanded of him; and God had taken him at his word. God gave him no sign, no consolation to say, 'Well done! That is what I wanted.' He had left him to stand by his own convictions right to the last.[6]

Paradoxically, it is this reading of the story which is vindicated by the resurrection of Jesus. Because only Jesus is known to us to have been raised from the dead, and raised in that particular and significant way, our own resurrection and eternal fullness of life are not its central message. It does indeed give us strong and reasonable grounds to hope for these things, but only if we take into our own earthly living what first and foremost it is about. What the Resurrection proclaims[7] is the vindication of the Crucified, the one who did the will of God perfectly by doing it in God-forsakenness, and who thereby established love and holiness in God-forsakenness as the state of being closest to the heart of God.[8] This is what it means to fulfil the will of God in a flawed and random universe. God has said to us, 'I will not be the world's puppet-master on your behalf. My will is that you should find your way to the goodness and truth, the courage and sacrificial love which are eternal, by accepting the nature of the universe in which I have placed you, and by staking your life on these things for their own sake. But I have given you a sign that this is my will in the Forsaken One whom I raised from the dead.'

But in this very moment of illumination the Cross points beyond itself by forcing on us a question which will not be denied: if all this is so, then is not Jesus better than God? Is not the one who has endured God-forsakenness rather than abandon the way of love that God requires more admirable than the One who endorses him, but does so from within the eternal security and blessedness of being God? Such a question arises only because of the Resurrection, but the Resurrection makes it unavoidable. If God has so put his seal on Jesus alone out of all the world, God cannot stop us drawing the inescapable contrast between Jesus and himself. If that contrast is not justified, then why? Is there something here which actually raises God to Jesus' level? Where is God in the Jesus story?

This significance of the Cross, which is indeed truly 'crucial' for faith's understanding of Jesus, is already plainly so in at least three of the four New Testament texts (considered at the end of the previous chapter), in which Jesus is linked to the very being of God.

In the early Christian hymn quoted by Paul in Philippians the whole and sole point of Jesus' emptying himself of divinity, and being born into the human race, is to submit to a slave's death on the Cross.[9] In Hebrews the key opening passage alludes only briefly to the Cross. But not only is expiation through Jesus' sacrifice on the Cross the theme of the whole letter; the general necessity of Jesus' sufferings is brought out quite explicitly early on. It is only through suffering that the Saviour is made perfect; it is by death that he frees those whom evil holds in thrall by the fear of death; it is his sufferings that enable him to help other sufferers; and, as in the Philippians hymn, it is because of his sharing in the common death of all humanity that he is now crowned with glory in heaven.[10]

Similarly in Colossians the divinity of Jesus and the Cross are brought tightly together. The statement that 'in him all the fullness of God was pleased to dwell' continues at once: 'and through him God was pleased to reconcile to himself all things . . . by making peace through the blood of his cross'.[11] In the second chapter of the Letter, after a reinforcement of the earlier link between Jesus and God,[12] the writer goes on to express the liberation from sin and guilt effected through the Cross in words which interweave both God and Jesus as agents in the process so closely that at certain points it is hard to be sure which of them is meant.[13]

Only in the Prologue to the Gospel of St John is there no

mention of the Cross alongside the affirmation of Jesus' divine origin and nature. That for John, as for the rest of the New Testament writers, the death of Jesus was the necessary completion of his life in obedience to the Father is indisputable. But John is the gospel author for whom the note of suffering is muted. His Jesus is never the victim, always the victor: 'No one takes my life from me, but I lay it down of my own accord. I have power to lay it down, and I have power to take it up again. I have received this command from my Father.'[14] Jesus is in himself 'Resurrection and Life'; and not only for him but for those who believe in him death is already a nullity.[15]

The only possible answer to the question 'Where is God in the Jesus story?' is the one toward which the greater part of the New Testament is pointing: 'God was in Christ reconciling the world to himself'.[16] For those who believe in the Resurrection there can be no other answer.

The argument may be set out as follows. Either God was the power behind Jesus' resurrection or he was not. If he was not, then the Easter story is mere fantasy and we should all stop wasting our time thinking about it, because only 'what everyone calls God' is a sufficient cause for such an event. If, however, he was the power behind the Resurrection, then we have another choice to make. Either God was, in some way, himself the personal subject of the historical human life, suffering and death of Jesus, or he was not. If he was not, then he is less good, less worthy of our reverence than Jesus himself (or indeed than many other martyrs for love, truth and justice); and in that case, whether he exists or not, he cannot be God for us. In effect, if he was not, there is no God. But if he was, then at last humankind has reason to believe in a God one can respect and love, a God who is alongside his creatures, not detached from them or indifferent to them. The full classic Christian doctrine of the Incarnation is the only basis on which moral and rational belief in God, a God worthy of the name, begins to be possible.

The implications of Incarnation doctrine

We come now to the heart of the argument of this book.[17]
One of the tragedies of Christian history has been that the
Church has never fully grasped the true implications of this
central article of her faith, but too often has preached and lived
by a version of God which contradicts all that that faith entails.
We who are Christians have misread our own role and pursued
triumphalist and exclusive policies which have largely obscured
the good news with which we were entrusted. We have insisted
on images of God which are absurd and morally perverse. But
at last there are welcome signs that the Church worldwide is
starting to come nearer to the way made plain by God in Jesus.

The first and fundamental truth implicit in the Incarnation
is that *the whole human family is God's family.* This is so by God's
unilateral act. All members of our species are, however distantly
and indirectly, related. We are one enormous family, spread
through time and space. God chose to become a member of
this family and by so doing adopted us all as his relatives. This
is not a symbolic or 'poetic' truth; it is sheer historical fact. All
the human beings who have ever lived or ever will live can
claim blood-relationship with the Son of God.

When Christians talk about the Church alone as 'the family'
or (in more biblical terms) 'the household of God',[18] it is not
only untrue, therefore, but it denies the heart of their own
faith. On this planet God's family is humankind – and, by right
and natural extension, all those other living creatures and the
environment on which we are dependent, for which we are
responsible, and with which our own lives are bound up. The
New Testament teaches that 'God so loved the *world* that he
gave his only Son . . .' and that 'in Christ God was reconciling
the *world* to himself'.[19]

It is significant that, as we noted earlier,[20] when God became
incarnate he did so in a society that had nothing corresponding
to what we mean by a 'church', and that in the whole record
of Jesus' teaching he speaks of the Church only in two places
in one gospel, both of which are suspect as inauthentic on
other grounds.[21] The kingdom or sovereignty of God relates to
the community as a whole in all its aspects.

Once we really take in what God has done in the Incarnation, we are also forced to rethink some traditional Christian positions on the subject of *faith*. In the first three gospels Jesus' teaching is essentially that a right human relationship with God turns on trust in God. In John and the rest of the New Testament trust in God means believing in Jesus: 'You believe in God, believe also in me'.[22] Faith in what God is offering the world in Jesus is what brings safety on the day of judgement, and admittance to eternal life. The words from St John quoted earlier, 'God so loved the world that he gave his only Son', continue, 'so that all who believe in him should not perish.'

Traditionally, therefore, what brings a person within the circle of the saved is a conscious act of faith by which Jesus is accepted for who and what he truly is. Before that act of faith one is outside, lost; after coming to faith one is inside, eternally blessed.[23] But the Incarnation should make us ask whether this is a large enough understanding of our real relationship with God.

The Incarnation has made an objective change in the situation of every human soul. Faith, then, is not the spiritual movement by which we change our own condition, or make ourselves eligible for God to change it. It is the dawning wonder of realisation that it has been changed. God changed it while we were not looking:

> It is all grace. It is not even that there is a door which Christ has unbolted, and we, standing outside it, have to stretch out our hand, lift the latch, and walk through. We are already inside. When our Saviour became man and undid the sin of Adam, he did not command the cherubim with the flaming sword to return to heaven, so that we could re-enter Eden. He picked up the walls of Eden, and carried them to the farthest edge of Ocean, and there set them up so that they now girdle the whole world. All we are asked to do is to open our eyes, and recognise where we are.[24]

And it is this recognition, of course, which transforms the whole of life.

The point about faith is that it is seeing things for the first

time as they really are;[25] and the way they really are, despite all
the horrors and suffering and wickedness, is 'gospel' – that is,
'good news'. There is a God; and God is love; and that love
is not exclusive. It is for everyone and everything. It is a love that
comes alongside the creation, shares the life of the creation at
the humblest possible level. It is not conditional on some mini-
mum degree of value in ourselves, as though God were like
those disastrous human parents who withdraw their love if the
child does not measure up to the standards they think appropriate. When we suddenly see the world this way round, as one
does when a pattern perceived till now as black on white
switches to white on black, a unique and fundamental joy
enters the soul, that joy of which Jesus said that no one will
take it from us.[26] Faith is access to that joy, awareness that the
source of that joy is the truth, and the spiritual discipline in
the teeth of doubt, disappointment, distress and even death
itself by which we hold onto that truth.

Faith in the Incarnation brings another source of joy by
changing the way we see *the human race*. Merely pondering the
human story and observing the human condition we are likely
to waver between optimism and pessimism, either hopeful or
despairing about our species and its future. But the Incarnation
gives us simpler and more fundamental grounds for judgement:
humankind is such that, as a human, even God could be true
to himself.

Much has been said earlier, and more will have to be said,
about the flawed and destructive features of human nature. We
are capable of evil so atrocious as to be unbelievable. But the
very fact that most of us find such evil atrocious, that we balk
at believing it, is evidence that we have a capacity for good, a
goodness capable, as we know, of the sublimest selflessness,
compassion and generosity. The Incarnation tells us to have
confidence in that goodness, because the Incarnation is God's
own vote of confidence in us. Human nature has divine and
eternal potential.

Incarnation faith thus means that we look with new eyes on
every other human being. We should expect to learn truth,
receive wisdom, experience love in any quarter. St Paul says of
Jesus that he is 'the image of God', alluding to the first creation

story in Genesis, where men and women are made 'in God's image'.[27] This image, therefore, rightly understood, is Christ-likeness, which is 'Godlikeness' in human terms, and is an endowment of humanity as such. It may be savagely disfigured, it may not develop to its full glory – every person is different. But it is there. Theologically, it is the definition of being human, and is certainly not to be looked for only in Christians. It is a potential, realised perhaps in everyone in some degree, of the whole human race; and it flourishes wherever authentic goodness and love are to be found.

The transformed vision of humanity which faith in the Incarnation inspires also entails a new perspective on *religious faiths* in general – that is, on all total accounts of reality, whether religious in the conventional sense or philosophical, theist, athe-ist or humanist. If to believe in the image of God in human beings must also be to believe that anyone may have insight into truth and goodness to offer, we should expect to learn from all that is best in the thought and life of other men and women, whatever their creed or culture, whatever the age in which they lived. The Incarnation, so far from nullifying faiths other than the Christian, in fact commands us to approach every honest and humble science of reality with expectation.

To say this is not, however, to endorse fashionable nonsense about all faiths really saying the same thing, or all paths leading in the end to the top of the same mountain. Such talk is insulting to all believers, and devalues rational thought in general. The God of Hinduism is not the same as the God of Islam; the reality of the theist is not the same as that of the atheist. Only in a world where all hope of discovering truth has been abandoned do people comfort themselves with the illusion that there is no ultimate difference between Yes and No.

Yet wherever human souls have known the authentic anguish of the quest for truth, of wrestling with the reality of the world of other beings around them, of their own inward life, and of the complexity of relationships, there will be insight: insight into good and evil, into the adventure of living together in peace and justice with nature and humankind, into the mystery of the spiritual. These are the regions we need to explore together in hope. To start from our various doctrines of ultimate reality is to start from the wrong end – not because precious truth is not to be found there, but because these are the frameworks with which each tradition tries to make sense of the whole, and each framework represents an evolution from a long history. People will indeed move from one framework to another if their own has palpably failed. But those who still find their own framework satisfactory are not going to change simply in response to verbal arguments or personal experiences that come out of a different pilgrimage.

All faiths and philosophies believe that they express, so far as is possible in human thought, the nature of ultimate reality, and these understandings are, to a greater or lesser degree, all different. But each one is also linked to a strategy for the good life, and it is this concern which creates the common ground on which dialogue is possible. Because the subject matter is human existence, it is possible to empathise with the experiences of the other person or community, and thus to begin to understand their values and objectives.

Eventually some sort of common profile of the good life, some agreed elements of what it takes to be fully and properly human – what a Christian would call 'Christlikeness' – might begin to emerge. This would in turn feed back into the 'ultimate reality' framework, enlarging and improving it. This process, ultimately, is the only way in which discourse between faiths about theological truth can profitably be approached; and its outcome cannot be predicted in advance. As a Christian I am convinced that in the end faith in the Incarnation would come to be seen by all as one key truth for our human relationship to ultimate reality – not least because of its unique value for enabling dialogue to take place with mutual respect. But if this does happen, it will only be because it has imposed itself 'by virtue of its own power',[28] power which will quietly have commended itself in new and deeper ways to the Christian parties to the dialogue as well as to others.

For the way to the ultimate goal of Godlikeness, the kingdom of God in earthly affairs, can hardly be limited to the spirituality and practice of the Christian Church as history has known that so far. In every generation, it is true, there have been women and men in the Churches who have been gloriously Christlike in the terms of their own day, and have inspired others to be the same. But, surveyed overall, the Church as an institution has failed dramatically to show and commend the Christ-ideal either to its members or to the world. There is therefore little reason to think that the world's growth in Christlikeness would be effectively fostered if everyone were persuaded to join the Christian Church as it is. The way forward for the Churches in relating to other belief systems has to be twin-track: to increase Christlikeness, both individual and corporate, within their own lives; and to co-operate with all people of goodwill, so far as these are prepared to do so, in discovering and promoting what Christlikeness means in the life of the world today. Only when these stages have been worked through will other faiths be able truly to hear the story of God in Christ and to take into their own religious understanding its unique and supreme contribution. This would also open the eyes of Christians to un-Christlike elements in their own lives and institutions to which they had so far been blind.

There are other implications of Incarnation faith which are more specifically internal to the Churches, and these will be considered in the next chapter. Here we must first turn to a cluster of other issues of major importance for Christian belief, those traditionally gathered under the heads of suffering and atonement.

Suffering

Why, some have asked, is it we who are supposed to ask God for forgiveness? Surely it is God who ought to ask forgiveness of us. If God really is 'in Christ, reconciling the world to himself', then let him first reconcile the world to the inevitability of extreme and meaningless suffering and to the presence of evil, for both of which he must be ultimately responsible.

Along with the evolution of the more elaborate complex adaptive systems[29] came something qualitatively new and supremely important: freedom. Freedom is the capacity to determine one's behaviour, at any rate in part, by a process of observation and memory, reflection, prediction and choice. Once the necessary biological threshold has been reached, it develops because it is by far the most potent way of coping with an environment such as ours. But when you have creatures with a margin of freedom living in social groups, eventually they arrive at what we call ethics.[30]

Ethics is the application of a particular kind of criteria to the business of choosing what to do, and it is the nature of these criteria that they cannot be reduced to some other sort. To say, 'this is good' or 'this is right' is not the same thing as saying, 'this works' or 'this is natural'. It is also characteristic of ethical thinking that it claims priority over other considerations. It takes for granted that if there is a clash between, say, what justice requires and what material advantage suggests, then justice should win.

This primacy of the good in our value systems has had a further effect, distancing us from less developed animals. It has set us at odds with the universe out of which we came. The cosmos functions in some respects in ways that conduce to what we regard as moral good and in others in ways the results of which seem to us evil. So, because the very idea of good implies that good ought to prevail, we are bound to find the universe wanting. It ought to be uniformly good, and it is not. In particular we ourselves, who have this sense of good, ought to be good, and manifestly we are not. These perplexities, and the quest to resolve them, are the key issues which have shaped all the great world faiths. In faiths which centre on a personal Creator this moral unease with the cosmos is by far the most serious embarrassment for the believer.

Some recent scientific thinking mentioned earlier[31] would, if confirmed, change the question we need to ask. If it is true that any universe would have to be broadly the same in character as the one we have got, then the accusation, 'Why did not God make a better universe?' has to be modified. It now becomes, 'Why, knowing what a universe would have to be like, did God make one at all?'

It is tempting to see in this modified question the chance to resolve the problem by drawing up a kind of balance sheet.[32] Do the gains outweigh the losses? Only in a world where pain is possible can there be such things as courage, adventure, responsibility for others, choice of the good for its own sake and, in the end, love. Presumably you also need a world of this sort if beings are to exist who can experience sheer pleasure as well as pain, who can enjoy thought, discovery, creativity, who can not only delight in beauty but add to it.[33]

Yet there are so many points such a balance sheet approach does not meet. The possibility of suffering may create the need for us to care for each other, and so in some sense be the matrix of selfless love. But for most of human history effectual care has been beyond our scope. Only in the last hundred and fifty years has medicine begun to offer real hope of reducing disease and relieving the worst kinds of pain. For hundreds of thousands of years authentic, selfless love existed, but in its helplessness was itself another form of anguish. Was that suffering justified by the fact that one day, when the technical means had been discovered, compassion would motivate vast increases in knowledge and so in our ability to help each other? The crux of the problem is the vast and unending misery from disease and disaster which is part of the system, for which no creature is morally responsible, and of which any beneficial effects in the long haul of evolution are too remote to have any meaning for individual lives.

Too often this central issue is glossed over by those who speak in defence of the state of things as though the great bulk of suffering was due to our human misuse of free moral choice. It is certainly true that humanity makes things far, far worse both for itself and for other creatures than need be. But here again we have to ask how much of that evil has been due not to genuinely free decision but to ignorance, to psychological illness or distortion, to fears and pressures inherited through the evolutionary process. There is also a legitimate question to be asked as to what levels or types of suffering are to count as intense enough to create a moral problem. Civilisation itself lowers the threshold of acceptable pain; the values of a culture largely determine what suffering we resent. But these can never be more than marginal adjustments. Such nibbling away at the issue from various sides will not resolve the complexity of human suffering; and it has nothing at all to say to something far simpler, namely the unavoidable pain from natural causes that attends the lives of other sentient beings in the wild.

Nor can we meet the challenge by claiming beneficial effects for suffering. Yes indeed, if we understand the causes of a particular suffering, we or others may learn how to avoid it in future. It is also true that a life without adversity, discomfort or disappointment is unlikely to produce a character that is brave, sympathetic and unselfish. Having things too easy can make one as uncaring and ungenerous as having them too hard. But the idea that really serious suffering is necessarily good for the soul simply does not correspond to experience. To animal pain such an idea is obviously irrelevant anyway. For most humans, even if they escape the deepest levels of self-absorption, bitterness or despair, chronic suffering builds a dark and narrow cell, in which their spiritual energy is largely taken up with sheer endurance.

Some, often children or youngsters, do respond to tragedy and disaster in ways that inspire us and command our admiration. We visit them in hospital, let us say, and come away feeling that we are the ones who have been blessed. No doubt, too, more of us could and ought to rise to our particular challenges in this way. But to argue, as is sometimes done, that suffering is there to ennoble and refine the personality (or, in religious terms, to make us holy) is to get things upside-down. Because some people manage to achieve heroic beauty of character in winning a victory over suffering, that does not make suffering a morally acceptable or universally effective method of training souls up to spiritual perfection. It would make as much sense to say that, because Milton triumphed over his blindness to compose *Paradise Lost*, blinding people is the way to produce great epic poets.[34]

The real theological problem is not about pain or deprivation in every form, but about those manifestations of them which serve no moral or spiritual purpose, and which are crushingly excessive or randomly unequal in their distribution. Some anguish, some loss we could tolerate or understand. The universe we have seems not only out of control in this regard, but by its nature bound to have become so.

This leads directly to one further theological dilemma. If this is the only kind of universe there can be, how can God provide a different sort of existence for creatures beyond this one, where sorrow and pain and death will be no more? What meaning can we attach to biblical and traditional imagery of a new creation, a 'world to come'? If, on the other hand, there can be such a cosmos, why did God not create it in the first place?

And yet, and yet, it is probably true to say that 99 per cent of people, despite all the suffering and evil in their own circumstances and in the world generally, would rather have existed than not.[35] This has little to do with the hope of a better life to come beyond death, even though that can well be, where there is faith, a comforting thought to sorely tried souls. It is more likely a distinctively human expression of the will to live, which in many species increases the chances of survival. In human beings, however, the deepest, stubbornest reason for preferring existence to non-existence has always been the value we set on our own identity. The first time the thought crosses the mind of a child, 'If my parents had never met, I would never have existed', it comes as something almost unbelievable. How can I, this very special me, be no more than an accident? By the same token it is those who, for whatever reason, cannot believe in their own worth who are most likely to take their own lives or to succumb in extreme conditions.

In looking for some response to all this from the standpoint of faith the first thing we have to accept is that there is not going to be an account of reality which explains everything. All is not for the best in the best of all possible worlds. The root of the conflict is that, on the one hand, we have good reasons for believing in the existence of a loving God but on the other, we have this morally enigmatic universe. It is easy enough to make a comfortable little synthesis if you deny one or the other half of the problem: either, 'There is no God, and all the so-called pointers to his existence are tomfoolery', or 'There is nothing wrong with the world; every evil is actually a good if seen from God's angle, or is sent by God to further some good purpose which we in this life cannot detect'. Those, however, who are genuinely open to the human experience of reality in all its aspects cannot be satisfied with either easy option.

There is a lesson to be learned from the life of Jesus which is directly relevant here. We saw it as a mark of Jesus that he refused to do evil that good might come. But, because Jesus was God, it follows that God as God will also never do evil that may come. Those, therefore, who say to the victims of some terrible tragedy, 'It is God's will', or 'He sent it', or 'One day you will see it was all for the best', simply do not understand the message of the Incarnation.

The universe is ambiguous and, so far as we can tell, is bound to be ambiguous. If we try to find ways of proving that it is not, we end up in sheer irrationality, calling black white, making the terms 'good' and 'evil' meaningless; and that price is too high even to think of paying. Perhaps each individual component of the world is in itself in some sense good. As the writer of the Book of Job saw and celebrated, a crocodile is, considered simply in itself, a wonderful thing.[36] No doubt the same can be said of black widow spiders, molten lava, lightning and bacteria, even perhaps of viruses. Evil springs not from them in themselves but from particular interactions between them and other entities, from their being in certain places at certain times. Moral defect attaches to the system as a whole. That is the way things are, and very possibly the way they had to be. If so, then this is something that not only we but God also have to accept.

What the Incarnation says to this is that God does not merely accept it and preside over the result in insulated protection from its costs. He himself experiences what it is like to live in such a world. In the case of Earth, he enters that experience as human. Elsewhere in the cosmos he will have done or will do the same in whatever life form is locally appropriate, as need arises.

> Who can tell what other cradle
>   high above the Milky Way
> still may rock the King of Heaven
>   on another Christmas Day?
> Who can count how many crosses
>   still to come or long ago
> crucify the King of Heaven?
>   Holy is the name I know.[37]

But is that all that can be said? Our knowledge of the universe tells us that each world on which sentient, rational, spiritual life exists must come to an end; and that the same holds good for the totality of things. Is death, is the extinction of all truth, beauty and goodness to have the last word?

Here again the truth revealed in Jesus gives us more light by which to tread. It may not be possible to create an evil-free, death-free universe from scratch. Nevertheless the Resurrection shows us that there can be such a life, such an order of existence, but that there is only one way to it, and that is the road that runs through death. Death, seen from our side, is indeed what it seems, the destruction of identity, of value; and it is inescapable because it is part of the logic of a space-time universe. If it is to be overcome, that cannot be done by going round it – there is no way round. It has to be done from within, by enduring it. But this is possible, not because of any unkillable element in ourselves, but because God is everywhere, and even death is not a place where he is not; and to all who enter that place he offers a share in his own immortal being.

The life, death and resurrection of Jesus tells us that existence in some such universe as this, with all its seeming God-forsakenness, is in fact the only way to the true life, the good existence which we crave. We have first to be, and that means being here. We can then pass through non-being to the being that is eternal. But that has implications for the way we live now. What the experience might be of making the passage to the way we are to live then, is something addressed, albeit all too briefly and inadequately, in the final two chapters. For the moment let us hold onto the fact that God himself has lived with the enigma of evil. He asks of us nothing he has not been prepared to share. But he offers us that which, when received, will make all our necessary anguish as a dream forgotten within moments of waking: 'When a woman is in labour, she has pain, because her hour has come. But when her child is born, she no longer remembers the anguish because of the joy of having brought a human being into the world. So you have pain now; but I will see you again, and your hearts will rejoice, and no one will take your joy from you'.[38]

Atonement

But if the heart of God is sacrificial love, if his way of being human is to refuse to do evil that good may come, why should he be interested in creating a new life beyond death for more than a very small proportion of the human race? With all our imperfections and our active wrongdoings what place can there be for most of us in God's new evil-free, death-free world? This is something far deeper than the question of punishment for the sinner and reward for the righteous that it is often made out to be. It is a question of where we belong, where – being the sort of people we are – we can be at home. Will the kind of life for which God re-creates us be fullness of life for us or not? Has God in and through Jesus done anything to overcome that lack in us, to make it possible for us to breathe the spiritual air of his kingdom?

That is the real issue behind what Christian theology has traditionally called atonement or reconciliation. It is the matter of bringing flawed and damaged creatures like ourselves into harmony with God and his values and with the divine society which in eternity he builds upon them. It concerns, therefore, a process of change and growth which it is clearly best should begin here and now.

One obstacle to that beginning has always been a sense of our own unworthiness, of not being the kind of people who are fitted for companionship with Jesus or his true followers. We are not even the sort of people of whom we ourselves approve. Hence, historically speaking, the main focus of atonement theology has always been an account of how God is held to have dealt with this particular problem. The result, as we shall see, has been an unhappy narrowing and distortion of the good news about God and his relationship with us in Jesus.

The traditional idea of atonement and the one which for many is the most important single touchstone of authentic Christian belief may be summed up as follows. God is both just and merciful. He is holy but he is also love. So, while he has to deal with our sins as justice demands, which would mean excluding us from his kingdom, he also longs to welcome us to communion with himself. His solution, reflecting both his justice and his love, was that the penalty for all the sins ever committed by anyone, past, present or future, should be paid for us by God himself in the person of his incarnate Son. All we have to do is to claim the benefits of this suffering on our behalf by acknowledging humbly and thankfully what God has done for us in Jesus; and this acknowledgement is the heart of what is meant by 'saving faith'.

A further point needs to be mentioned if this idea of atonement is to be fully understood. Sins against God have been said, theologically, to carry an infinite guilt and therefore to require an infinite penalty to expiate them. Since no creature, obviously, can pay such a penalty, someone who can suffer infinitely must do it for them; and that means God himself. This argument derives from earlier centuries, when the heinousness of an offence was measured not just by the offence itself but also by the honour and status of the person against whom it was committed. An injury to the king (*lèse majesté*) was far more serious than one to a commoner. An injury to God, therefore, is infinitely serious, because his honour and status are infinitely great. Even though the cultural conventions on which this theology was based have been abandoned, the idea that sin as an offence against God calls for an infinite penalty is still unthinkingly preached today.

For many millions of believers the assurance that this penalty was paid by Jesus once and for all has been the heart of the 'good news', the Gospel. It was this which made the burden fall from Christian's back,[39] and which has done the same for countless others, bringing joy, liberation, and the start of a new life. It is therefore with a fear of desecrating what for some readers may well be a holy of holies that one ventures to renew criticisms of this position which, though they have been around since the twelfth century,[40] have never been adequately rebutted. Yet the task of criticism *must* be attempted yet again, for there are many other millions who have been appalled by this teaching and for whom it has been a major reason for rejecting – or never accepting – the Christian faith. Let it also be said, however, that the intention behind such a critique is not to deny the centrality of the Cross or the objective nature of the change which the Cross has made in our relationship with God.

The first and obvious difficulty is that though this action on God's part is alleged to serve the claims of justice it does nothing of the kind. A penalty can be paid only by the guilty; what is suffered by the innocent is not punishment. The self-sacrifice of a substitute is an act of love, not of justice.

A deeper objection concerns the nature of retribution. What is punishment for? Fundamentally it rests on a kind of moral intuition that someone who makes others suffer should suffer in their turn. It is a question of fairness, which is what also requires that the punishment should be proportionate to the crime.[41] Many societies today would also say that it should be proportionate to the offender's moral culpability: the person under extreme provocation, for example, or mentally incapable of understanding what they were doing should receive a lesser penalty or in some cases none at all. There is, therefore, an objective aspect to retribution: the need for the moral account to be somehow balanced. But there is also a subjective purpose: that of conveying to the offender how society regards his or her actions and if possible of bringing the guilty person to see them in the same light.

Retribution, then, is not relevant to the innocent. Their personal moral balance sheet does not need to be adjusted, nor have they done anything of which they ought to be ashamed. It also knows nothing of punishment proportioned to some supposed greatness in the victim of the offence. It is concerned only with the offence itself and with the inward state and outward circumstances of the offender.

But there is another idea popularly attaching to retribution which is directly related to Christian atonement theology. This is the idea that punishment in some way removes guilt. The assumption is that retribution expiates guilt and so enables the offender to start a new life on level terms with everyone else. In religious language, sin and guilt are 'taken away'; the sinner is 'washed clean'.

Leaving aside the question whether this could ever be done vicariously – which, if all depends on punishment, it obviously could not – it needs to be said that retribution cannot and does not affect guilt. When I have, say, served a prison sentence, no more punishment can be imposed on me for that offence. But that is not because I am no longer guilty of it. A line has been drawn across that particular page; my debt to society has been paid. But for the rest of my life the guilt of that offence attaches to me. I am still the one who did that. It is part of the story that makes me what I am. Other people may choose to 'forget all about it', and not to treat me for ever as the one guilty of that particular act. But the fact remains: retribution does not take away guilt.

Another point needs to be made which is too often ignored in Christian teaching. No one has authority to forgive sins committed against another. Society may properly punish them as crimes against the community, if that is what they are. But so far as the relationship between offender and victim is concerned, that can be repaired only by them. In what sense, then, can God be said to forgive my sins? He can do so in respect of the harm he himself has suffered – for instance, in the damage I may have done to his good purposes in the world, or the hurt I may have caused him because of his love for those I have injured. But even God has not the right to wipe the slate clean on others' behalf in respect of what I have done to them. Standard Church teaching is that if we express sincere sorrow to God for our sins, then all is put right with regard to everyone else. But this easy comfort is false because it is unjust. Not even God can, for example, forgive on behalf of those who suffered in the Holocaust and all those millions more whose lives were scarred permanently by their sufferings. Reconciliation, to be complete, must wait upon forgiveness by the victims.

Perhaps this is the ultimate meaning in Jesus' teaching that God will not forgive our sins, unless we forgive those who have sinned against us. If all are eventually to be reconciled, that means that each of us will one day have to forgive all those who have wronged us. Reconciliation cannot be complete unless it is universal. If God has forgiven all the harm done to his purpose of love, by myself as well as others, then I cannot be in tune with his mind and heart unless I forgive the harm done to me. It is not that God is punishing me for refusing, or twisting my arm. It is just that if I refuse I am still outside the new world of reconciliation. I am unreconciled myself, and blocking the reconciliation of others.

Judgement and forgiveness

It will be seen, therefore, that any reconstruction of the ideas of atonement or reconciliation calls for some careful thinking on the related themes of judgement and forgiveness.

The traditional picture of judgement is shot through with anomalies and contradictions. First of all, it asks us to believe that God's attitude toward us changes radically the moment we die. While we are in this life, forgiveness and reconciliation are available whenever we are truly sorry and forgive others. But, it would seem, as soon as we die, love and mercy are out. From then on, unrepented serious sin committed in this world excludes us for ever from the joy of life in the family of God – and that is the mildest interpretation of 'eternal damnation' or 'punishment'.

For a Christian such a picture ought to be, in the strict sense of the word, unbelievable. How can it be true that a God who has adopted every human person, regardless of their goodness or badness, as a member of his family, who knows human life from the inside, will suddenly change the whole basis of his relationship with them? He himself would have to become a totally different character. The Israelite prophet knew better; 'For I the Lord do not change; therefore you, O children of Jacob, have not perished'.[42]

A somewhat different account of judgement makes it all depend on faith. Those who believe in God and Jesus are safe; those who do not are lost. In some versions this means specifically believing in expiation of sin by the death of Jesus on the cross; in others acceptance of the faith of the Creeds, or a simple intention to believe what the Church believes.

This at once raises the question of all those who have never heard the Gospel, or have never heard it in a form which could commend it. To them we must add the many who have been turned from belief by the confusion and corruption and cruelty of the Church, and its insistence on 'tithing mint, dill and cumin' rather than living out 'justice and mercy and faith'.[43] Then there are the many more who have not been able to reconcile belief in God with intellectual integrity. Surely no honest Christian, one who has struggled with the kind of difficulties for faith that we have been examining, will cast the first stone at them! And if we cannot do that, will the God who vindicated the one who died in God-forsakenness, do so where we refuse?

Both these visions of judgement force us to face the same question, one implicit, indeed, in the very understanding of faith from which the present work began: how can anyone be judged justly on the basis of their faith and life here, when in this world the evidence of what to believe and how to live is so uncertain? Only when we come into the clear light of the kingdom shall we be in a position to decide, and only then will it be fair to judge us on whatever decision we make.

For that open encounter with God will be the first chance we shall ever have had to learn the full truth about ourselves and about our relationships with other people and other creatures, and so the first chance to face what it is we have to repent, and why. In meeting Jesus – God in human terms, the only terms that make sense to us – we shall see in his eyes and through his eyes whatever of authentic guilt and sin there is in our story,[44] with all right allowances made but with nothing fudged, none of that 'understanding' which is mere collusion in the guise of love. And what we see will include any offence against reason and truth which meant that our belief or dismissal of belief was not in fact the pure integrity we had assumed, but perhaps no more than going with the crowd, fear for our reputation, childish rebellion, or shrinking from this or that ethical demand.

If God does not change, then his dealing with us in judgement will be the same as it has always been: perfect holiness, absolute truth, but also that loving offer of forgiveness which has always been there, and always on the same terms. Some might say that this would de-gut the whole idea of judgement, make it meaningless. But is this so?

What do we mean by 'forgiveness'? First, there is an essential distinction to be made, but one often overlooked. Forgiveness is not the same thing as reconciliation. Reconciliation is what comes about when proffered forgiveness is humbly and sincerely accepted. For a relationship to be created anew, both parties have to accept what needs to be done and to make each their own distinctive contribution in the light of that.

What is the contribution of the one who forgives? To begin with, there has to be complete openness and honesty. The wrong done has to be spelled out in all its wrongness, without exaggeration but also without pretence or insincere diminution. Only so can offenders know what genuine blame attaches to them. Humanly this is impossible; but God will convey total truth in love, and that is judgement – as it ought to be.

Next, what is the offer made by forgiveness? It has two elements. One is internal to the person forgiving: a willingness to accept the change in her or his own situation brought about by the wrong done, and to start from there to reshape life on these new terms, without repining, without holding the altered circumstances against the offender. The old good has gone, and cannot be recovered. Now a new good must be built. In trivial matters this may not be too difficult; but where serious, perhaps disastrous harm has been done, it calls for heroic generosity and love. How many ever achieve it? If sufficient time is allowed – as it should be, for this is a process of change and growth in a damaged plant, and cannot be hurried – wonderfully more than one might suppose. What does this mean for God? It must entail at least two things. First, God has to evoke in the created order; a new way forward to his kingdom and the Resurrection is our assurance that he can do this, and that for God no evil will ever have the last word. But secondly, the Cross tells us that for every seeming success of evil in all cosmic history God willingly pays the price in crucified love.

The other element in forgiveness is the offer to the wrong-doer of a new partnership. Here again, the old good cannot be revived. There has to be a new creation, at which offender and victim have to work together in the new conditions. What that means for the injured has just been described. For the guilty the demand can be severe in a different way, because he or she has to learn to face with genuine sorrow the full truth of what has happened; and that includes the truth that she or he has been the sort of person who could be responsible for that. 'Father, I have sinned against heaven and before you; I am no longer worthy to be called your son'[45] – no, and never will be worthy, but will be welcomed with joy nevertheless.

Forgiveness does not do away with retribution. On the contrary, if received in humble recognition of the truth and with the gratitude owing to someone who has voluntarily foregone just rights against us, it gives rise to the only exactly appropriate retribution there can be: the inward anguish of soul of those who at last understand and feel what suffering they have caused to another, and are concerned for that other and not for their own good standing, either in their own eyes or those of the world. This is the true retribution which the formal retribution imposed by society aims to inspire in the offender, though too often without success.

From that encounter with the divine and human Jesus which will be Judgement Day for each one of us there are, therefore, various possible outcomes. Our analysis so far has had in view those who are unaware (as to some extent we all are) of their own guilt and so have to be brought to awareness, thence to penitence, and thence to that inward sorrow for sin which is necessary and inescapable retribution. But some are already conscious of their sins; they are penitent, they do not try to evade a just inward sorrow. These do not have so far to travel spiritually – in the case of some only a very little way. But what of those who will not accept the truth?

Anyone with the least imagination would shrink with horror from the thought of what the truth about themselves must mean to a Hitler or a Stalin or any other of history's monsters. Yet, if it can be done at all, the human, crucified Son of God is the one who might be able to fan into flame whatever ember of genuine humanity remains even in such as these and as their Good Shepherd to lead them through their inconceivable wilderness of remorse. But suppose the truth, hugely horrific or merely very ordinary, very petty, is refused? What happens then? Does rejection of God mean a fall into non-being? Or is there some divine equivalent of humanity's judicial penalties, some pain of alienation from the good, which may in time lead the guilty to come to themselves in a far country, and turn back to embrace true retribution: 'treat me like one of your hired servants'?[46] What is certain is that the God who has taken every human soul into his family will not give up on anyone. In that case a stage of punitive pain, leading, love would hope, to acceptance of redemptive suffering, is more likely than the final writing off implied in annihilation.

Which leaves one question: is there any way of escape for the truly penitent sinner from the pain of authentic inward retribution? If we have to accept that whatever we have done is part of our story for ever, how can we ever be delivered from the anguish of remorse?

The answer points us to the deepest of all truths about our deliverance from evil, which is that we have to learn to accept it as a gift from others. If they truly wish to go forward with us in joy and peace, then for us to cling to our inner torment is to yield to the final and most subtle temptation to put ourselves first – to want somehow, impossible though it is, to justify ourselves, to be perfect in our own eyes at last. Paradoxically, we become our true perfected self only when we stop trying to make ourselves perfect, and receive ourselves as a gift from those who love us as we are, for what we are. We are truly, inwardly washed, when we let ourselves be embraced as clean.

This point cannot be reached without first going through all the stages on which we have just reflected. There is no short cut, no ladder on the board from the bottom row to square 99. But the process turns out in the end to have involved all those elements which Christian tradition has in the past schematised as justification by faith alone, salvation by grace through faith, particular judgement, hell, purgatory, and heaven. They become meaningful, however, only when we relate them to ourselves and to each other not in the framework of some impersonal judicial procedure, but in terms of a personal relationship of holiness and love.

Which raises one final consideration. This picture of judgement and atonement with reconciliation is not simply a matter between God and the individual soul. It involves all those who are in any way caught up in or affected by our personal history. They all have their part to play in bringing us to the truth and its purifying pain, and in delivering us, when that has done its work, from its righteous retribution; and we have the same service to do for them. For those whom death has robbed of the chance of reconciliation in this life what joy it will be when each of us receives our liberated, perfected self as a gift not just from God but also from all those fellow creatures who have been bound up in the bundle of life with us,[47] and whom the Spirit of God has made children in their Father's likeness.[48]

Postscript

In the light of the Incarnation, Cross and Resurrection we see that this process is already beginning here and now. We are inside as we are, sins and all. What we need is to learn to live in this new environment.

This is possible only because the Cross and Resurrection have changed the whole scene for every one of us, changed it objectively. Jesus endured the Cross and the grave at human hands, yet still came back with his word of goodwill to be carried to all nations. Because and only because of that we know that God's purpose of love toward us is indomitable. He died – the eternal Son of God died – so that all of us, Christian or not, could know this for a surety. If he had not died, we could not have known. He died for us all. And that means he died also for me.

5

The Way and the Truth and the Life

> The grace of God is not in the man who does
> not love his enemies.
>
> Archimandrite Sophrony, *St Silouan the Athonite*,
> Pt 2, Ch. 1.

> In place of the rigid ancient law, humanity must
> hereafter with free heart decide for themselves
> what is good and what is evil, having only Thy
> image before them as their guide.
>
> Fyodor Dostoevsky, *The Brothers Karamazov.*

Following Jesus began as a way of being a Jew, and flowered into a way of being human.

The central and passionate concern of Jesus' life and teaching was God, the creator and sustainer of all things, the *abba*, Father, of every human soul, known uniquely to Israel through his care for them in their history, and now about to establish his sovereignty of holy love over all the Earth. The urgent priority, therefore, for any community or individual was to live human life in the spirit and by the values of the divine kingdom and so to be at home in it as truly children of God.

There was, then, no new 'doctrine' about God in Jesus' own message. That came as Jesus' earliest followers reflected on where God had been in Jesus' own story, and on the liberating change which that story had brought about. The proof of that change was to be plain to everyone in the transformed conduct and relationships of those who followed Jesus.[1]

The heart of earliest Christianity, therefore, is the flourishing of Christlikeness in human life, not in imitating this or that detail of Jesus' own behaviour, but in being governed by the same Spirit that had filled his earthly existence.

The inward dynamic of this Christlike life was joy, a joy that flooded every Christian as he or she drank in what God had done in the Cross and Resurrection of Jesus. In a universe seemingly helpless under the amoral tyranny of chance and necessity[2] they had found God in one who, a sufferer like themselves, had broken the power of pain and evil from within their torture chamber. Formerly, awareness of their own brief mortality had slewed all principles and values toward self-preservation and the satisfaction of their own needs and desires. But now death was no longer the horizon circumscribing their existence and dictating their notion of being human.[3] 'Do not fear those who kill the body,' Jesus had said, 'and after that can do nothing more'.[4] Their perspective reached far beyond death to a new and greater life; and the right way to live here and now was in preparation for and continuity with the life to come.[5]

Being the community of Jesus' disciples has always had these two aspects: the transformation of human life into Christlikeness; and the story which explains why this transformation is the disciple's joyful and enthusiastic vocation. Telling that story is what Christians refer to as 'evangelism' or 'evangelisation', passing on to others the 'good news' which has opened their own eyes to the true blessedness of the human situation, and to the full moral and spiritual potential of human existence. But without the transformation of life into Christlikeness the story on its own means nothing. It is mere religious rhetoric, convincing and deserving to convince no one.

The primary vocation of Christians, therefore, is as men and women in solidarity with all other women and men to help bring out the true Christ-image of God in each human soul and to foster and serve the values of the kingdom in human society. The top item on the agenda of every Christian congregation should be to help the life of the human community of which it is a part become more truly what it is, the life of the family of God. Every person in our neighbourhood, in our workplace, in any association for any purpose whatever, is a son or daughter of God, a sister or brother of Christ. The believing Christian is not more so than any other person. He or she is simply the one with the joy and privilege of seeing every person in this new and wonderful light, because the truth of the Incarnation has shown that this is so.

It is natural and right for a Christian to speak of growth in Christlikeness, for Jesus himself is said to have exhorted his followers to love one another as he had loved them, and to follow his example.[6] But behind this lay Jesus' fundamental principle that the vocation of all human beings was to live as children of their 'Father in heaven', just as the heart of his own calling was to live as God's 'son'.[7] The essential quality in all human conduct and relationships is to be this family likeness to God, or, in the good old English word, 'godliness'.[8]

Jesus' life was one in which God was able, morally and spiritually, to be himself. What Jesus was, God is. But it was also one particular human life in a particular time, place and culture. Had that not been so, it could not have been authentically human; but precisely because of that particularity it could not embody all the possibilities for a Godlike humanity. For one (very obvious) thing, it could not embody what it is to be a Godlike woman – which explains many of the current concerns of feminist theologians.

The vocation of each human soul is to live out his or her unique image of God, to be Godlike in the way one's own inheritance, history and circumstances make possible. A remarkable contemporary Christian thinker, Dorothy Daldy,[9] has described this in the phrase 'creative obedience within one's own personal given'. This definition happily combines the three factors that contribute to Godlikeness in each and every life: the controlling model of God's own character ('obedience'); the particular opportunities and limitations of each person's historical situation (the 'personal given' or datum); and the freedom to be Godlike in one's own way and according to one's own endowments ('creative'). The concept as a whole also reflects an essential aspect of God himself; for even God must be obedient to his own inner nature and can exercise creative freedom only within the terms of cosmic reality as he has determined that. Even God is not free to do just anything.

All this means that within the universe there are many ways of being Godlike. What we see in the 'saints', the outstanding followers of Jesus down the centuries, is but a small sample, though one in which Christians ought always to seek inspiration for their own development. But we need also to look beyond that circle of consciously Christian godliness.

The vision of human life which we have seen in Jesus is normative because of who he is. But it can be so only in its controlling principles: its attitudes to people and other creatures, its values, everything that defines what we may call its 'spirit'. When we find that spirit in those who are not Christians, it does not cease to be Christlikeness. On the contrary, it is essential to celebrate these Christlike qualities in those of other faiths and philosophies for what the Incarnation tells us they are: godliness, 'Godlikeness', the true image of God.

It is a distasteful triumphalism on behalf of the institutional Christian Church when such people are described (as was at one time fashionable) as 'anonymous Christians'.[10] They are not Christians; they are Jews, Muslims, Sikhs, Hindus, Buddhists, humanists or whatever. Pretending that they are really Christians is an unconscious way of refusing to face the authentic virtue of the faiths they do profess. Given the behaviour of the Churches to those outside their ranks in the course of history, outstandingly but not exclusively the Jews, such an attitude is offensive and arrogant, even though not intended to be so. The right Christian attitude is to acknowledge humbly that godliness is to be looked for in all human beings.

Indeed, it is only because godliness may be met with in anyone, anywhere, at any time, that the vocation of Christians to work with all men and women to bring out the true image of God in every individual and in society is possible at all. The Christian contribution to this collaborative enterprise will sometimes be to stand for ethical imperatives which come from Jesus but which others have either rejected or never understood. But at other times it will be to recognise in someone of another allegiance a deeper perception of what godliness requires than that of the Christian collaborator, even though not expressed in Christian terminology.

People can collaborate only on what concerns them all, and that is our shared human existence: personal and family life, work, community, culture, the global network of nations. In the course of Christian history there has been an immense amount of beneficial social action in this field by individuals and Churches; but it has traditionally been carried out as an independent, Christian operation. If Christians are now to co-operate more and more with others, then they have to accept that virtually all the nations of the world are either secular and pluralist or committed to some other faith. In the once Christian west, for some fifty per cent of people the very idea of God is either discredited or of no everyday relevance. There is a general impression that traditional Christian beliefs have been debunked; and the snatches of Christianity that are picked up tend to be either bland and self-evident uplift or extremist versions of the Gospel which come across as offensive or incomprehensible. In such a world the cutting edge of the good news is not normally going to be its story about God and Jesus – that comes later for those who want to know the reason for Christian ethical witness – but its vision of godliness.

Godliness in the life of the world: Christian ethics

The discipline of Christian ethics may be defined as the systematic study of what is entailed by this concept of godliness when worked out in the life of the world. Christian ethics is not, and must not become, a system of behaviour for Christians only. Its norms, values and attitudes are meant for humankind as a whole. It starts from the assumption that all human beings are in the image of God. This clearly cannot mean that all men and women are already Godlike – the unimaginable depravity, cruelty and selfishness to which human beings can sink proves that this is not so. What it does mean is that every person, by virtue of being human, has the potential to grow into godliness in their own way; and the image of God is fully formed in them when their particular potential for Christlikeness, for living in the spirit of Christ, is realised.

To give even the most skeletal survey of this ethical field in one section of one short chapter is clearly impossible, but a few illustrations may give some idea of the way in which this concept of godliness can be applied to ethical issues.

First, consider the question of humanity as a *community of women and men.* No man can ever know what it is to be a woman, and no woman can ever know what it is to be a man. One is not more truly and fully human than the other; each is fully human in a different way. There are vast areas of common ground – in intelligence, intuition, aptitudes and imagination – which enable men and women to communicate and collaborate at profound levels. Almost any statement in the form 'women are *A*, whereas men are *B*' can be challenged with some instance. But there are also characteristic differences, though these need very careful definition, for much superficial nonsense is talked on the subject. Current wisdom seems to give a fair account of the situation, when it says that masculinity and femininity are not clear-cut mutual exclusives. There is a spectrum from a theoretical total masculinity at one end to total femininity at the other, and everyone is at some point in between. But it still remains true that a man's experience of being human is not ultimately accessible to a woman, nor hers to him.

When we come to consider the bearing of godliness and the image of God on this aspect of human life, our starting point must be the statement of Scripture that all human beings, male and female alike and equally, are 'in the image of God'.[11] But this being so, the fact that men and women live their common humanity differently must mean that the image of God, the potential for godliness, cannot in itself be gender-specific. The point may be made concretely in this way. The Blessed Virgin Mary expressed in her feminine being the same image of God as was seen uniquely and perfectly in her divine and human son.

Our authoritative vision of the perfect image of God is found in Jesus, in the spirit by which he lived. Anyone in whom the image of God is coming to fulfilment, who is growing in godliness, is Christlike. It does not depend on gender. As Jesus said, 'Whoever does the will of God is my mother and sister and brother.' This also invalidates the claim that women cannot preside at the Eucharist because the president must be an 'icon' – that is, an 'image' of Christ.[12] In the only sense that matters both women and men equally can be 'images of Christ'. Furthermore, if men and women have different experiences of what it is to be human, to be in the image of God, and therefore distinctive understandings of God himself, then if they are to be helped to live in true godliness, not only as themselves but also in relationship with one another, both will need the ministry of godly women as well as men.[13]

The thought of all the women in the world who in many societies are denied any sort of equality of status with men leads naturally to the question of *human rights*. The content of human rights is too vast a subject to be entertained here; but a word may be to the point concerning the Christian contribution to the prior ethical problem of deciding who are entitled to these rights.

The standard answer is 'any member of the human species'. Rights must inhere in the bare fact of being human. Any other basis would not be sufficiently absolute to offer protection.

In theory this is admirable, but in practice those who wish to get round it merely decree that this or that category of persons either is not fully human or has forfeited the right to be considered as such.

Slaves have always suffered in this way. The ancient practice of declaring someone an 'outlaw' also stripped them of their rights. In this century more people than ever before have been imprisoned, tortured and executed, all without just process of law, simply because the officials of some regime declared them enemies of the state, or 'subhuman'. The Nazi killings of gypsies and the 'subnormal'; Stalin's starving and massacring of the kulaks; Pol Pot; Tibet; the Sudan; Rwanda – the list goes sickeningly on. Out-topping all, the supreme horror of our 'civilisation', the Holocaust, in which the genocide of six million Jews was 'justified' on the grounds of their alleged 'degeneracy'.

But some who rightly shudder at such atrocities may well never think twice about another gross violation of human rights, namely the abortion of a foetus which would be viable if allowed to go to full term.[14] The killing of such a foetus has, shockingly, been sanctioned by some Christian leaders, partly on the grounds that until the baby is born it does not have the full rights of a human person, and therefore the needs or wishes of others have precedence over its right to life.[15] Similarly, those who argue that a woman should have an abortion if she so desires, because she alone has the right to decide what to do with 'her own body', are refusing to recognise the unborn child as another human being. But the foetus is not the mother's own body; it is already someone else's body. Killing that someone has, therefore, to be camouflaged by pretending that as a fellow human she or he does not exist.

The concept of human rights does indeed presuppose some definition of humanity; and that is a matter on which all ethicists need urgently to work together, especially in view of some of the projected advances in biological and medical science. But does not the Christian understanding of both humanity and God have things to say which significantly reinforce and extend human rights?

Theologically, a human being is a creature made in the image of God, that is, having the potential in some degree, however limited, for Godlikeness. Since the heart of God's own being is love, it follows that wherever there is the most rudimentary capacity for something we can call 'love' – that is, an affective bonding with another being – or even simply 'joy' in the sense of pleasure in existence, then however limited the person in question, or however great the support they need, the image of God is present in him or her. It must also certainly be presumed to be present in any viable unborn child. Tragically there are rare cases where, though the child after birth can go on living, all the brain centres relating to any specifically human existence have been destroyed or do not function; and it may then be that there is no ethical duty to prolong the child's life. But in most cases of profound handicap, mental or physical, we do not have sufficient access to the person's subjective state to have the right to say that he or she is not in God's image; and it is our duty to reverence that image, and do all in our power to maximise its potential.

Secondly, however monstrous a person's life may have been, we know that God's purpose of love toward her or him never ceases. Whatever the cost to God, however seemingly hopeless the prospect, such a person is still precious to him. Bearing in mind, therefore, what was said in the previous chapter about the dynamics of atonement and forgiveness, godliness requires that we should treat every person, however depraved, as a human being, and do whatever we can to bring out the image of God in that person.[16]

This reflection calls to mind a sinister argument gaining wide currency today, that there can be no rights without responsibilities. This is manifestly false: a newborn infant has rights but no responsibilities, and so does a victim of severe psychotic illness. Citizens in breach of their responsibilities can be denied particular rights, such as liberty, to a carefully controlled degree; but even the convicted criminal has basic human rights which must not be taken away. The argument quoted is sinister precisely because it could be used to deny human rights to anyone of whose activities the state disapproved.

The Christian will want to reinforce the idea of rights from another direction. If godliness imposes on me a duty to behave toward others in certain ways, then I must grant them the right to expect certain standards of behaviour from me. They may not realise this, and if they do they may not reciprocate, but these things are irrelevant. Godliness toward others can never be conditional on their godliness toward oneself, because that was not how God behaved in Jesus. It is especially important for a community or nation to remember this unconditional nature of ethical duty, if it is to retain any moral principle.

The kind of rights deriving from this duty of godliness toward others can be seen if we consider the idea of *wealth*.

What do we mean by wealth? Is it gross national product, or any of the various measures of the money supply? Does it include, say, the market (or replacement) value of the infrastructure, or simply the total of liquefiable or accessible assets? What is the real wealth of a business, if a market fluctuation can shrink it by millions of pounds, or of a nation, if a currency crisis can diminish it by billions?

One way to answer this question is to ask what are the true sources of wealth creation. There are in fact two, and only two: people; and the planet on which we live. On human skill, wisdom and inventiveness and on the way humans manage and deploy the resources of the Earth we depend for wealth in all the various ways in which that may be defined. Because this is so, wealth itself, in the most fundamental sense, consists in these two things: humankind, and its tiny, beautiful and marvellously endowed environment.

This chimes with the biblical picture of humankind as created to be God's steward, living off the world but also caring for it on God's behalf.[17] The human dominion mentioned in the creation story[18] was never originally intended to sanction callous and selfish exploitation. Human beings are presented in the beginning as vegan, and their tyranny over other creatures comes with the descent into sin.[19] When God's perfect kingdom is restored, relations between all species will be ones of peace.[20]

For the godly, therefore, authentic wealth creation includes an absolute moral obligation to help every human life achieve its best potential. Things like genuine community life, proper food, decent housing, employment, health care, education, freedom and equality under the law, security, and peace are not luxuries to be paid for provided enough 'wealth' can be created first. There is no wealth creation in the true sense without them. Any godly and rational ethic for business and industry will recognise the duty to make a contribution to these needs – through such things as fair commodity pricing, equitable wages and conditions, health care, training, work-sharing and flexitime – in addition to paying reasonable taxation, before trying to maximise profits. Where godliness is not given its best chance to grow, whether in individual or community life, what results is not wealth but the waste and destruction of wealth.

So too with the environment. The human vocation is to protect, conserve and optimise the amazing wealth God has given us through the evolution of the cosmos, to understand its delicate mechanisms and balances, to cherish it and develop it within the terms of its own nature. We have the brains to do that; we lack the moral will. Instead we ravage the ecosphere, exploiting it to indulge the rich, and to allow bare survival to the poor to whom the rich deny justice.[21] Any truly godly spirit must cry out against the great Babylon[22] of the runaway trans-national consumer society which is the engine of this destruction, and labour for its replacement by an order of things which is at once economically efficient and more just.

Linked to these concerns is the relationship between *humankind and other animals*, a subject which, sadly, is a good illustration of the way in which secular people can be far ahead of many Christians in godliness. Some Christians indeed actively denigrate animal welfare work on the grounds that 'people are more important'. But caring about animal suffering does not imply indifference to that of humanity. The merciful whom Jesus called 'blessed'[23] will exercise compassion wherever suffering is to be found.

Disregard of animals has traditionally been justified on the theological grounds that animals do not have souls. This is a somewhat barren approach today, when the concept of 'soul' in humans is itself under radical revision. But, if we think instead in terms of the image of God, then it is not unreasonable to argue that, since humans are in that image because they have evolved to a certain stage, then we should expect to find at least fragments and foreshadowings of that image in earlier stages. In certain primates particularly we find phenomena analogous to thought, learning, social organisation, individual relationships, fidelity, grieving and sacrifice. To some degree such analogues are widespread in the animal kingdom.[24] Our links with the higher animals are not purely biological, and the sense of kinship with them which some intuitively feel is not mere sentiment or nature mysticism.

Animals, however, do not have value simply because of affinities with or usefulness to humankind. The Bible itself makes this seemingly modern point. The Book of Job portrays wild animals inhabiting worlds of their own and living lives indifferent to ours. Humans are but one small part of an immense drama in which God rejoices and which they must approach with reverence and awe.[25]

The immediate crux, however, of our relationship with animals today is the incalculable suffering we inflict on them to serve our own interests. Chief among these by far is the production and distribution of food. Independent scientific assessments have stated again and again that battery and broiler units, intensive indoor veal and pig rearing, live animal transportation, and slaughterhouse practice combine to inflict pain and misery, fear and distress on hundreds of millions of sentient creatures every year. Other major areas of cruelty include unregulated scientific experimentation, trapping, whaling, hunting and the abuse of working and companion animals.[26] There is indeed much animal suffering in the wild, though it is impossible for us to weigh the good and evil in such an existence. But that argument is no excuse for adding to any hardships they may endure, and is totally irrelevant to the issue of suffering inflicted on animals that would never have existed had we not bred them for our own purposes. We give them life to make that life a torment.

Others have objected to the phrase 'animal rights' on the grounds, already criticised,[27] that animals cannot have rights because they have no responsibilities. But animals do have rights in relation to humankind, because humans have a duty of godliness. We have the brains to feed ourselves, conduct research and enjoy our pleasures, without multiplying the suffering of other creatures of God; and as God has given us the ability, so we have the duty, and animals have a 'right' to that duty from us. We also have a duty not to desensitise and brutalise other human beings by requiring them to be cruel on our behalf.

It will be apparent by now how important it is that Christian ethics are concerned with the spirit in which life is lived far more than with detailed rules. Its absolutes are the need for human lives to show 'the fruits of the Spirit' – love, joy, peace and the rest[28] – and such primary virtues as justice, courage, self-discipline and prudence.[29] Wisdom in ethics is to learn from the past in order to predict for the future whether particular conduct will promote these things or diminish them. The answer to such a question may not always be what is conventionally accepted.

This may be illustrated from a burning controversy within Christianity today, that concerning *homosexual relationships*.

The traditional Christian norm of sexual behaviour is clear and simple: full sexual relations are in place only within a heterosexual marriage which is in intention lifelong. This, the final judgment of Scripture[30], is still official teaching in the great majority of churches.

This ideal can be commended for wholly positive reasons. The principle of 'total intimacy, total commitment' gives the joy of sex a security in which deeper love can grow. This bonding resources man and wife both for parenthood and for many other roles in life. Fidelity safeguards the integrity of families within the community. Self-discipline leaves everyone freer and more confident in other kinds of relationship. It also reduces society's obsessive preoccupation with sex on which corruption and perversion feed.

Over and above all these, the ideal also fosters authentic Christlikeness in daily life. The marriage vows – 'for better, for worse, till death us do part' – breathe the very heart of the love which took Jesus to the Cross.

This ideal has admittedly never been fully achieved, even within the Church itself. Nevertheless its basic elements were once widely accepted as valid ethical goals. Today, however, western ex-Christian society[31] no longer regards it as either practicable or desirable and many church members have succumbed to that ethos. Whatever gives each individual pleasure is seen as their 'nature', not to be denied without harm to their personal fulfilment. The moral rider that one's own gratification should not harm others is no defence against wishful self-deception. Sex is 'good for you', so how can I be exploiting my partner? Prostitutes are on the game 'because they like it'. Divorce is 'better for the children', however much research proves the contrary. Paedophiles claim they give the child a 'rewarding and valuable relationship'. And so *ad infinitum*.

Christians ought to care passionately about this human damage, and strive to reverse it by word and example and by public action. But if they are to be ethically coherent they will need to reappraise the issue of homosexuality.

To the detached observer the most obvious feature of Christian sexual teaching is that it is an ethic for heterosexuals. Given that the overwhelming majority[32] of the human race is heterosexual, that is reasonable enough. But it means that this ethic can be fairly applied to homosexuals only by classifying them as deviant heterosexuals;[33] and that, in the light of increasing knowledge, is no longer reasonable.

From an evolutionary point of view homosexuality does not make much sense. It certainly does not promote the survival of the species; and at the individual level it is at odds with bodies not well adapted to meet its needs.[34] Its origins are still obscure, as the current preference for multiple- or variable-cause explanations indicates.[35]

In the circumstances to argue, as is often done, whether homosexuality is contrary to God's purposes in creation or part of that creation's rich variety is unhelpful. Like many other developments in Nature it is simply a fact. What matters is to ask how it can best be enabled to further God's purposes; and here again the key concept is growth in godliness.

Even a modest acquaintance with those living with HIV or AIDS will discover outstanding instances of Christlikeness. The sacrificial devotion of many gay men to their sick or dying partners and the courage of the sufferers themselves witness that their love has been a means of grace by which they have grown into true godliness. They have redeemed suffering and evil, and refused to be defeated by death.

Many heterosexuals can testify that the physical expression of their love in a faithful partnership has helped them become better people. If my neighbour reports exactly the same experience through the physical expression of his or her different sexuality and I condemn that as evil, am I not in great danger myself of condemnation for hypocrisy? Will I not be much safer to be guided by Jesus' own advice: 'You will know them by their fruits'?[36]

However excellent the Christian heterosexual ethic, it loses credibility when it is misused to dictate the way of godliness to homosexuals in their different situation. The first requirement is for the Churches to learn from Christian homosexuals what the Spirit is saying to them about growth in Christlikeness. When the listening does begin, a common mind on basic principles may freely emerge and in God's time lead to an authentic Christian homosexual ethic, accepted as such by the Church.

It is curious to reflect how at different periods in Christian history particular rules emerge as touchstones of authentic discipleship. Absolute truthfulness, for example, never achieved that status in mainline Churches, while avoiding divorce and remarriage unquestionably did so. Yet both have equal backing in words of Jesus.[37] Saddest of all, perhaps, has been the failure of the Churches to give that status to Jesus' injunctions against violence.[38] In early Christianity *non-violence* was very much a part of Christian ethos and practice. But the use of force too soon erupted in internal Christian quarrels and, after the Roman empire became officially Christian, the bar on military service also lapsed.[39]

The ethical difficulties of total pacifism are well known and keenly felt, not least by myself. But even the 'just war' criteria developed by medieval and later theologians, had they been enforced by the Churches on their members, would have made most of the wars in western history impossible. Yet not only was this seldom done, but the Churches actually embraced violence as an instrument of policy in, for example, the Crusades, the torture and execution of heretics (hypocritically handed over to the secular power for the purpose), and in unquestioning support for wars of national aggrandisement and colonial expansion. True, protesting voices have never been silent,[40] and minority groups within Christianity have been faithful to Jesus' command.[41] But might not a more consistent witness, over time, have brought humanity as a whole to renounce war and violence? How shall we who are Christians answer that indictment in the presence of God?

But underlying every betrayal has been the same sin: the refusal to accept that the heart of the image of God is *sacrificial love*.

The human person cannot mature in isolation. We become fully human through relationships with other people and creatures. All are the grace of God to each other. Godliness is the art of living in a mutual giving and receiving which makes not only each self but the whole communion of selves-in-the-world an image of God.

That communion cannot run simply on justice. Justice draws the lines below which we must not fall. But people's inevitably conflicting interests and desires can rarely be reconciled with absolute justice. Compromise there has continually to be; and that means indeed as much justice as possible but also a balance of sacrifice. All parties have to give up something which justice might have awarded them; and that, however modest, is an act of love.[42]

The same quality of sacrificial love enables us to bear the

cost of resisting temptation or humbly seeking forgiveness. Some it leads to cruel martyrdom for the cause of godliness. But whatever the particular demand, this road through the narrow gate of the Cross is also the way into unending fullness of life.

One might think that the Gospel of the Cross and Resurrection would therefore be enough to convert men and women to this sacrificial love as the law of their own lives. But while this has always been so for some, millions more have believed yet apparently seen in their faith no reason to adopt such a quixotic and impractical rule of conduct. At the same time such a life has been gloriously displayed in many of other faiths or none. The lesson is surely that sacrificial love as the law of true life has to be accepted for itself.[43] Godliness has to be loved for its own beauty, not simply as the moral of a faith-story. Understanding this is the key to the Church's primary vocation in the modern world.

The role and character of the Church

The New Testament and later theology have been almost over-preoccupied with thought about the role and nature of the Church. The purpose of this section is simply to draw attention to one particular, neglected source of insight.

In much the larger part of the Church worldwide the ordained ministry – the clergy – consists of three 'orders': bishops, priests and deacons. The historical processes by which this system emerged were complex, and need not concern us here. What is often overlooked is that the end result is a profound symbolic expression of Christlikeness and of what should be the character and calling of the Church as a whole.

The term 'bishop' (in Greek *episkopos*) means 'overseer', 'superintendent', 'guardian'. At one point in the New Testament, in a letter which later speaks of Jesus as the 'chief shepherd', it is linked with 'shepherd' as a designation of Christ.[44] In John's gospel Jesus speaks of himself as 'the good shepherd', who gives his life to guard the sheep of God.[45]

The Letter to Hebrew Christians characterises Jesus as the

eternal High Priest, superseding the priesthood of the Jerusalem Temple;[46] but in doing so it also crucially transforms the concept of priest. In both Judaism and paganism priests were consecrated to make offerings, animal or other sacrifices, to God or the gods. Jesus brought no object, however valuable, to God, only the consecration of himself to God's purpose.[47] Priesthood thus comes to mean the offering of self and life to God on behalf of others in sacrificial love; and it is in this sense that priesthood is to be the vocation of all Christians.[48]

The term 'deacon' (from the Greek *diakonos*) means 'servant', and this is a role to which Jesus himself in the gospels lays claim.[49] It is also one he impresses on his followers, basing his command on his own example. In one account this servant role is also linked explicitly with the sacrifice of his life.[50]

The Church's ordained ministry in this threefold form thus comprehensively symbolises both Jesus' own vocation and that of all Christians. As shepherd: the task of guiding God's children in the right way, feeding them with the truth, and guarding them from spiritual harm; all at the cost, if need be, of one's own life. As priest: responsibility for that true worship of God which, whatever its ritual expression, is nothing without the substance of lives consecrated to sacrificial love of the whole world, including our enemies. As servant: commitment, whatever the cost, to the needs of others, especially the poor, outcast and oppressed, and to the promotion of authentic godliness in the affairs of the world.

Once grasp this spiritual character of the ordained ministry and there is no difficulty in answering the question, 'What are the clergy for?' It is to enable the whole Christian people to fulfil their Christlike calling to live as shepherds, priests and servants of the world. There is no problem, for example, in reconciling a priestly ordained ministry with the 'priesthood of all believers'. The ordained priest is there to help all Christians become priests in the true sense. Bishops and deacons are there to help all Christians understand and practise true godliness and to do so in humble respect for and collaboration with the image of God in all human beings.

In the practical life of the Church, of course, this is never a neatly compartmentalised scheme. All three orders find themselves doing a bit of everything – but this is hardly surprising, seeing that the three roles began life as aspects of the unified calling of Jesus.[51] Increasingly too the ordained share all three with lay people. But what is vital is not to lose sight of the purpose of it all: that through the same threefold character in their own lives all Christians, acting as salt in the food and leaven in the dough,[52] should help all humankind to be, in sacrificial love, shepherd, priest and servant of the Earth and all its inhabitants.

The sacraments

For their work the Church's ministers are entrusted with two resources by which time can be, as it were, transcended, and men and women in each generation brought into spiritual contact with God in Jesus. These resources are the sacraments and the Bible. Of sacraments, two are acknowledged by almost all Christians[53] to be fundamental and supreme, as deriving from commands of Jesus himself: baptism and the Eucharist.

Baptism is the ritual act by which a person is admitted to membership of the Church worldwide. The action is simple, if strange to the outsider. Either water is poured over the candidates, or they are immersed in it; and this is done three times, in the name of the three Persons of God the Holy Trinity – the Father, the Son and the Holy Spirit.

Over the centuries, starting from the New Testament itself and, in particular, the writings of St Paul, many ideas have attached themselves in Christian tradition to this rite of baptism. The chief of these, and their undergirding by the primordial significance of water, have been summed up in these words, written to be placed by the font in a parish church:

> Water means cleansing:
> in it we wash and are refreshed.
> Water means life:
> without it we die.
> But water also means death,
> for in it we drown.

> To this stone basin, called the 'font',
> we bring those, young or old,
> who are to be made Christians,
> Christ-spirits in the world;
> and we pour water over them with prayer.
> We ask for them God's cleansing,
> not just from dirt but from evil.
> We ask for them God's perfect life
> which physical death cannot destroy.
>
> But that life has to be found
> through another kind of dying,
> dying to self and being born
> to a new life of love for others,
> just as Jesus died for others on the Cross
> and came back to us in love and greater life
> on the first Easter Day.
>
> So by this font we keep the Easter candle,
> praying that the new lives which begin here
> will be, like that of Jesus, lives of love,
> and one day find their home with God
> for ever.

The fuller understanding of Incarnation doctrine for which this book has argued does not invalidate these insights, but it does put them in a different perspective.

Traditionally, baptism has been seen as the point at which God takes the believer out of the doomed world and receives her or him as God's child into the number of those for whom the gate to eternal life is now open. Clearly, however, if God has already adopted the whole human race as his family,[54] baptism ceases to be the moment at which God does this, and becomes instead a grateful celebration of what in Jesus God has done.

This shift brings with it liberation from some anxieties and controversies which have long debilitated the Church both internally and in its relations with fringe members. The old fear, for example, that a baby dying unbaptised could not 'go to heaven' now survives for the most part only as a vague,

uneasy memory in some people, but where it is found a right
Incarnation doctrine can lay it to rest.

More common and more serious are the disputes that rend
denominations and congregations over infant or believer's baptism. In New Testament times, some argue, only adults were
baptised, and that only after proving their acceptance of core
Christian beliefs.[55] So, therefore, it should be today. Those who
support infant baptism do so on condition that already baptised
Christians are found to sponsor the child, supplying the child's
deficit of belief with their own proxy faith, and standing surety
that when old enough the child will ratify what has been done
in her or his name – or at least that they will do their best to
ensure that this happens. Those who reject infant baptism are
equally concerned to allay fears that the child may suffer in
some way from not being baptised. Following Scripture, they
see the Church as a community which God has bound to
himself by a covenant of love and mercy. A believer's children,
therefore, will be accepted by God during their childhood as
within that covenant relationship, though on reaching adult
years they will have to make their own faith commitment and
seek baptism.[56]

This is all a bit complicated, and not easy to commend as a
picture of a generous, welcoming God. Of course an adult
seeking baptism will be a believer; if not, he or she would not
be asking to be baptised. But with regard to infants, God in
Jesus has already taken each one as his child from the moment
when she or he was conceived. So far then from being obliged
to refuse baptism, the Church is acting very wrongly if it does
not in the sacrament joyfully give thanks for that fact and
welcome the new human being into its company. As time goes
by, if the Church is able to do its job, the growing soul will
learn the truth about this relationship in which every man and
woman is loved and adopted by God. If in adulthood such
people decide that they cannot believe that, they are free to go
their own road. But God's love for them does not change. They
are still his children, whether they believe or not; and they will
not have to return to belief in order to re-enter the family, for
they never left it. They only left the Church.

Turning now to that other great sacrament, the Eucharist,

the technical background for what will be said here has been set out in Appendix B.

The act at the heart of Christian community prayer and worship is one that all cultures use to mark occasions of special feeling or corporate significance. With it we celebrate our joys and achievements, we share our griefs, we pledge our fellowship, we remember those who have influenced our lives for good in the past, we launch new ventures in hope for the future. It is the act of eating and drinking together; and even in our post-modern western society that is still something so fundamental to human culture that its symbolic potential is virtually inexhaustible.

In Jesus' culture that potential was even stronger, and he and his friends had, like everyone else, made use of it all their lives. Shared meals – from time to time in the Temple, regularly in the home – were expressions of their relationship with God and with one another. What more natural than that on this last night together, wrought up by danger and impending disaster, he should have asked them, whenever they met again in this way,[57] to remember him in prayer before God. They were to take a loaf of bread, break it, say a blessing, and share it; later, to take some wine, pour it out, say a blessing, and drink it.

The broken bread and poured out wine were prophetic signs[58] of the death that was soon to consummate his life in the service of God and God's kingdom. The prayer was to be a thanksgiving for that life and death and a plea that God would bring in the kingdom as soon as possible. By all eating the broken loaf and sharing the wine poured into the cup they would be committing themselves to that cause, the cause for which he had given his life, and pledging themselves to serve it as his disciples by the methods he had used, crowned, if need be, by dying on their own crosses.

After the Resurrection some of them seem to have experienced Jesus present in his new life especially vividly on those occasions when they were praying in this way.[59] If one believes in the reality of the Resurrection, this is wholly to be expected; and there can be very few Christians in the world today who would deny that the Son of God in his risen life meets with his friends when they celebrate the Eucharist.

What could be more profound – and yet more simple – than this act of prayer together which sums up the whole truth of our human condition? Here we receive, expressing our dependence on God in Jesus for the sources of true life. Here, in response, we give, the simple products of the earth and of human labour expressing our unity in the joyful offering of ourselves for the purposes of godliness in the world. In breaking the bread and pouring the wine before God we remember with thanksgiving the life and death without which humankind could never have known the reality of God's love for them. In receiving them back we are touched by the eternal love of the one who died, now present with us in our own living and dying, and making them a foretaste of eternal life. As Jesus' friends we renew the commitment of our baptism, and pledge ourselves afresh to him and to each other to live by his Spirit and to help all the other human children of God to do the same.

Is that not in essence what Jesus wanted? Does it not also express the whole liberating, healing transformation that God brought about in him for humankind? Is it complicated? Can it not be grasped with joy by anyone? Is it not in effect what all Christians in their inward devotions experience in this sacrament? So why is it that the Eucharist, which was meant to be a source of unity in discipleship, has become the cause of division?

The answer is that the words which stand at the heart of every Eucharist – 'This is my body', 'This is my blood' – became the occasion of one of the greatest tragedies in the history of the Christian Church.

'Tragedy' is surely the right word, for it is hard to see how the evils which ensued could have been avoided. By fifty years after the Resurrection the split between the Jewish people and the Christian community was virtually complete. New converts were overwhelmingly Gentile, and the words of Jesus in Greek rang very differently in their ears from the way they would have done to a Jew. The word 'is', which would not even have been there in Hebrew or Aramaic, to Greek-speakers meant 'really is', and the sense of what Jesus had said seemed plainly that in a miraculous way those who ate the bread and drank the wine ate the flesh and drank the blood of the Lord.[60] By the beginning of the second century CE the eucharistic bread and wine have become the 'medication', the 'drug', that cures you of vulnerability to death, and makes you immortal.[61]

To do the impossible and sum up many centuries of Christian history in a word, the Churches have been riven apart over the issue of the sense in which the bread and wine 'are' the body and blood of Jesus. Some of the most sophisticated metaphysical theories of all time have been deployed to answer that question and, for the greater part of the worldwide Church, are official teaching. This makes them a major obstacle to unity, and such they are likely to remain.[62] All one can say in extenuation is that at least this is a step forward from the times when Christians imprisoned, tortured and burned each other for holding different views on this subject.

Yet at least in those past times the theologians had the excuse that they thought sincerely that they were interpreting what Jesus meant. Today the advances in New Testament studies have demolished that excuse. There can be few specialist New Testament scholars in the world who would now argue for the old interpretation of Jesus' words. The issue is settled. Why then do the Churches not get together and start again on defining what they believe about the Eucharist? For the reason touched on earlier (in Chapter 2): that none of the mainline Churches has ever yet been able to say officially 'We were wrong' on a matter of doctrine. Even the fact that many of the faithful are uncomfortable with the understanding of the sacrament suggested by traditional teaching, and that many more outside the Churches are baffled and even revolted by it, is not motive enough for a review. Where would be the virtue in faith, it is said, if believing were easy?

One other problem about the Eucharist needs to be faced. It began, as we have seen, in the context of a genuine meal; and that may well have remained its setting for some time.[63] But more and more it became a ritual act. The bread and wine of the eucharistic prayer were not received on the occasion of sharing other food but simply by themselves within an act of worship. So we arrive at the situation today, where what is received is no more than a tiny piece or wafer of bread and a sip of wine. Nor are they eaten and drunk in a way that bears any resemblance to ordinary eating and drinking. The powerful fundamental symbolism of the shared meal has gone, and with it something crucial to the whole Christian Gospel and calling: the recognition that everyday life is itself holy, sacramental in character.

It is, no doubt, unavoidable for practical reasons that when the whole Christian community in one place comes together for the Eucharist what happens should not be much like a regular meal. This makes it difficult devotionally to see the Eucharist as the offering to God of our commitment to godliness in the human reality of home, workplace and neighbourhood. One change, however, could do more than anything else to bring back that sense of reality. Why should the Churches not get back to their roots in the Jewish world of Jesus, and make the eucharistic prayer both in the general congregation and also in the home – or any other appropriate meeting place of Christian disciples – part of a meal when friends of Christ gather to eat and drink together?

For this to make its full impact the observance would need to be performed by people themselves as an integral element of their normal life. To hand it over to a consecrated priest would at once imprison it again in the sphere of the technically religious. As was said earlier, the Church needs its ordained ministers; and one of their tasks is to guide all Christians in their approach to the sacraments, so that these are indeed points at which life is transformed and people are put in touch with God in Jesus. It is absolutely right, therefore, that a priest should be the normal president at the Eucharist when the whole congregation meets together, not only for the reason mentioned but also because he or she is an official representative of the wider Church. But if the Eucharist is to regain its true place in human life it must be open to all Christians to celebrate it as their thanksgiving for and recourse to the love of God both in daily normality and in times of special need or danger.[64]

The Bible

Throughout this book there has been constant appeal to the Bible, either to bring Jesus to life, or to illumine fundamental insights of Christian faith and life. All Churches acknowledge the supreme position of the Bible as an authoritative witness to Christian truth. It was mentioned as one of the two great resources available to the ordained minister in the task of enabling Christlikeness, the image of God, to flower in each disciple and in the community as a whole. But there is no doubt that it presents serious difficulties to many readers, not only because of the archaic culture from which it comes but also because of the many elements in it which are far from the vision of God and godliness which we have been given in Jesus. Before coming to our final summary reflections on the faith of a Christian, therefore, what can be said about the most valid and valuable way of using the Bible?

The Bible is not in itself a compendium of all we need to know about God. It points beyond itself, demanding to be completed. It springs out of a past in which God has already been at work; and it points ahead to a deeper knowledge and to a fulfilment which it glimpses from afar. As Jesus says in St John's gospel, 'When the Spirit of truth comes, he will guide you into all the truth . . . and he will declare to you the things that are to come.'[65] That process is still not complete.

To take the Bible seriously must be to take history seriously; and that means not talking simply in terms of a book, a set of printed pages, a fixed and static thing, but seeing that book as the product of the life of a people, a community. Historical process is about people, their stories, their thoughts, their dreams. And this brings us to another key fact about the Bible.

The Bible, as indicated earlier, is a collection of extremely varied writings. It contains laws, legends, history, songs, love poems, prayers, hymns, prophecies, practical wisdom, genealogies, manuals of religious ceremonial, mysterious visions, letters, and those unique compositions, the gospels. Its contents cover thirteen centuries: a work song and a tribal lay date from about 1200 BCE; the Letters to Timothy and Titus may have been written around 80 or 90 CE. How many hands have contributed to it we shall never know. The laws collected in Exodus, Leviticus, Numbers and Deuteronomy represent the accumulated work of generations of different groups of priests. The prophetic books contain pieces added from various sources over two hundred years to develop their main themes, not to mention all sorts of marginal comments which have got into the text. King David was indeed a composer of Psalms, but the Book of Psalms is the work of many poets, Temple and court singers and revisers. Proverbs is an anthology. Nor should we forget the countless scribes who copied the texts, making thousands of tiny changes – most of them unintentional, no doubt, but some their personal flash of insight about God, when they found themselves thinking in exasperation about the author, 'Now why didn't he put that in?'[66]

The most appropriate definition we can give of the historical and literary character of the Bible is that it is an archive, a collection of documents, in this case mostly religious documents, written for various purposes in the life of a community, a society. An archive is not a single overall panorama, giving us an observer's account and interpretation of events. It is the material actually thrown up in the course of those events, the controversies and hopes, tragedies, triumphs and humdrum daily duties. In the Bible we are not, so to speak, told by a commentator to believe that God was involved in this pilgrimage of a people. Instead we empathise with the efforts people made to recognise his involvement at the time, with all their blindnesses and misconceptions and self-serving as well as their leaps of faith and heroic commitment.

What is more, believers relate to this archive as themselves members of that community, still continuing today. In the Magnificat[67] Christians sing, 'As he promised to *our* forebears, Abraham and his descendants for ever.' The history reflected in the Bible is an earlier period of Christian history, as it is of Jewish and Muslim history; and Christians have developed it in their own distinctive way, just as Judaism and Islam have developed it in theirs. We are all 'Peoples of the Book', because we acknowledge the historic people of the Book as our own fellow pilgrims and spiritual ancestors.

When we look at the portion of our story which gave

rise to that Book, our dominant reaction ought to be one of amazement. It begins with a loose tangle of barbarous clans, who thought that their tribal god required them to slaughter every living thing, women, children and animals included, in every town they captured, and who were suckers for any new fertility cult that caught on among their neighbours. Yet this people grew into a nation with an exalted monotheistic worship of a universal God of justice and mercy, and with an ethical way of life which commanded the admiration of many thoughtful minds in the Graeco-Roman world. Weak, dispersed and persecuted they might be; but spiritually and morally they had succeeded where all other societies or philosophies had in serious respects failed. What was to be their destiny?

The answer, as Christians believe, is that they had been prepared by God to be a people within which he himself could share human existence. The final records from the archive speak for those who were caught up in this miracle, the first generation of those whose lives were totally reconstructed by what had happened. The reason why the Bible alone mediates the truth uniquely necessary for the fulfilment of humankind is that it alone puts us in touch with this event, beside which all other events are less than the jottings of a newspaper's society diarist. Moreover it places this event within the stream of history, giving it a home in a particular people, Israel, and thus according their journey of spiritual discovery a unique and universal significance.

Seen in this light, the imperfections of the characters in the drama and of their ideas of God and human behaviour are not only not a problem, they are enormously encouraging. To begin with, most people today are at some recognisable point on the same pilgrimage. We have the same doubts about the meaning of life, the same anger at its injustices, the same moral perplexities and failures. The curses of the Psalmist, the anguished cries of the prophets, are often closer to our inmost feelings than we dare admit, for then we would have to face the fact that we are not so 'Christian' after all. But if we are prepared to be honest the Bible is a source of tremendous hope. It tells us that, given half a chance, God can work his purpose out even through people like us. The God of the Bible comes to us in the nitty-gritty of the actual moment, and speaks to us through our own inadequate words and broken situations. Truth, it says, was not in the end to be found in the abstract concepts of pious uplift. It came in the unique historic actuality of one particular human life, death and resurrection and in what, as a result of that, you and I and any other human soul can make of our lives as we try to get them more and more lined up on God and on his kind of love as revealed in Jesus.

If we belong to the 'People of the Book' – if their history is now our history – that is because, by being born as a human being, God united the whole human family to theirs. 'Salvation is from the Jews', as the Gospel of St John says;[68] but the way that salvation came meant that it could never be confined to Jews. The final records in the biblical archive show us the followers of Jesus struggling to come to terms with their dawning realisation of this.

Here again, therefore, the Bible points beyond itself. There can be no true understanding of it which treats it as somehow 'the Church's book', and so makes God 'the Church's God'. God is the God of all creatures; and, through the medium of all languages, the Bible, which begins with the creation of the universe and of humankind, and ends gazing ahead to the final perfecting of all things, is a book for all people. Its authority is unique, because in the story which created it humanity has access, not just in the mind but in the heart's experience, to the one truth crucial to human living. The Bible promises us that, as time goes by, everything we learn about the cosmos and ourselves will fit together round that truth, thus endlessly enlarging our understanding and adoration of God and our love for him. All we have to do is to trust the Spirit which spoke through the prophets and rested on Jesus to be with us too in each generation.

6

Let God be God

For my thoughts are not your thoughts, nor are
your ways my ways, says the Lord. For as the
heavens are higher than the earth, so are my ways
higher than your ways, and my thoughts than
your thoughts.

Isaiah 55:8–9

There we shall be still and see; we shall see and
we shall love; we shall love and we shall praise.
Behold what will be, in the end, without end!
For what is our end but to reach that kingdom
which has no end?

St Augustine of Hippo, *City of God*, XXII.30.

When all the evidence has been marshalled, and all the arguments examined, the question to which we most long for an answer remains: what is God in himself? What is God like?

As we have seen, the story of Jesus is crucial; he is our window onto God's heart and mind. But we cannot simply say, 'God is like Jesus'. Jesus was human like ourselves; his deity was hidden. What is more, when he lived in our history, he did so as one who had a human relationship with God, his divine *abba*. We cannot merely blow up our image of Jesus and project it onto the backcloth of the universe and call it 'God'.

Prayer and the knowledge of God

The place in our lives where we have our most direct experience of God is in our prayer. What happens when we pray?

In one way of prayer we focus ourselves on the thought of

God, helped perhaps by Scripture or other reading, and we just wait for him. The time may be full of distractions, we may have no sense of God at all; but our effort at attention to God is a pledge of our love and trust. Sometimes, in a way seemingly unrelated to our own efforts, we experience a mystical joy, a sense of being taken out of ourselves, and we feel sure that God has been with us. In retrospect we are often aware that he has also been with us when there was no joy at all, only boredom and weariness. But such experience does not give us much idea what he is like.

There is, however, another kind of prayer, the one on which Jesus laid most stress. Here we are not primarily thinking of being with God, of getting to know him directly. We come instead in dependence and trust, asking some blessing for the needs of others or ourselves. But, despite Jesus' encouragement, we have our hesitations. Billions of impossible or incompatible requests are hurled at God every day from this planet alone! What do we suppose is happening when we pray in this way?

First, we need to rid ourselves of a wrong mental picture. Because in Jesus God meets us as an individual human person, we understandably imagine God in himself as a 'super-person', a larger, more complex version of the same thing. But God is nothing of the kind. 'Person' is a concept derived from our experience of ourselves. Humans are persons, living in relationship with one another, but each limited and different. But God is not limited. He is a spiritual power and presence, over, in and through the whole cosmos, but having his being quite independently of space-time, not conditioned by it. We can relate to him as person to person, in the way proper to human beings, because in his love for all creatures God chooses to relate to each one in the way appropriate to its kind. But we must not, because of that, make the mistake of imagining him as simply a superior version of ourselves.

When someone makes a request in prayer on behalf of another, at once a three-cornered relationship is activated: the person praying, the person prayed for, and God. Because God is not determined by space-time – he did, after all, create it – he is not, like matter, distributed through the universe, but is present as himself to every creature in it. We and those for whom we pray are thus immediately close to one another, for all of us are directly in touch with God.

One way of thinking about such prayer, therefore, is this. The greatest power in the universe to cherish life, give strength, heal body or mind, evoke better insights, wiser counsels or more godly behaviour is the loving and creative spirit of God. But in most cases it may well be that God's spirit needs, to use a technological metaphor, a pathway along which to access the person or situation calling for his help. Our human love and concern, and our natural psychic networks with those involved, may supply that, if made available in love for him to use.

This model has the advantage of corresponding more closely to experience than some other accounts. We all know that even the most heartfelt prayer does not necessarily mean that what we want to happen will come about. Sometimes it does; perhaps more often it does not. But, in many cases where it does not, we find that things in fact went better than those concerned had feared or expected.

That is not proof that prayer is effective. There can be no such proof. But it does fit in with some other considerations. What, for instance, were the real possibilities in that situation? We know the result we wanted to see, and it may well have been in itself something good. Its very simplicity may have been an index of the depth and sincerity of our caring.[1] But if it was not within the potential, say, of that aged body or broken mind, of that group of people with their particular history, of that environment, then even God could not make it happen. God's love can bring about only what can be done. That will often be something more wonderful than human action alone can achieve, but it will still be within the existing potential. If we are amazed, it may simply be that neither we nor those prayed for had any idea what that potential was. It may also be true that what God can achieve is greater or less in proportion to the faith and the genuine love we put at his disposal – Jesus seems to have implied something like that.[2] But experience enables us to say with some confidence that there is no loving prayer that does not enable some blessing; and that there are some blessings that will never come without someone's prayer.

That is why one of the greatest vocations of the Church is

to be in continual prayer for the human community and the environment of which it is a part. It is for Christians to be in such solidarity with their neighbours at a human level that they know what should be taken to God in prayer, and that they ensure that it is taken, without fanfare,[3] and regardless of whether those in need are Church members or not.

Is this to say that God does not in fact work miracles? That he can help forward only what is within a situation's natural potential, known to us or not? Christians could hardly take up that position when their faith rests on an act of God which burst the bounds of all natural potential.[4] What picture can we compose to help us place miracles within our general understanding of the world in relation to God?

If most answers to prayer can be thought of as God's Spirit evoking a situation's full natural potential – what was already there, but unknown to us – by a 'miracle' we mean the input by that same Spirit of something that was not already there. God is not just the manager of the universe but its Creator. He brought it into being as a new thing and he can do new things with it and in it, if he so desires. Whatever God introduces in this way will clearly be compatible with the total scheme and function within it; but it will be the feeding into the cosmos of something which it could not have produced for itself, but which God knows is needed at that strategic point for the cause of the kingdom. Miracles will never be many.[5] When they happen, they may not always be easy to recognise or to distinguish from ordinary answers to prayer. But that they should happen at all is in no way discordant with our general understanding of the universe and of God's relation to it.

Returning to the matter of petitionary prayer, that too has important things to tell us about God in himself. The heart of such prayer at the human level is authentic love for those prayed for, love that truly cares and identifies. It is the experience of those deeply practised in such prayer that their own imperfect love gets taken up into a greater love, indwelling them and reaching out to the world in a way far beyond their own powers. There is no doubt in their minds that in this they have experienced God's presence in their souls, and that his nature is love.

God and suffering

Yet there is a problem here. Love as we know it, authentic love, means that whenever the one loved endures harm or evil, the lover suffers with them and for them. But the theologians have traditionally asked: can God suffer? If, they have said, God's natural state is perfect blessedness, then any change from that, such as suffering must involve, will be for the worse. But God, as the sum of all perfection, cannot change for the worse. Therefore God cannot suffer. Again, to suffer is to be acted upon against one's will. But only something stronger than oneself can do that. Since there is nothing stronger than God, God cannot suffer.

It is important to be clear that the theologians are here talking about God as God, as pure divinity, not about God incarnate. Indeed, it was partly for philosophical reasons such as these that Christian thinkers early argued that one of the motives for the Incarnation was to enable God to suffer.[6] In this way the inability of God to suffer as God – his 'impassibility', to use the technical term – was safeguarded, but the divine generosity of the Cross remained.

This, however, did not meet the real difficulty. Suffering as we know it requires a physical organism capable of feeling pain. This applies even to what we call 'mental' suffering: temptation, anxiety, fear, sympathy, anger, jealousy and many other states all affect us through the bodily misery to which they give rise. The Incarnation was an act of love in which God showed himself willing to share suffering as experienced by us or by any comparable sentient physical being. But that would not be suffering in the sense in which God would experience it if he could suffer as God.

We know that the better someone is the more cruelly evil breaks their heart, because they are more aware of its real nature. So, but even more terribly, it must be with God. If it were not, God would not be Love.

But is that the right way to put it? Perhaps the reason that theologians had a problem lay in their logic. If you define blessedness as the absence of suffering, then a God who lives in perfect bliss will lose that bliss if he suffers. But is that the true definition of blessedness? If we start instead from the axiom 'God is Love',[7] then perfect blessedness consists in being love, and love of its nature is liable to suffer. In that case God's blessedness would be imperfect if he could not suffer.

We reflected earlier that any creation capable of producing life and, more wonderful still, beings in God's image is going to be vulnerable to pain and evil. God's purpose in creating, however, was the increase of joy – that beings other than himself should exist to enjoy the blessedness that he enjoys. That looks like a contradiction impossible to resolve. But God knew, as we know now from the Cross and Resurrection of Jesus, that the only road to that blessed and eternal life has, for creatures, to run through the gate of death. In creating, therefore, God was making a conscious choice. Because his creatures, for their own ultimate fulfilment, would have to suffer, he was also committing himself to suffering both as God and, in order to help these other beings on their way to blessedness, as one of them. Yet he knows that his purpose of the increase of joy will be achieved in the end; and because he is Love the unimaginable anguish which that purpose entails for him is still blessedness unimpaired.

This understanding in terms of creation also disposes of the other argument for God's impassibility, namely that he cannot be acted upon by anything stronger than himself. Any power the creation has to cause God to suffer is God's own power, for he alone gave it existence and holds it in existence. God, being Love, chose that the creation should be able to hurt him, because that was the only route to its own ultimate perfecting. No one and nothing imposed that on him.

When we talk of God suffering as God, it is impossible to form any notion of what that involves.[8] God's nature in itself is and must remain an impenetrable mystery. But we can say that it must be so, because this is the nature of love as revealed in Jesus.[9]

God as Trinity

The same applies to another mystery, that of God as Trinity. How it can be so is beyond our thought. That it must be so is clear.

The background is the story of Jesus. The gospels show him, as we have seen, living in dependence upon and loving obedience to God as his Father. Likewise they describe him as empowered by God's own Spirit, sent by the Father and thus distinct from the Father; and this is the same Spirit which from the beginning Christians have claimed to experience indwelling their own lives.

Once the Church had been inspired to acknowledge Jesus as God, it became clear that the God at work in the life, death and resurrection of Jesus was something far more than the single divine figure of traditional imagery. The relation of Jesus to his Father and the relation of the Spirit to the Father and to Jesus echoed in human terms what was eternally true in God himself. This is precisely what we find John expressing in his gospel, when he has Jesus talk as the eternal divine Son about his co-operation with and obedience to the Father. This was the divine reality behind the earthly events.

Because of our natural and incurable tendency to think of God in terms of ourselves we easily fall into picturing the Trinity as a team or committee of three individuals; and even the greatest representations of the subject in Christian art inevitably reinforce this.[10] But theologically we must resist the temptation.

We are 'individuals' because we are physically packaged. God is spiritual. When we say that Jesus is God, we mean that he is fully God: the fullness of God is in him,[11] not just one third. So likewise with the Father and the Spirit.[12] If this seems at first like pure paradox and mystification, the theologian has a simple reply. Modern science and mathematics also produce concepts which contradict our ordinary commonsense and seem utterly impossible; but we accept them because we are convinced that only these seeming absurdities do justice to the evidence. We do not say, 'This in human language makes nonsense, therefore it must be false.' We recognise that human language can only point in the right direction, and outline the defining limits of an answer. The same applies to our words about the Trinity. Reality in itself is beyond our scope and so, unsurprisingly, is its Creator, God.

Eternal life

The same applies to our final topic, the goal of God's own endeavours and of the pilgrimage of faith: eternal life.

What do we mean by 'heaven' or 'eternal life', and what are the true grounds for desiring it? I was once asked whether, if it could be proved that there was no God, I would wish I had lived my life differently. The reply, so far as memory serves, was this: 'No, I would not want to have lived my life by different values, because I believe that those by which I have at least tried to live are right in themselves anyway. But I would be very sad, because it would mean that truth, goodness, beauty and love are not eternal and will not triumph in the end.'

The reason for wanting there to be a 'heaven' is that the last word may rest not with evil or nothingness but with goodness and love. To the degree that we care about that we shall long for heaven as it really is.

If there is, in the worst of sinners, even the faintest residual wish or hope that the world and their own selves need not be as they have made them – perhaps no more than the echo of something good and happy of which in childhood they once had dreamed – encounter with Jesus will mean at least a chance of starting out on the long, long task of regrowing their whole personalities from those tiny withered seeds. That task will call for help not just from God but also (as we were thinking in Chapter 4) from all those whose lives theirs have touched in any way. To seek help, reconciliation and healing from all those they have injured will be as appallingly hard for them as it will be for those others to give it. But the giving will be as necessary for the perfecting of their victims as the receiving will be for the sinners.

In differing degrees the same process will be necessary for everyone. But there will be much more to come than just receiving our selves, cleansed and renewed, as divine Love transforms the other people in our lives, and enables them to make that gift. That is but the preliminary stage,[13] preparing the ground for the image of God to grow in each of us as it is enriched by the godliness of all those around us.

And what a glorious multitude that will be! Souls of every land and time, every race and faith, all longing for that fullness of life which comes from loving and rejoicing in God's whole resurrected creation and from being oneself loved and a source of joy. Nor will our fellow citizens in heaven come only from this Earth. From wherever in the cosmos the image of God has taken creaturely form they will come in, so that all may find in each unending cause for wonder and praise.

> But in the eternities
> Doubtless we shall compare together, hear
> A million alien gospels, in what guise
> He trod the Pleiades, the Lyre, the Bear.
> Oh be prepared, my soul,
> To read the inconceivable, to scan
> The infinite forms of God those stars unroll
> When, in our turn, we show to them a Man.[14]

And more mysterious even than these, yet perhaps intuitively recognised, will be the creatures of quite other orders of being, reflecting and serving their Creator in different ways – those spirits to whom not just Christians but believers of other faiths have given the name of 'angels'.

Coming back to our human selves, what of those who had no chance to live, those dying in infancy or before birth? Or again – and one of the most agonising cases of all for relatives or friends – those whose whole personal being was destroyed in this life by, for example, dementia or Alzheimer's or Creutz-feldt-Jakob disease? Long before they die, it may feel to others that already they no longer exist. What is there to go on through death to Resurrection life?

Such questions raise the whole issue of what we may call the 'mode of being' of creatures in eternal life. Even here we depend on the loving will of the Creator to sustain the cosmos from which we derive our existence. Because we are products of that ongoing physical system, our ultimate dependence on God is hidden from us, but it is none the less real for that. When we die, the intermediate physical support for our personal being ceases and the only power that keeps us in existence is the one that was actually doing so all the time, namely God. We then 'transfer', so to speak, to that spiritual mode of being which is God's, for it is entirely in God's loving mind and will that we exist. There God clothes us in whatever spiritual 'body'[15] expresses our personal reality; and that can and will change 'from glory to glory'[16] as the image of God grows in us. Moreover, being in this way with all other creatures 'in God', we shall be exempt from the conditions of space-time, and it will make no sense to talk of growth and change taking a longer or shorter period. It will simply be part of the interchange that is the nature of life in 'the land of the Trinity'.[17]

This freedom from space-time means that what God holds in being beyond death will not be simply the person as he or she happened to be at that moment. A parable may help here. When someone dies and an obituary is written or an address given at a memorial service, we do not speak only of the cancer victim or the frail old body longing for release. We try to distil what that person was by bringing together facts and facets from their whole life story. What God delivers from death is something like our picture of the person we remember, only real and complete.

Similar considerations apply in the case of psychiatric disorders and many other disabilities. So many conditions which 'spoil' a person's nature are physical in origin. When the remorseless pressure of the body is removed, what emerges will be the person, known only to God, whom she or he longed and tried to be. Likewise, when the destructive emotional inheritance underlying a neurosis is no longer part of a person's environment and she or he enters the realm of divine truth and love, there may be a marvellous unfolding of unsuspected beauty.

As for the infants, they will not have had the chance to 'make their own souls' amid the joys and agonies of life. They are, as it were, almost entirely potential. But in the rich exchange of God's people in heaven they will develop from the starting point of their innocence into a very special kind of perfection.

How the rest of creation will one day take its place in the divine order[18] it is problematic even to speculate. Nevertheless it is logical to assume that it will, and that the relationship with other types of creature, damaged by our tyranny and selfishness, will be healed. Even as they are, in the grip of imperfection and dysfunction, the innumerable life forms and other elements in the cosmos give glory to God by the wonder of their being. And there will surely be a special place for those friends in whom, as we saw,[19] there are fragments and foreshadowings of the divine image.

Today the message most strongly heard from the doctrine of the Trinity is that all true being is 'being-in-communion'.[20] The full flowering of the image of God in creatures is possible only when they are living in communion with all other beings; and the deepest meaning of the image is revealed not in any individual but in the communion of which the individual is a member. Thus the full significance of the image of God even in Jesus is not disclosed until we know him in the family of the Trinity.

The Church of God, as the New Testament constantly teaches, was meant to be an exemplar of this being-in-communion. Instead Christians who share the same creeds, the same Scriptures, the same sacraments, the same ministry, and who acknowledge the same Master and Saviour, have become a byword for division and fighting and rejecting one another. It is doubtful whether there has ever been a pretext for Christian disunity which was not utterly trivial compared with what the disputants had in common. How are we Christians ever to find the humility to seek pardon of all the fellow human beings our quarrels have betrayed?

To speak of the Trinity as a family is a metaphor which, at its best, conveys both a communion of shared mutual commitment and also the idea of a group open to welcome new members. In the Incarnation the Holy Trinity made that welcome plain; and in eternal life every creature is one of that family. For many women today, however, that imagery is spoiled by the overwhelmingly masculine character of the Godhead as expressed in the figures of the Father and the Son, and in the traditional use of 'he' to refer to God. Doctrinally there is no gender in God. The masculinity of the incarnate Jesus is, as we saw earlier,[21] no bar to recognising that the fullness of the divine image includes all that is godly in both women and men. In time, we must pray, the Holy Spirit will show us how to combine in general devotion the authoritative language of Scripture with these other insights already pioneered by such as St Anselm and Mother Julian.[22]

'Perfect in love'[23]

But these difficulties belong only in this life, where we see in a mirror dimly.[24] In heaven we shall see 'face to face'; and then we shall be like the One we see.[25] That likeness and that vision will be complete when the heart of our own being is identical with the heart of the being of God, namely Love.

There is a strand in Christian devotion which, though almost a cliché in the tradition, strikes the average believer as artificial and unconvincing. It is the idea that our true destiny is to be detached from all love of creatures, and to give all our love to God alone. A related theme is that when we do some act of loving service to another we should do it 'as to Christ' or to Christ 'in' that person.[26]

This is strange, and surely misguided. There are two fundamental commandments: to love God; and to love our neighbour as ourself – not to love our neighbour for God's sake, but to accord him or her equal value with our own soul. Do we suppose that God loves us only because we are brothers and sisters of his Son? If so, how did he love us enough to send his Son in the first place?

Love that loves the beloved not as what they are but for some other reason is not authentic love. If we are to be in the image of God, it will be shown in the fact that we love all other beings in themselves. Then our love will be like God's love,[27] and our whole self will be in harmony with his.

That is why all the citizens of 'the high courts of heaven' care not only for each other but also for us who are still on pilgrimage toward that 'better country'.[28] One day we shall learn a little of the blessings which that love, which traditionally we call 'the prayers of the saints', has brought us. For how could they think only of themselves, when God is concerned for many whose destiny still hangs in the balance? The saints' love, like his, will be costing and sacrificial; but also, like his, it will be perfect joy, for true love can find no joy in ceasing to love, whatever the cost.

There in eternal life they 'see' God because their will is at last one with his. One day, when creation has finally run its course, and the kingdom comes, that will be true for all of us. But eternal life can begin for us here and now, in so far as we bring our own being into harmony with his universal and unalterable purpose of love.

In the case of that perfect love whereby countless happy angels and men shall each love the other no less than himself, each one shall rejoice for every other as much as for himself . . . All will enter into your joy . . . (for) surely, they will rejoice in the degree that they will love.[29]

Appendix A:

The nature of Jesus' resurrection, and the evidence for it

The resurrection of Jesus is central to the argument of the present work; but to avoid obscuring the main lines of that argument it seemed best to place a summary of the evidence for that event in this Appendix.

General grounds

The general grounds for belief in Jesus' resurrection have not changed in centuries, and they are three.

1. *Jesus is remembered.* Had the story of Jesus ended with his death by crucifixion, it is highly unlikely that the world would ever have heard of him. At most he might have received the sort of passing mention given him in the authentic text of Josephus.

2. *The disciples regained hope.* The crucifixion left Jesus' leading disciples in a state of crushed disillusionment (Luke 24:11, 18–24; John 20:11–15, 19). Yet within six weeks they were enthusiastically proclaiming him as Israel's Messiah (Acts 2:36). Some decisive experience must have triggered this transformation; and it must have been one which set not only the death on the cross but its attendant criminal shame and its condemnation by the biblical Law in a wholly new light. Experience of Jesus risen is the only explanation, other than fraud, in the field, and if true could certainly be expected to have this result.

3. *Contemporaries found the disciples persuasive.* Conspiracy to deceive is not plausible, because from the start the disciples were willing, even eager, to face ostracism, persecution and death for preaching the Resurrection (Acts 4:1–3, 19, 29–31; 5:17–18, 27–33, 40–1; 6:8–15; 7:52–60; 8:1–3; 9:1–2). Clearly

they were convinced of the truth of their claims, and able to convince others.

Documentary evidence

The fact of the Resurrection is, of course, attested by almost every book in the New Testament. In addition to the four gospels and Acts, the letters of St Paul (except Philemon) make constant reference to it, and discuss its significance from many angles. Of the remaining texts 1 Peter and Revelation give it most prominence. Hebrews, Jude and the three letters of John, while making no explicit reference, speak a good deal about related themes, such as Jesus' exaltation into heaven, and the gift to us of eternal life. Only in James and 2 Peter may there be said to be no allusion at all; and even here there are passages hard to explain unless the Resurrection is assumed (Jas. 5:7, 14; 2 Pet. 1:11).

The documents directly relevant, however, to the nature of Jesus' resurrection and to the disciples' experience of it can be reviewed under six heads: Paul's First Letter to the Corinthians; the four gospels; and Acts together with certain passages in Paul's other letters.

1 Corinthians

Scholarly consensus dates the material in this letter, which may in its present form be composite, between 52 and 54 CE – that is, not more than twenty-five years after the crucifixion. In 15:3–6 Paul writes: ' . . . I handed on to you as of first import-ance what I in turn had received: that Christ died for our sins in accordance with the scriptures, and that he was buried, and that he was raised on the third day in accordance with the scriptures, and that he appeared to Cephas, then to the twelve.'

The words 'handed on' and 'received' are semi-technical terms, and refer to the process by which converts were instructed (cf. 1 Cor. 11:23). Authoritative forms of words were used to guarantee basic teaching (cf. Rom. 6:17). Stylistic features, as well as Paul's explicit reference to what he had himself 'received', suggest that he is here quoting the instruction he was given about Jesus' resurrection after his own conversion – that is, between 33 and 36 CE – and which he had used verbatim when instructing the Corinthians. These verses thus take us back to some five years only after the events they relate.

Note that the four statements are on a par: 'was raised' is meant as factually as 'died', 'was buried'. The same applies to 'appeared' (literally, 'was seen'), which carries no overtones of an 'apparition': compare the English usage, 'I was waiting outside the station when Jill appeared.'

In this skeletal 'creed' we find all the elements developed in other sources: 'was buried', in conjunction with 'was raised', implies the empty tomb; 'appeared' refers to the kind of experiences reflected in Matthew, Luke and John. Specifically, for Cephas (Peter) see Luke 24:34; for the Twelve see Matthew 28:16–17; Luke 24:33–6; John 20:24 and Acts 1:21–6. Paul supplements the official formula with a reference to a meeting with 'more than five hundred' disciples at one time, with James (possibly Jesus' brother: see Gal. 1:19), and with 'all the apostles' (membership uncertain: see, for example, Rom. 16:7), before rounding off with the appearance to himself, regarded by him as the validation of his own unlikely apostleship, and evidentially the equal of all the others mentioned.

St Mark

The customary dating of Mark's gospel in the late sixties CE has been questioned by some recent scholarship, which places Luke in the mid-fifties, and Mark therefore earlier than that. Traditionally Mark is said to have derived much of his material from Peter. It is reasonable to assume that Mark's gospel represents the author's theological presentation of oral tradition from the first Christian generation.

The authentic text of Mark, as we have it, ends at Mark 16:8, and contains no account of meetings with the risen Jesus – only a young man who tells three women who have come to anoint the body that he has risen. The youth shows them that the tomb is empty, and commands them to pass on the message that 'his disciples and Peter' will see Jesus back in Galilee (16:6–7).

St Matthew

Matthew's gospel is agreed by the majority of scholars to be later than Mark, even though early Church tradition holds it to be the first to be written, c.41 CE. In my own view it is later than Luke also.

Matthew's Resurrection material is close in outline to Mark, but elaborates it. This time two women come simply to view the tomb. While there, they see the stone door rolled away from the tomb by an angel during an earthquake (Matt. 28:2). His appearance terrifies and paralyses the guards placed at the tomb by the 'chief priests and the Pharisees' (27:62–6; 28:4). Like the young man in Mark the angel tells the women that Jesus is risen, shows them the empty tomb, and sends them to the other disciples with the same message about Galilee (28:5–7). On their way, however, the women now meet Jesus himself, who repeats their instructions (28:8–10). The guards report to their superiors what has happened, but are bribed to keep silent and to say that the disciples stole the body while they were asleep. This, Matthew adds, is the story spread 'among the Jews to this day' (28:11–15). Meanwhile, the 'Eleven' (i.e. the twelve apostles less Judas, who has killed himself: 27:3–10) go to Galilee, where Jesus meets them, though even then they can hardly believe (28:16–17). The gospel ends with Jesus' command to make disciples of all nations, and the assurance of his presence with them in power till the divine consummation of world history (28:18–20).

St Luke

If, as seems probable, Acts was written during Paul's house arrest at Rome (Acts 28:30–1) – that is, in 61–3 CE – then

Luke's gospel, to which the opening words of Acts refer (1:1), must be earlier. It too, therefore, represents an account of the Resurrection based on the stories of the first Christian generation.

Nevertheless it has highly distinctive features. The visit of the women (number unspecified: Luke 24:10) to the tomb to anoint the body, the stone rolled away, and the tomb empty are, with minor variations, as in Mark and Matthew; but this time two men in dazzling clothes (i.e. angels) tell them that Jesus is risen (24:4–6), and there is no message about going to Galilee, only a reminder that Jesus said all would happen as it has (24:6–7). The women report to the Eleven and the other disciples, but are not believed (24:9–11). An additional note not in all manuscripts (24:12) tells of Peter running to the tomb to check, in terms close to John 20:3–10.

Luke's special material now follows. Two disciples walking home from Jerusalem to Emmaus are joined by a stranger who asks what they are talking about and, on hearing the news of Jesus' death and the report of the empty tomb and the angels' message, then proves to them from the Old Testament that all this was in fact the destiny of Israel's Messiah (24:13–27). On reaching Emmaus the disciples invite the stranger to lodge with them for the night. Over supper he breaks and blesses bread, and they suddenly recognise him as Jesus, whereupon he vanishes (24:28–31). At once they rush back to Jerusalem, where they find the other disciples and learn that Jesus has appeared to Peter (24:32–5).

Jesus then materialises in the midst of them, so that they panic and think him a ghost. He invites them to touch him and discover for themselves that he is not, and then eats some fish to prove the point (24:36–43). After expounding the scriptural prophecies relating both to himself and to the mission of the Church, he commands them to wait in Jerusalem for the power promised by his Father (24:44–49). He then leads them out to Bethany, blesses them, and ascends into heaven, after which they return in joy to Jerusalem (24:50–3).

Luke is insistent, against Mark, Matthew and John, that all the Resurrection action takes place in Jerusalem. The story could not have happened in one day as narrated (note 24:29), and in any case conflicts in this respect with Luke's other accounts in Acts (Acts 1:1–11). The emphasis on Jesus' eating food is also strange. Underlying themes here reappear in John.

St John

The date of John is notoriously uncertain. It seems to come from a time when Jews and followers of Jesus are defining themselves in hostility to one another. Jewish Christians are probably being expelled from the synagogue and persecuted (cf. John 16:2 and many narrative details in this gospel), which some have seen as pointing to a date after 70 CE (but see Acts 6–8). John also has an idiosyncratic approach to history (see pp. 89f., 165), in which outward words and events and the hidden divine action from which they spring merge in the telling. John can nevertheless be sharply emphatic about factual details which are vivid to him, or which he thinks specially significant, or perhaps where he believes other narrators to be mistaken. It is, therefore, unsafe either to dismiss his account as of no evidential value historically or to follow him wherever he diverges from other versions.

John's Resurrection narratives are placed both in Jerusalem (Ch. 20) and in Galilee (Ch. 21, this being in the nature of an appendix to the whole work: see 20:30–1 and 21:24–5). Whether each chapter derives from the evangelist in the same way is open to debate.

In the Jerusalem stories it is Mary Magdalene alone who discovers the stone rolled away and assumes from this that the tomb is empty (20:1–2). The fact is confirmed by Peter and the 'disciple' who run to the tomb, enter, and find only the grave-cloths (20:3–9). They then leave, but Mary remains and is rewarded by the first encounter with the risen Jesus, which she afterwards relates to the other disciples as Jesus has commanded her to do (20:10–18). That evening Jesus appears among the disciples in a locked room and shows them the marks of his wounds (20:19–20). He endows them with the Holy Spirit and grants them authority to give or withhold the forgiveness of sins (20:21–3).

The apostle Thomas, absent on this occasion, refuses to believe until he too has seen and felt Jesus (20:24–5). A week later Jesus appears again, and Thomas is convinced. Jesus pronounces a blessing on those who believe without such proof, clearly meant by the evangelist to be taken as referring to future converts (20:26–9).

The Galilean episode in Chapter 21 consists of two connected stories. Peter and six other disciples have apparently returned to Galilee, and at Peter's suggestion they resume their old occupation as fishermen (21:1–3). After a night without success a man on the shore tells them where to cast their nets and they catch a huge shoal (cf. a similar story set during Jesus' ministry: Luke 5:1–11). The beloved disciple realises that the man is Jesus, and on reaching land they find a breakfast prepared at which Jesus presides (21:4–14). The second incident concerns a private talk which Jesus has with Peter after the meal. He draws from Peter a threefold avowal of love, thus wiping out Peter's threefold denial before the crucifixion (18:15–18, 25–7), and gives him a threefold charge as pastor of Jesus' flock (21:15–17). Jesus then utters a veiled prophecy of Peter's martyrdom, but ambiguously refuses to disclose the future of the beloved disciple (21:18–23).

The Acts of the Apostles

The material in this work falls into two distinct categories. The first is a brief preamble (1:1–11) leading up to Jesus' ascension into heaven. Like the ending of Luke's gospel (Luke 24:44–53), it stresses the command to the disciples to wait in Jerusalem until they are empowered by the Holy Spirit for their mission (1:4–5, 8). Unlike the gospel, Acts speaks of a period of 'forty days' (1:3: a standard biblical phrase for a significant period of time) after the first Easter Day, during which the risen Jesus met with the disciples and gave them further teaching.

The second set of material is quite different, consisting of the story, told three times (9:1–8; 22:6–11; 26:12–19) of an appearance of the risen Jesus to St Paul on the road to Damascus, an experience which led to his conversion. Luke is mentioned in at least one authentic letter of Paul's (Philem. 24) as a colleague, and from the narrative seems possibly to have been present at at least the third of the three tellings of the story. In any case, if a friend of Paul's, he must have had opportunity on many occasions to hear his account.

These episodes are strikingly different from those in the gospels. Some features are strongly reminiscent of the story of Daniel and the angel in Daniel 10:5–9. The two phenomena related are a brilliant light, which causes Paul temporary blindness, and a voice addressing Paul. The three accounts are not consistent in every detail. In Acts 9:7 Paul's companions hear the voice; in 22:9 they do not. There are also discrepancies over what is supposed to have been said to Paul: in 9:6 he is simply told to go to Damascus and await further instructions, which are never made explicit; in 22:10–15 the Lord's command is the same, but Ananias, the Christian disciple who baptises him, tells him that God has chosen him to witness to the whole world; and in 26:15–18 Jesus himself tells Paul of his commission to preach to the Gentiles. But what is stressed is that this experience was an encounter with the risen Jesus in person (9:5, 17; 22:8, 14; 26:15–16), however different from those in the gospels.

Paul's letters

Finally there is the evidence in Paul's letters. In 1 Corinthians 15:8 Paul mentions the appearance of the risen Jesus to himself as on a par with those included in the teaching he received, but neither there nor anywhere else in his letters do we have a description of that appearance in his own words. He does, however, give one account of his dramatic move from the Pharisaic to the Jesus party within Judaism, a move which Acts links with the Damascus road experience. In Galatians 1:11–12, 15–16 Paul claims that the gospel he preaches came to him by direct revelation from Jesus Christ, and that God, who had destined and called him for this very purpose 'was pleased . . . to reveal his Son in me, in order that I might preach him among the Gentiles.'

The words 'reveal his Son in me' have been much debated. Do they imply a purely interior and spiritual new apprehension of Jesus as alive, and of his nature and mission? From what Paul says elsewhere we know that there was a mystical element in his spiritual life, and that he had ecstatic experiences and also inner converse with Christ (2 Cor. 12:1–10; cf. Acts 22:17–18; 23:11). Is the Galatians account, therefore, an alternative and more authoritative version of the story in Acts? But it is possible to exaggerate the conflict between the two sources. Acts and Paul himself are in agreement that there was a moment of radical disclosure for Paul, which completely altered the perspective of his faith, and convinced him that Jesus was Messiah and living Lord, God's saviour of Gentiles as well as Jews, and to be preached as such. Whatever elements went to make up this spiritual revolution in him, the fact that he also insisted to his Corinthian converts that his own meeting with the risen Jesus was such as to stand alongside the experiences of the other apostles seems to call for something of the type described in Acts; and Galatians cannot be said to rule this out.

The other possible source of light from Paul himself on the nature of his experience of the risen Jesus is what he has to say about the Resurrection life that Christians themselves can expect. In Philippians 3:20–1 Paul explicitly says that at his second coming Jesus 'will transform the body of our humble state to conform it to the body of his glory'. 'Glory', in Paul as in the Bible generally, connotes the radiance of divine light, the vision of God. The other key passage, in which he uniquely spells out his thinking on this subject, is 1 Corinthians 15: 35–49. Paul here is concerned to stress two themes: the continuity of person between our life here and in the Resurrection world, and the amazing transformation which our being will undergo. The Resurrection life is one that decay cannot touch, that is spiritual not physical, that is not earthly but heavenly. What we have become will be revealed in glory (cf. 2 Cor. 4:16–17). Paul's thinking was no doubt influenced in part by conventional ideas of the nature of heavenly existence, with its angelic beings and the radiance of God himself. But it would surely be perverse not to see also the impact of his own experience of encounter with the risen Christ.

Summary of indications

What can be derived from these fairly diverse accounts? If what we are trying to do is to reconstruct the original sequence of events, or to fit all the pieces as they now are into some complicated jigsaw, then we have no hope of success. For one thing each gospel writer has recorded only those items of tradition which he found significant for his particular theological presentation and has organised them into his own reconstruction. We may, therefore, be morally certain that other details which we might have found illuminating have been lost. For another, the timelag between the events and the writing of the gospels must mean that the individual pieces of material had had a history of their own, which had elaborated and nuanced them before they ever got to the evangelist. Even if they might have fitted together when they began their career, they are not going to do so now.

What we can perhaps hope to do is this. We can summarise the main features of the narratives as we have them, especially those elements that occur in more than one source. Then we can ask various questions. Does this look like something the first Christians could have made up wholly on the basis of their existing religious ideas? If not, what is distinctive about it? What kind of experience might have given rise to these new ingredients, bearing in mind that, if the basic claim has any truth in it at all, they were going to have to struggle to make sense of that experience, using the conceptual resources available to them? Reconstructions of the actual course of events do have their place in this exercise, if only as a way of explaining how certain discrepancies might have arisen; but they can never be conclusive.

Taking that as our approach, we may note the following core elements within the divergent memories and traditions.

1. *No one witnessed the resurrection.* One negative factor is of importance: it is never claimed that anyone saw the actual resurrection – the stories all relate to what came afterwards. Only in the later apocryphal writings such as the Gospel of Peter, which were not accepted as canonical scripture, are attempts made to imagine the event itself. The statement that

Jesus rose from the dead is therefore something inferred from other experiences.

2. *The first reports that something had happened came from the women disciples.* The first hint of what had happened is picked up by a woman disciple or women disciples who visit the tomb early on the Sunday morning. The names vary somewhat in the four gospel accounts, but Mary of Magdala is in all of them (Matt. 28:1; Mark 16:1; Luke 24:10; John 20:1).

3. *The stone had been rolled away.* There is also agreement that they found the circular stone blocking the entrance to the rock tomb rolled back, leaving it open (Matt. 28:2; Mark 16:3–4; Luke 24:2; John 20:1).

4. *The body had gone.* Further investigation, by the women or others, shows that the body is no longer there (Matt. 28:6; Mark 16:6; Luke 24:3, 6; John 20:2–8, 13, 15).

5. *There were meetings with the disciples.* Subsequently there are a number of meetings of various disciples with Jesus alive (Matthew, Luke, John and Paul; Mark records only that there was to be such a meeting, and later editorial attempts to complete the gospel seek to supply this deficiency).

6. *Some disciples were uncertain.* All the gospels state or imply doubt, hesitation or frightened inability to respond by some or all disciples present on one occasion or another (Matt. 28:17 – the Greek should perhaps be translated, 'they [presumably the eleven apostles] worshipped him but were uncertain'; Mark 16:8; Luke 24:11, 37; John 20:24–5).

7. *The encounters with Jesus were not simply visions.* Jesus is heard to speak, and in a majority of cases dialogue is mentioned or implied (Matt. 28:9, 18; Luke 24:17–27, 29–30, 38–41, 44–8; John 20:15–17, 19, 21–3, 26–9; 21:5–6, 10, 12, 15–19, 21–2; and Paul as related in Acts 9:4; 22:7–8; 26:14–18).

8. *There is ambiguity as to the mode in which Jesus is present.* This is so even within individual narratives. By touch and sight he seems to have a physical body like that of other people (Matt. 28:9; Luke 24:30, 39–43; John 20:20, 22, 27; 21:13), but that body is also said to be capable of appearing and disappearing, even in a locked room (Luke 24:31; John 20:19, 26). In this connection there are two particularly puzzling passages. The first is the one where Jesus asks to be given food, so that

he can prove that he is not merely a ghost, as he proceeds to do by eating a piece of cooked fish (Luke 24:41–3; John 21: 9–15 may imply that Jesus shared the breakfast, but this is not made explicit). The second is Mary Magdalene's meeting with Jesus in the garden of the burial, when it is implied that she attempts to touch him but that Jesus forbids her, because 'I have not yet ascended to the Father' (John 20:16–17).

9. *There are varied accounts of Jesus' appearance.* Most stories suggest that Jesus appeared clothed, but they report different guises at different times – a feature that distinguishes these narratives from ordinary ghost stories (Luke 24:16, 31: as a traveller; John 20:14–15: as a gardener; John 21:12: as a casual passer-by). The invitation to see and touch the scars in the hands and feet (Luke 24:39–40; John 20:20, 27) presents no difficulty if Jesus was clothed, but in the case of the spear wound in the side we are presumably meant to infer that clothing was removed to make this possible (John 20:20, 25, 27: John's is the only gospel to mention this wound to the body).

10. *The witnesses failed to recognise Jesus at first.* Linked with these variations we have the theme of non-recognition: at first encounter even those who knew Jesus well may fail to identify him (Matt. 28:17, perhaps; Luke 24:16, 31; John 20:14–16). One passage suggests that awareness of who he was might be purely inward, not from outer resemblance (John 21:12). Note also Paul's question as recorded in Acts 9:5; 22:8; 26:15: 'Who are you?' – part of the unvarying core of Luke's Damascus Road narrative. (In this connection note especially 1 Cor. 9:1: 'Am I not an apostle? Have I not seen Jesus our Lord?' This must refer to seeing the risen Lord, as it is linked to Paul's right to be called an apostle, which implied among other things being a 'witness to the Resurrection'. Paul claims not merely to have heard Jesus, therefore, but to have seen him.)

11. *The location of the meetings with Jesus varies between accounts.* Luke sets all the meetings in or around Jerusalem. Matthew and Mark have Galilee as the key location (the appearance of Jesus to the women in Matt. 28:9–10 may be the evangelist's way of incorporating the tradition that Jesus did appear to a woman or women disciples on the first Easter morning, but the encounter serves little purpose except to reinforce the

angel's promise in v. 7 of a meeting in Galilee). John, however, places significant meetings in both Jerusalem and Galilee; and the gospel in its present form insists (21:1, 14) that the Galilee lakeside meeting was a 'third' encounter, subsequent to the two Jerusalem appearances to 'the disciples' (20:19–29: the meeting with Mary Magdalene is clearly discounted for this purpose).

The weight of the material is against Luke's all-Jerusalem scenario, which may owe something to a theological presentation concerned to emphasise Jerusalem as the starting point of the Church's mission, spreading out from there to the Gentile world and Rome, its capital, symbolised by Galilee (cf. 'Galilee of the Gentiles': Isa. 9:1, cited in Matt. 4:15). Jesus 'is going ahead of [the disciples] to Galilee' (Mark 16:7), as Luke sees it, in the sense of leading them in their mission to the whole world (Luke 24:46–7; Acts 1:8; cf. Matt. 28:19–20).

Contemporary expectations

How far might the disciples have been influenced by current ideas of resurrection, either in their recalling and recording of their experiences or even in determining the character of those experiences in the first place?

There seem to have been two different meanings attached at that time to the idea of 'rising from the dead'. One is reflected in certain gospel passages where people are said to have speculated that Jesus was one of the ancient prophets risen from the dead – Elijah or Jeremiah or some other – or even John the Baptist (Matt. 14:2; 16:14; Mark 6:14–16; 8:28; Luke 9:7–9, 19). The background to these popular notions (reminiscent of traditions in many cultures that some great hero of the past would one day return to rescue his nation) is almost certainly to be found in the prediction at the end of the last of the prophetic books in the Old Testament that God would send Israel 'the prophet Elijah before the great and terrible day of the Lord', to endue the community with a spirit of reconciliation, and so avert God's consuming judgement (Mal. 4:5–6). There was no particular problem here, so far as resurrection was concerned, because Elijah was believed not to have died but to have been carried alive and bodily into heaven (2 Kings 2:11: there are many intentional echoes of this story in Luke's narrative of Jesus' ascension: Acts 1:6–11). When John the Baptist began his call to Israel to repent, some saw him as the fulfilment of this prediction (Matt. 11:13; 17:9–13; Luke 1:17). After John's execution (Matt. 14:1–12; Mark 6:14–29; Luke 9:7–9), as attention focused more and more on Jesus, so the Elijah identification seems to have been transferred to him; and the references to other prophetic figures may be no more than generalisations from that. The equation of Jesus with John the Baptist is bizarre (see Herod's dismissal of the idea, Luke 9:9), but if historical may have arisen from some feeling that Elijah's God-promised mission could not have been summarily cut short, and that his spirit had now taken over another vehicle.

These traditions are clearly not relevant to any concept of resurrection proper, which is the other meaning we have to consider. That was thought of as an act of divine new creation (2 Macc. 7:28), part of a larger universal restoration, when the whole universe would reflect God's righteous will (Acts 3:21: cf. Rom. 8:20–3). As to the form of this resurrection life there were various ideas. What may be the earliest Old Testament reference to resurrection (Isa. 26:19) seems to envisage a renewal of ordinary life, though in conditions of peace and happiness. A more certain and explicit picture (Dan. 12:2–3) foresees a selective resurrection: the outstandingly righteous are raised to glory and eternal life, the wicked to punishment (in non-canonical literature compare 1 Enoch 50–51). The former are thought of as beings of radiant light. Similar imagery is used in the Wisdom of Solomon (3:7), in 2 Esdras (7:97, 125) and 1 Enoch (104:2: cf. 62:15–16). Some pictures of this future life set it in the world as it is now, only perfected (e.g. 1 Enoch 24–36; 51:4–5; cf. Rev. 20:4–6, the millennial kingdom prior to the new heaven and earth). In these works the interim state between death and the future life at the Last Day seems to be a purely spiritual existence.

It is not really possible to glean from these sources how people imagined the Resurrection life in detail, if indeed they did. All that can perhaps be said is that there were two basic conceptions. One was essentially of earthly life as we know it, but freed from want, disease, sin, war and death, and set in a perfected physical environment (comparable to the views of Jehovah's Witnesses today). The other was modelled on ideas of angelic existence, in which radiance, light and fire were the medium of personal presence (cf. Luke 20:36).

Each of these conceptions seems to have left its mark on the stories of Jesus' resurrection, the one in the extreme physicality of some features in Luke and John, the other in the dazzling light of Paul's encounter, as told in Acts, and in the stress on the 'glory' of resurrection in his own letters. But the other elements in the stories – notably those of disguise and of the ability to come and go mysteriously while in bodily, not spiritual form – seem to have no precedent in tradition. A reasonable conclusion is that actual experience has here and there been related or recollected in line with conventional expectations of what resurrection ought to be like, but this only underlines that there had first to be an event which demanded to be understood as resurrection.

Post-mortem appearances, in some respects similar to those of Jesus, were attributed in antiquity to the Neo-Pythagorean philosopher Apollonius of Tyana, who died at the end of the first century CE. The sources for his life are, however, relatively much later than those for Jesus, the principal biography not appearing until 220 CE; and most scholars regard the stories about him as influenced in part by conscious attempts to set him up as a rival to Jesus. There certainly seem to be no grounds for assuming any influence in the opposite direction – that is, of stories about Apollonius affecting the New Testament accounts.

Alternative explanations

All down the centuries alternative stories have been constructed in order to provide a naturalistic explanation of the Resurrection narratives. These alternatives are of two broad types: those which allege that Jesus never died, so that the question of resurrection does not arise; and those which argue that the disciples' experiences were wholly interior and psychological.

In early Christianity various groups claimed that Jesus escaped death on the cross, his place being taken either by a human substitute or by a phantasm which deceived the onlookers. The motivation here was purely theological: it was unfitting that a divine or near-divine being should undergo suffering and death. Likewise it is the teaching of Islam, as laid down in the Qur'an (Sura 4, v. 157), that Jesus was not put to death, though the authorities were left under the illusion that he had been. What really happened was that 'Allah lifted him up to his presence'; and Jesus will appear on the 'Day of Resurrection' (i.e. the Last Day) to be a 'witness against them'. For Islam it is unthinkable that God would allow the true Messiah, a prophet second in honour only to Muhammad himself, to be put to death.

In modern times the motivation has been rather different, concerned to avoid the need for a miraculous resurrection by saying that Jesus was taken down from the cross alive, cared for, and revived. (Interestingly, some modern Muslim popular apologetic offers such a reconstruction in refutation of Christian claims, even though the passage from the Qur'an quoted above would seem to exclude the need for this.) Attempts to interpret the New Testament evidence in this sense are often ingenious and immensely elaborate, so elaborate in some cases as to be more difficult to believe than a straightforward miracle. They also have to minimise the severity of Jesus' sufferings in the crucifixion itself, in order to make his survival clinically plausible. The fact that he is said to have died more quickly than expected (Mark 15:44 ff.), while his fellow victims had to have their end hastened (John 19:31 ff.), is held to be suspicious, despite the emphatic insistence of John's gospel that its apostolic source was an eyewitness of the fact that Jesus was dead, and that his body was stabbed with a spear to make sure (John 19:33–5). While, however, the details of the accounts can be assessed and reassessed interminably, all such theories have to overcome two simple objections: (1) that a merely resuscitated Jesus could not have given rise to the traditions as received; and therefore (2) that there must have been a conspiracy to deceive – which indeed most writers who are of this mind assume.

Since early Christian times the deception theory has been

countered by pointing out how improbable it is that the disciples would have persisted in it when it meant persecution and martyrdom. Nevertheless, the lengths to which human nature will go in deception or self-deception mean that we have to consider the possibility that Jesus or the disciples or both were so determined to save face that the price to be paid for this religious confidence trick did not deter them. Or are we to assume that Jesus had become so unhinged by his ordeal that, in his survival against the odds, he believed he had been raised from the dead? But even if he had gone mad, the disciples had not. What did they do with him? Seclude him for his perhaps few remaining days? Kill him? All these options have been taken up by one theorist or another at some time. The fatal objection is that they are all so utterly out of moral character with either Jesus himself as presented in the gospels and in the oral traditions behind them or – if we assume that the alleged teaching and behaviour of Jesus are in fact the idealistic creation of others – with the spiritual calibre necessary to produce the best of the New Testament texts.

Modern psychological theories avoid these pitfalls, since they start from the presumption that Jesus did die. They are concerned rather with the possibility that the Easter stories express a sincere but purely inward conviction on the part of Jesus' friends.

In its simplest form this conviction would be that Jesus had indeed been serving the cause of God, whatever the verdict of those in power or, seemingly, of the divine Law itself (Deut. 21:22 ff.); that he had given his life for it; and that God therefore had his spirit in his keeping, and would in due time vindicate his servant as he would other martyrs. In itself there is nothing improbable in holding that this was the disciples' situation; but what that state of mind could never have done is give rise to the Easter stories. Jesus and his friends came from that persuasion within Judaism which believed that the dead would be raised and the righteous rewarded *at the Last Day*. Given time to get over the trauma of Good Friday, therefore, the natural thing would be for them to come to believe that that reward awaited Jesus. What their tradition would never have done was to lead them to expect a premature resurrection at once. In fact it would have militated against their expressing their conviction in such a form.

We are driven, then, to conclude that the first disciples did have experiences which were the root from which flowered their resurrection beliefs. The questions that remain, though it is hard to find precise terminology to do them justice, may be put like this. Were these experiences generated wholly from within their own psyche, or did realities external to them trigger the experiences? If the latter, were their accounts true in essence to those external realities? Were those realities veridical – that is, did they communicate a true state of affairs in the divine and human orders?

As to the question whether the experiences were generated wholly within the psyche of the disciples, individual or collective, the same issues arise as over the view that the disciples believed that Jesus' soul lived on and that he would be raised at the Last Day. Internally generated experiences can draw only on images and concepts already available, consciously or unconsciously, within the memory store. This material may be organised in new creative ways, responding to the needs and desires of the person or persons concerned, but will not normally run counter to what is within their scope or expectation. To cite a famous example: that Bernadette Soubirous should have had a vision of the Blessed Virgin was not surprising; what was outside the naturally explicable was the message she claimed to have received – 'I am the Immaculate Conception' – and it was therefore right that investigation should focus on whether or not she could already have heard of that terminology in connection with Mary.

We have already looked at the ideas about resurrection that might have formed part of the disciples' mental stock at that time. What can we say about their psychological state, and the needs and desires that might be influencing them?

After Good Friday they would have been in the first shock of bereavement at the loss of a beloved friend, mentor and leader. To grief would most likely have been added revulsion at the cruelty of his death, depression at its shame, and anger at its injustice. Compounding and complicating these feelings must have been their sense of guilt and remorse at having failed him, as they saw it, at the moment of crisis. In addition they were men who had left their home communities, thrown up their jobs, branded themselves as dangerous in the eyes of many of the most influential leaders of their society, and uprooted themselves from a whole way of life, in order to stake everything on following Jesus to the glorious destiny they believed he had promised them. What they needed was not just consolation in bereavement but something that would convince them that their sacrifice had not been in vain, assure them that their failure had been forgiven, and enable them to put the past behind them by giving them a new cause for which to live.

We cannot but be struck, therefore, by the way the Easter narratives show us these needs being met. A special gesture of reconciliation is extended to Peter, who had denied Jesus three times (John 21:15–17). The risen Jesus is at pains to help his friends understand that his death had been necessary, even in its particulars (Luke 24:25–7, 44–6). Matthew, Luke and John all tell of a new mission entrusted to the disciples (Matt. 28: 18–20; Luke 24:47–9; John 20:21–3; 21:15–19). Does this not suggest that the experiences were indeed generated from within the psyche of the disciples by a process of wish-fulfilment, that they were a way of coping with unbearable strain? In the case of the collective encounters with the risen Jesus, is it not possible that these were stimulated by the telling of prior individual experiences such as those of Mary Magdalene (John 20:11–18) and Peter (Luke 24:34), both of whom may have been carrying the heaviest emotional burdens?

When, however, we look at the texts more closely, other factors have gone to shape them. Take first the story of Peter's reconciliation in John 21. Within the New Testament Peter's status is ambiguous. During Jesus' lifetime he seems to have acted as the spokesman and leader of the innermost circle of followers; and in Matthew 16:18 ff. he is said to have been nominated by Jesus as the rock on which the future community of the disciples is to be built, and the holder of supreme authority within it. But the parallel passages in Mark and Luke (Mark 8:27–30; Luke 9:18–21) make no mention of this; and the gospels all tell of disputes within the inner circle as to which of them should really be leader (Matt. 18:1–5; 20:20–8; Mark

9:33–7; 10:35–45; Luke 9:46–8; 22:24–30; cf. John 13:12–17). There is not space here to cover the evidence in the rest of the New Testament concerning Church leadership; but suffice to say that Peter's position is one of special but not exclusive or universal eminence, and was in certain respects the focus of debate (e.g. cf. Galatians 1:18–19; 2:11–14). Given this situation, the narrative in John 21 undoubtedly takes on a Church-political as well as a pastoral and spiritual dimension. It is in part concerned with establishing Peter's right to lead despite his threefold denial of Jesus. The question and answer about the destiny of John (21:20–3) may also owe their place in the tradition to the existence of a network of churches in Asia Minor which had looked to John as their patriarch, but within which his authority had been challenged (cf. 1 John 2:18–19; 2 John 7, 10–11; 3 John 9–12).

Similar considerations apply to Luke's account of Jesus as explaining the necessity of his sufferings. Attention has already been drawn to Luke's impossibly crowded timetable for the first Easter Day. When these verses (24:25–7, 44–6) are unpacked, we find that Jesus is supposed to have taken first the two disciples walking to Emmaus, then the whole group back in Jerusalem, through all the Old Testament passages predicting his Passion. As with the case of the Petrine leadership, the story in Luke is heavily geared to attributing to Jesus himself authorisation for later theological developments in a way which, in the context of the first Resurrection appearances, is highly doubtful.

Other material in the Easter stories may perhaps be included in this category, for example the granting of the power to absolve or retain sins (John 20:21–3). In Matthew we can make a similar distinction with regard to the episode of the Temple guards (27:62–6; 28:11–15), included to counter a rival Jewish version of events, and the reference to the Gentile mission and baptism in the name of the Trinity (28:19). All these passages are skilfully crafted to deal with later Church concerns; and their literary character marks them off from the basic accounts of the disciples' experiences of the risen Jesus, where the primitive oral tradition can still be discerned.

That all these ideas and more stemmed eventually from the

root fact of the Resurrection is undeniable. It is also perfectly
clear that as a result of whatever were the authentic Easter
experiences the disciples did believe themselves forgiven and
accepted by Jesus and by God, despite their failures; that they
came very quickly to see a divine purpose in Jesus' crucifixion;
and that they took on with fervour a charge to proclaim this
divine purpose. All this is indisputable in the light of the New
Testament record as a whole and of the history of the earliest
Church. The value of separating out from the Easter narratives
those elements which read back a more advanced stage of the
process into its beginning is that it allows us to focus on
the primary and more mysterious ingredients. These, as we
have seen, are the ones least likely to have been generated
within the psyche of the disciples, because they correspond to
none of the expectations natural to Jews of their time and place.

One further possibility, however, needs to be considered.
There are in the gospels a number of places where Jesus is said
to have predicted his own resurrection 'on the third day' or
after three days (Matt. 12:40; 20:19; Mark 8:31; 9:31; 10:34;
Luke 18:33; John 2:19–22; cf. Matt. 26:61; Mark 14:58 ff.).
Might it not be that these strange predictions, possibly recollected only subconsciously (cf. Luke 24:7), could have given
rise to the necessary intense psychological expectancy precisely
at the right moment? Perhaps most commentators today would
say that it is wholly unnecessary to introduce this further com-
plication for the simple reason that the passages concerned are
clearly a reading back into the gospel story of post-Easter
hindsight and that it is most unlikely that Jesus ever said any
such thing. But if one means to face honestly all the queries
that can be raised about Jesus' resurrection this one has to be
included. What can be said about these passages?

There certainly are puzzles about them. That Jesus might
well have said, in connection with the death he more and more
clearly foresaw, that he would rise again presents no problems.
He believed in the resurrection; he believed that his death, if
it came, would be in the service of God. What more natural
than that he should also believe, and say, that at the resurrection
of the righteous he too would rise? The difficulties come from
the time element, the 'third day'.

The clues to the source of this idea point in two directions. The first line goes back toward the Old Testament and the 'sign of Jonah' (Matt. 12:38–41; Luke 11:29–30, 32). In Luke's version of this material there is no mention of resurrection. Jonah is simply a sign from God to the people of Nineveh, who repented at Jonah's preaching; and the implication is that Jesus is a sign to his contemporaries for the same reason, his preaching of repentance. Matthew has this interpretation too, but first expounds the words about the 'sign' of Jonah as follows: 'for as Jonah was in the belly of the whale three days and three nights, so shall the Son of Man be in the heart of the earth three days and three nights (cf. Jonah 1:17)'. This raises the additional difficulty that Jesus was not in the grave three days and three nights; but the likelihood is that this alleged saying of Jesus is really a product of the early Church's search for Old Testament predictions of the resurrection, which proved extremely unrewarding and gave some very forced results.

The other line is more significant but, if possible, more obscure. It concerns the tradition that Jesus claimed that if the 'temple' were destroyed he would rebuild it in three days. John quotes this in the context of Jesus' driving the money changers out of the Temple and says categorically that Jesus was talking about the temple of his own body and that the disciples did not understand this until they recalled it after his resurrection (2:19–22). Interestingly both Matthew and Mark relate that at his interrogation before the council Jesus was accused of having said the same thing (Matt. 26:61; Mark 14:58 ff.), but that the testimony was inadmissible because the witnesses could not agree. The accounts also vary between 'after three days', 'in the course of three days' and 'on the third day', the latter presumably being an attempt to bring the saying into line with what actually happened at Easter. A solution of the problem may never be possible. Jesus is said to have predicted the total destruction of the Temple (Mark 13:2; Matt. 24:2; Luke 21:5–6) and it is easily conceivable that in response to exclamations of horror and incredulity he made some remark to the effect of 'Don't worry, God could enable anyone to put it up again in three days, if they had faith!' Informers could easily have got tied up over that one! But speculation is futile. All one can say is that the mysterious traditions about three days or the third day, whatever their original context, may have led to modification in the tradition of originally more general assurances by Jesus of faith in his own resurrection. For our present purposes it must suffice to say that recollections so confused and obscure are not a very convincing clue to anything strong enough to give the disciples an expectation of Jesus' immediate resurrection in the teeth of all that they had been taught about resurrection in general. Far more probable is it that words which originally belonged in a wholly different context have been transferred to Jesus' resurrection because of what actually happened.

This topic of expectations, however, does direct our attention to the most striking evidence of all that the disciples' experiences were a response to a reality outside themselves. As has already been noted several times, those Jews who believed in a resurrection of the dead all looked for it, whatever its detailed form, at the end of present history, when God would inaugurate the new age in which his will of righteousness and love would be sovereign. Now one of the most firmly established features of primitive Christianity was its insistence that the end of the present age was to be imminently expected, an insistence that eventually became an embarrassment to succeeding generations. From the writings of St Paul we can see that one major reason for this conviction was the assumption that Jesus could only have been raised as part of or in association with the general resurrection. God would not raise one person in isolation. If Jesus had risen, the rest must follow soon: he was the 'firstfruits', the firstborn from the dead (1 Cor. 15:20–3; cf. Col. 1:18). In short, the early Christian teaching that the end of this age was to be expected at any moment sprang from the testimony of certain followers of Jesus that after his death they had met him in a mode of life which could be described only as that of resurrection. We are thus strongly compelled to believe that their experience was indeed of some reality other than themselves and to assume that that reality must have been of this particular kind.

What then did happen?

In conclusion, then, we need to say something in modern terms about the events of the first Easter and their character. For one thing, if no reconstruction of events can be achieved, such as might plausibly have given rise to the accounts we have, then that must weaken our assurance about the work of God allegedly mediated through those events. For another, we need some not too vaguely defined idea of what happened if we are to make valid use of Jesus' resurrection as a clue to the nature and purposes of God.

First, then, Jesus did die on the Cross. To accept this is entirely reasonable, bearing in mind the cumulative effects of his spiritual agony in Gethsemane; the physical violence to which he was subjected; the psychological ordeal of his examination, first by members of the council, then by Pilate; and the heartbreak of his sense of abandonment not just by his friends but, far worse, by God (Matt. 27:46; Mark 15:34). It was part of the cruelty of crucifixion in some of its versions that it demanded of the victim a continuous effort to stay alive. That Jesus should have reached the stage of seeing no point in making that effort and, in the words of Matthew's gospel, have 'let his spirit go' (Matt. 27:50) is only too credible.

Secondly, there are no good grounds for doubting that his body was taken down and buried in haste, before Friday's sunset ushered in the Sabbath, in a cave tomb made available as an act of piety by a Jew of some standing. Moreover, the place of his burial would have been known not just to his friends but more widely. There was neither attempt nor need to conceal it, nor indeed any possibility of doing so.

The accounts all agree that during the Sabbath the Law was observed, and no one made any move. This brings us to the morning of Sunday; and here we need to deal separately with the events round the tomb and what happened afterwards. Again there is agreement that as early as possible that morning a woman or women from among Jesus' disciples came to the tomb, and all four gospels name Mary of Magdala as either one of a group or having come alone. It was then discovered that the tomb was open – the circular stone which closed the entrance had been rolled aside – and the body gone.

Mark, followed by Luke, says that the women went to the tomb to complete the necessarily hasty burial arrangements of the Friday by anointing the body with spices; but if John is correct this had already been more than adequately done at the time of burial. Matthew merely states that the women came 'to view the tomb'. In John no motive is given for Mary Magdalene's visit, but from the fact that she returned later to weep her intention may have been a formal act of public mourning. If tending the body was the women's intention, it seems strange that they had taken no one with them to roll back the heavy door; and Mark seems to feel that point, and suggests that in their haste the need had been overlooked (Mark 16:3). There really is no way of discriminating between these differences in detail, nor anything to be gained by trying. On the crucial point there is unanimity: the tomb was empty.

In the view of some scholars the whole 'empty tomb' motif is a later legend, created to bolster the Resurrection story. Against this view may be cited the key role played by the women, an element most unlikely to have been invented without foundation in that culture at that time. As often pointed out, women were not accepted as uncorroborated witnesses in a court of law, a fact which may explain the care taken by both Luke and John to state that the women's story was confirmed by male disciples (Luke 24:24 – note the disparaging tone of 24:11 – and John 20:3–10). But if we do assume that the story is true and that the tomb was empty, we also need to define with more care than is usually given to the matter what the real significance of that might be.

To begin with, there are various possible explanations for the tomb's having been found open, but the resurrection of Jesus is not one of them, nor does the New Testament imply that it was. If walls and doors were later to be no obstacle to meetings with the risen Lord, why should the stone sealing the tomb have had to be moved? The simplest explanation is still that of Frank Morison in *Who Moved the Stone?* that it was rolled aside by the unnamed young man in the white garment, whom the women found sitting in the tomb on the right hand side (Mark

16:5). In all the other gospels he has been transformed into an angel or two angels, but there is no reason why he should not have been an ordinary mortal.

The tomb might also have been open if even earlier a person or persons unknown had come and removed the body. This was the immediate inference drawn, we are told, by Mary Magdalene (John 20:2). That would fit the detail of the folded grave-cloths and the separately folded head-cloth (John 20:6–7). But who could have done it? The enemies of Jesus, to prevent a cult of Jesus as a martyr from growing up round the tomb? But if so, why when the disciples began preaching the Resurrection did they not come forward and crush the superstition once for all? Sympathisers might have come by night, even during the Sabbath, if they had reason to hope that Jesus might not really be dead. If he were, then they would have replaced the stone and gone away, leaving the body. If he were not, then we are faced with all the difficulties already mentioned in connection with modern conspiracy theories.

What needs to be understood is that the fact that the tomb was open and empty makes it impossible ever to say for certain what happened to Jesus' body. The basic picture given in the gospels is quite compatible with belief that the body of Jesus' earthly life had been transformed by divine action into a Resurrection body; but there can be no proof either way. All we can derive from the empty sepulchre is a negative inference, namely that if the body had been there it would not be possible to interpret the disciples' experiences of the risen Jesus in terms of a transformed earthly body. The empty tomb, however, leaves all options open.

Turning from the events of that first Easter morning, we have to consider next the alternative pictures in the gospels of where the meetings with Jesus took place. The dual location in the traditions – Galilee and Jerusalem – cannot be wished away; there must have been something to occasion it. But that need not be precisely as described by Matthew, Mark or John. If we break Matthew and Mark down into simple movements of people, we get the clear impression that the disciples left Jerusalem more or less immediately for Galilee. The men, at any rate, are not said to have met Jesus in the capital that first

Sunday. John seems on the face of it to paint a very different picture. Chapter 20 tells of two meetings with the risen Lord in Jerusalem on successive Sundays, at the first of which the disciples are endowed with the Holy Spirit for leadership and mission. The chapter ends with what reads as a solemn conclusion to the whole gospel. For that reason Chapter 21, as we have it, forms a kind of appendix; and the editor responsible for including it also understood its contents as falling after the events of Chapter 20 (cf. 21:1, 14).

But the actual narrative in Chapter 21 gives a different impression. In v. 3 we read: 'Simon Peter said to them, "I am going fishing." They said to him, "We will go with you."' This is surely very strange after what is supposed to have happened in Chapter 20. The sense of strangeness is accentuated when we go on to read of the disciples' tardy recognition of Jesus on the shore and then the moving story of Peter's reconciliation. But if what is being related is the first encounter with the risen Jesus, and the events leading up to that, it all makes dramatic and psychological sense. The likelihood seems to be that a secondary editor or editors of John's gospel acquired these traditions after the main body of the work was complete and, given the all-Jerusalem setting of that work's concluding section, could find no other way of understanding them. But the natural interpretation of the material is that here we have stories relating to experiences in Galilee when the disciples had fled there soon after the discovery of the empty tomb.

That the inexplicable opening and emptiness of that tomb could have been the last demoralising blow which led them to escape while they could is not implausible. We would then have to say that, though Mary Magdalene and possibly others of the women met with Jesus on that first Easter day, the men did not believe them. It was in Galilee that they met with Jesus risen and as a result of those encounters were fired with the message of his vindication by God and all that flowed from that. They therefore returned to Jerusalem to make that message known at the very scene of Jesus' supposed defeat and to challenge those who had rejected him. (The existence of the Jerusalem church, led by senior apostles from the earliest days and acknowledged as the mother congregation of Christians is amply confirmed not just by Acts but by the letters of St Paul.) That there were further experiences back in Jerusalem, which have left their mark on the traditions we now have, is not an unreasonable supposition. That some of them should be linked with the gift of the Holy Spirit, with a growing understanding of the presages of Cross and Resurrection in the Scriptures, and with the primitive community's practice of breaking bread together with prayer in memory of the Lord (cf. Acts 2:42, 46) is hardly surprising.

When we ask about the nature of these experiences, we are inevitably on more problematic ground. Yet there are certain things that can be said with some confidence. To begin with, the meetings were experiences of two-way communication. They were also encounters in which the disciples felt their failures and sins forgiven and their relationship with Jesus fully restored; and the tradition that Jesus came to them with the greeting of 'Peace!' (John 20:19, 26; Luke 24:36) represents the simplest surviving account of how that assurance was conveyed. Then again, without being too rash, we can infer that the mode of Jesus' new being may well have been the strongest evidence that he had been vindicated by God. The way he was alive now seemed to be one endowed with powers beyond those of ordinary human existence, and yet he was still essentially the same person. It was as though the tangible, audible, visible medium of personality was now totally at the disposal of his and his Father's purpose and could do whatever was best suited to that purpose at any given moment. It was, in short, life fully in the Holy Spirit, humanity taken into the divine order. The actual details of the way the disciples experienced this must have been confusing at the time and hard to interpret; and it is certainly beyond us now to be dogmatic about this or that concrete aspect. But the amazing nuclear explosion of theological understanding of Jesus which we find in the New Testament within so short a time can be adequately explained only in one way: that it began from the eyewitness recollections of those post-Resurrection meetings of Jesus with his friends.

These meetings in time came to an end. That they were restricted to those who had been Jesus' friends in his earthly life and that there were no encounters with his enemies is not really a problem. The purpose of the meetings was not simply to prove that Jesus was alive but also to empower and commission those he had trained, so that they could take forward the cause of the kingdom. Jesus' opponents could never have understood the kingdom values which the Resurrection vindicated. Likewise the meetings came to an end because the work of the kingdom could not be fulfilled in the old dependence on Jesus as leader but only in the creative freedom of that life in the Spirit which was now his in all its fullness. The New Testament speaks of the boundary between these two stages in different ways: Matthew, as a promise of Jesus' being spiritually with his disciples always; Luke, as an ascension into heaven to await a return, though never, as Acts shows, losing personal contact; John, in terms of Jesus' abiding with his friends as they are to abide in him, and both in the Father. Again, the confidence in the possibility and realisation of these new relationships is something that takes its rise from the Easter experiences of the life Jesus now enjoyed. In the end, it is these transforming convictions which tell us most about the reality of Jesus' resurrection and are the best evidence for it.

Appendix B:

The Last Supper in the light of New Testament evidence

The source of the Christian Eucharist is the 'Last Supper', the final meal which Jesus shared with his closest friends. Matthew, Mark and Luke state that the meal was the Passover supper, John that the day of the Passover had not yet arrived, in which case the occasion may simply have been a fellowship meal. What matter for our present purposes, however, are Jesus' words and actions during or after the meal in relation to bread and wine, the words and actions that Christians narrate at the heart of every Eucharist.

The information in the New Testament concerning these appears to derive from three separate sources. The earliest may be the one in Paul's First Letter to the Corinthians, if his claim to have received this as a tradition coming 'from the Lord' (1 Cor. 11:23) means that, like the teaching about the Resurrection, it originated directly from the Jerusalem congregation. The second source is Mark, whose account has been used by both Matthew and Luke with their own variations. The third source is one which seems to have been special to Luke, since his story contains details not found in the others, notably two cups of wine, one before the bread and one after. John's narrative of the Last Supper makes no mention of any of these words and actions.

The only point on which all four accounts agree is that in relation to the bread Jesus said 'This is my body'. In substance, though not in precise wording, they agree that he linked the cup with his blood and with a 'covenant' or a 'new covenant'. Mark, Matthew and Luke have words about the blood being poured out 'for you' or 'for many'; and the same three record with variations a saying of Jesus that he would not drink wine again until the kingdom of God had arrived. Paul and Luke preserve the words, 'Do this for my memorial', Luke associating them with the bread, Paul with both the bread and the cup.

Mark, followed by Matthew, makes no mention of them. The manuscripts of all the accounts display complex variant readings, no doubt reflecting different versions of the words used in Christian teaching.

The story of what Jesus said and did has become for the Church an obligatory part of the eucharistic thanksgiving prayer, but it was no command of Jesus that this should be so. The natural sense of the phrase 'Do this for my memorial' is certainly not 'Repeat the words, "This is my body", "This is my blood".' In both Luke and Paul the command must refer to saying a blessing or thanksgiving before taking, eating and drinking. But what did Jesus mean by speaking thus of his own body and blood?

Consider first the cup of wine. Mark makes special mention of the fact that 'they all drank from it' (Mark 14:23). Matthew turns this into a command by Jesus: 'Drink from it, all of you' (Matt. 26:27). Paul and Luke both imply that all drank. The stress on this fact is interesting. In no way, sophisticated or simple, can the disciples have thought that the wine had somehow actually become Jesus' blood. Quite apart from the absurdity (Jesus was standing there) and the obscenity of the idea, the Jewish Law explicitly and repeatedly forbade the consumption of blood of any kind (e.g. Gen. 9:4; Lev. 3:17; 7:26–7; 17:10–12; 19:26; Deut. 12:16; 15:23).

The various ways in which the accounts phrase the words about the cup are also significant. Mark, followed by Matthew, has 'This is my blood of the (new) covenant', which cannot as it stands be translated back into Hebrew or Aramaic. The version in Paul and Luke ('This cup is the new covenant in my blood') could be so translated; but it is precisely this phrase which is the more oblique and distances itself from any simple identification of the wine with the blood. The kind of association it evokes is that of the cups of wine which were offered with certain sacrifices in the Temple (e.g. Num. 15:7, 10). The stress is on the coming death of Jesus, not on the wine itself.

A story in the Old Testament may be in point (2 Sam. 23:13–17). David was campaigning against the Philistines, and a Philistine garrison was holding Bethlehem, David's native town. One day 'David said longingly, "O that someone would give me water to drink from the well of Bethlehem that is by the gate!"' On hearing this, three of David's mightiest warriors broke through the Philistine lines and came back with water from the well and gave it to David. The story goes on: 'But he would not drink of it; he poured it out to the Lord, for he said, "The Lord forbid that I should do this. Can I drink the blood of the men who went at the risk of their lives?"'

This moving story may throw light on the thoughts of Jesus and his friends. When David called the water 'the blood of the men who went at the risk of their lives', no one thought that he meant that the water had turned into the blood of the three heroes. Where we might say that the water was now as precious as the lives risked to get it, the Hebrew mind expressed it more graphically; and the image carried enough force for the water to acquire the sacred and taboo character of blood. That being so, the water could be offered only to God.

The ancient folktale shows helpfully how a Jew might be moved to say such a thing and why. It also shows that the words need not at all imply that the water or wine was in itself in any way changed. Indeed, the fact that the disciples did drink what was proffered them by Jesus himself makes it even more unthinkable to suggest the idea in their case than in the old story. But the Old Testament supplies further clues to Jesus' full meaning.

Prophetic signs

Against the background of the Jewish Scriptures the most helpful comparison is with those actions of the old prophets which have been called 'prophetic signs'. These were actions designed to symbolise some coming event, such as victory over an enemy (1 Kings 22:11), future deliverance (Isa. 7:14–16; 8:1–4; Jer. 32:6–15), enslavement (Jer. 27:1–7), or the capture and destruction of Jerusalem and the exile of its inhabitants (Ezek. 4:1–7; 12:1–7). But such actions were not just a visual aid, intended to dramatise a prediction the prophet was going to make in words. They were performed at God's command, and meant that the event symbolised was God's will, and that it would surely come to pass and achieve his purpose.

It is entirely in keeping with Jesus' deeply scriptural faith that his actions with the bread and wine should have been of this kind. If we ask what the divine purpose was which Jesus' death, symbolised in this prophetic sign, was to serve, the most likely answer is that Jesus himself was not sure (cf. p. 77f.). He believed that his witness to and service of the kingdom of God had brought him to a point where the sacrificial offering of his whole life must culminate in his accepting the death which his enemies were plotting for him. His chief concern was that his closest friends should survive to carry on that mission, and he meant his death somehow to ensure that that would happen. (These points are spelled out in more detail on pp. 92, 94f.) The sharing of the bread and cup were to be the sacred means by which this commitment was kept alive, and his own life's work, sealed in death, continued.

The various elaborations – for such they must be – of what Jesus said, now lost to us, indicate how the earliest Church interpreted this death. All four accounts see it as the inaugur-ation of a (new) covenant, a new and binding relationship of life and peace between God and his people. Just as the covenant in the time of Moses had been initiated with blood in sacrifice (Exod. 24:8: cf. Heb. 9:18–20), so this better and eternal coven-ant began with the sacrifice of Jesus (Heb. 9:23–8). Paul and Luke record the death as 'for you', that is, the disciples; Mark and Matthew as 'for many', the worldwide but unknown number God would eventually save. For Matthew the death is also, like the sacrifices in the Temple, 'for the forgiveness of sins' (Matt. 26:28). All these different presentations are in har-mony with an understanding of Jesus' words and actions as a prophetic sign.

But what part do the eating and drinking of the bread and wine play in all this? Two passages in the New Testament are especially relevant here.

John 6: 'the Bread of Life'

Even though John has left us no account of the bread and wine at the Last Supper, it is quite impossible to read Chapter 6 of his gospel without hearing strong echoes of that tradition. Thus, in telling of the feeding of the five thousand, John uses the words: 'Jesus then *took* the loaves, and *after giving thanks distributed* them among those who were sitting down' (John 6:11). Most striking of all is the statement that eternal life depends on eating the flesh of 'the Son of Man and drinking his blood' (vv. 53–5). How are these words to be understood?

The chapter is a complex piece of writing and needs to be taken as a whole. In form it is an argument between Jesus and his Jewish hearers, an argument which, as in other instances in this gospel, becomes steadily more angry and at cross-purposes as the audience misunderstands Jesus more drastically.

We begin with the crowd who had been fed the previous day. They are searching for Jesus. When they find him, Jesus tells them that their real need is not for food to sustain bodily life but for that which will give them eternal life; and he is the one from whom this food is to be had (v. 27). To receive this food they have to trust in Jesus as the one sent by God (v. 29).

This introduces the theme of the bread from heaven. For forty years the Israelites had lived on manna on their way through the desert from Egypt to the Promised Land (Exod. 16:13–35; Num. 11:7–9). Jesus' hearers now ask for some miracle of that kind, and quote the psalm: 'He gave them bread from heaven to eat' (v. 31: cf. Ps. 78:24). Jesus takes up this image and replies that the true 'bread from heaven' is what God is offering them now – the one (i.e. himself) who has come down from heaven to give life to the world (v. 33).

The hearers now begin to lose touch with Jesus. All they can think of is some kind of supernatural food. They fail to notice that Jesus has redefined the word 'bread' as a person, namely himself. Instead they ask for the magical bread of their imagination (v. 34). Jesus tries again: 'No, no, you don't understand. The "bread" that gives life is me. It is those who come to me, who trust in me as my disciples, who will never hunger or thirst (v. 35). They will possess eternal life, because God's will is that I should raise them up at the Last Day' (vv. 39, 40).

The audience now latch onto a phrase Jesus has used several times, that he 'came down from heaven'. What is he talking about? They know all about him, who his parents are, and what town he comes from. How can he say he came down from heaven? Jesus' response is firm. If they do not understand, the reason is that God has not been able to draw them to Jesus. If they would learn from God, then they would trust themselves to Jesus; and anyone who can give that trust already possesses eternal life (vv. 41–7). The 'bread of life' is Jesus himself. Anyone who eats that bread – that is, comes to Jesus as the source of true life – will indeed live for ever (vv. 48–51).

Jesus now uses a phrase which stirs his hearers to violent altercation: 'the bread that I will give for the life of the world is my flesh' (v. 51). At first we seem to have moved from the idea that Jesus is himself the bread to the bread as something that he gives. But this bread is still his whole self in its human and bodily existence. The reference (enigmatic so far as the hearers in the story are concerned, but plain enough to the believing reader) is to the Cross, where through the surrender of his flesh to human death Jesus will fulfil the promise he has just been making, namely to win eternal life for those who trust in him.

His hearers, however, ignore the words 'for the life of the world', and concentrate on the 'flesh'. 'How can this man give us his flesh to eat?' (v. 52). This provokes from Jesus the retort: 'Very truly, I tell you, unless you eat the flesh of the Son of Man and drink his blood, you have no life in you' (v. 53). The expression is then intensified by using a word for 'eat' which has an emphatically physical ring to it: 'Those who "devour" my flesh and drink my blood have eternal life . . . for my flesh is true food and my blood is true drink' (vv. 54–5).

Two points about these verses need to be noted. First, the choice of any particular Greek word must always be the gospel writer's decision, not that of Jesus; and if we take in one feature of the Greek at this point, we should also give weight to another. The opening words are one of a number of examples in this chapter of the use of the present participle active, the force of which is to express a continuing state or activity. Thus, 'the one who keeps coming to me does not know hunger, and the one who goes on believing in me will never thirst' (v. 35), and, 'all who keep their eyes on the Son and remain believers in him already have eternal life' (v. 40). What all these instances convey is not particular discrete actions but constant states; and so, despite the aggressively physical-sounding language of vv. 54–5 and those immediately following, the writer clearly does not have in mind the individual occasions when Christians meet to receive the eucharistic bread and wine but the permanent day-by-day, hour-by-hour spiritual relationship of the believer with Jesus (cf. the relationship of the vine and the branches in John 15). To take the words as referring to actual eating and drinking, even in a sacramental sense, of the body and blood of Jesus is to fall into the same trap as Jesus' audience in the story. However extreme, the image is only an image for the wholehearted trust in and dependence on Jesus to which God seeks to draw anyone prepared to listen to him, in order that they may find true and eternal life (vv. 35–6, 39–40, 44–7).

A further indication that this is the true reading of the story comes in the conclusion. 'When many of his disciples heard it, they said, "This teaching is difficult; who can accept it?" But Jesus . . . said to them, "Does this offend you? . . . It is the spirit that gives life; the flesh is useless. The words that I have spoken to you are spirit and life"' (vv. 60–3). From that moment, we are told, 'many of his disciples turned back and no longer went about with him' (v. 66). When Jesus then asks the Twelve if they too are going, Simon Peter answers: 'Lord, to whom can we go? You have the words of eternal life . . .' (v. 68). It is the personal response, allowing Jesus' words to abide in the soul and keeping his commandments, which receives the Spirit into the very self and makes it a home for the Father and the Son (cf. John 14:17, 23; 15:7).

1 Corinthians 10–11: 'the fellowship of the body and blood'

The other New Testament evidence which needs to be considered comes in Paul's First Letter to the Corinthians. There are two passages which are relevant, and each can be translated and interpreted in more than one way.

The first passage (1 Cor. 11:26–34) follows directly on Paul's account of Jesus' words and actions over the bread and the cup at the Last Supper. The background is the disorder which seems to have prevailed in Corinth when the church there met for the Eucharist. It appears that, instead of sharing their food with poorer members of the congregation and waiting for all to arrive for the solemn meal which would culminate in the breaking of the bread and sharing of the Lord's cup, some people started at once, gorging and getting drunk in private cliques (11:17, 20–2). The practice, to which Jews were accustomed, of combining prayers and hymns and commemorations with a normal meal, had not exported happily to the different culture of the Greek congregation in Corinth.

After repeating the traditional teaching about the Lord's Supper, Paul develops his argument. The ritual of the bread and the cup is a proclamation of the Lord's death (v. 26), a statement which agrees well with the understanding of Jesus' actions as a prophetic sign. To share in the bread and the cup without reverence is to show that you care nothing for that death and so to identify yourself with those who perpetrated it and to share their guilt (v. 27).

Hence the need to examine oneself with care, to make sure of approaching the Eucharist in the right spirit (v. 28). The careless show that they make no distinction between this bread of the Eucharist, in which the breaking of the Lord's body on the Cross is proclaimed, and the breaking of bread at an ordinary meal. They do not 'discern' (i.e. discriminate, and so judge correctly) that when the loaf is blessed and broken it represents the body of the Lord in a symbolic enactment of the mystery of the Cross (v. 29). This is blasphemy, which inevitably is punished by God (v. 30). Part of the trouble has been the indulgence in food and drink, which has led to irreverence. If the offenders would satisfy hunger and thirst at home and then come in the right frame of mind and wait till everyone was ready, all would be well (vv. 33–4).

The second passage comes a little earlier in the letter (10:14–22), and the problem lies in v. 16. The key word in the Greek is *koinonia*, traditionally rendered 'fellowship' or, nowadays, 'communion' (that is between people). A different translation, adopted in some modern versions, takes it here to mean 'sharing': 'is it not a sharing in the blood/body of Christ?' The argument of the passage as a whole, however, points away from this latter interpretation.

This argument becomes clearer if we start from the end and work backwards. Paul has been reminding the Corinthians (10:1–11) of some of the sins committed by the Israelites in the desert on their way from Egypt to Canaan, and the punishments that followed. One of these offences was idolatry; and Paul warns his converts against the danger of their also sliding into idolatry by eating meat which had been offered in sacrifice in the pagan temples – in effect, most of the meat on sale in the market. The root of his objection is that by eating food which has been offered in this way they will be entering into fellowship with heathen gods who are in reality demons (vv. 20–1).

The key idea which unifies this whole passage is that of 'table fellowship', the bond which creates a sacred relationship between those who eat together. This played a large part in the culture of Israel and the ancient world generally, as it does in many societies today. The special horror of what Judas did is that even after he had received a mark of honour and affection in the form of food from Jesus' own hand he went out from that fellowship into the night of betrayal (Mark 14:18–21; Matt. 26:21–5; Luke 22:21–3; John 13:21–30; cf. Ps. 41:9).

Thus the pagan worshippers enjoy table fellowship with their gods, and with each other as fellow worshippers. So too in v. 18, where the reference is to Jewish sacrifices in the Temple, those who eat the offerings, whether priests or worshippers, are bound together with one another and with God as 'members of a fellowship (*koinonoi*) of the altar.'

It is in this light that we have to interpret vv. 16–17. V. 17

stresses the unity of fellowship between Christians who share in the Eucharist: as they all eat of the one loaf, so they themselves are one body, a theme which Paul goes on to develop at length in Chapter 12. Just as Jews are '*koinonoi* of the altar', so Christians have a '*koinonia* of the blood of Christ' and 'of the body of Christ' – that is, to paraphrase, a fellowship based on Jesus' sacrifice of himself for them all, and on their eating and drinking together the bread and wine that are the symbolic proclamation of that sacrifice.

An examination of the New Testament evidence, therefore, leads irresistibly to the conclusion that there is *no biblical warrant for the belief that,* by some kind of supernatural change, *the eucharistic bread and wine become* in some sense *the body and blood of Christ,* to be eaten and drunk by the worshippers. Not only is there no warrant, there is not even a trace of a tendency in that direction. The idea clearly never entered the mind of Jesus, nor did the New Testament writers misinterpret him in this way.

'Do this for my memorial'

It has been argued with some force that these words, even though they appear only in Paul and Luke, are an authentic recollection of what Jesus said at the Last Supper. It is clear that the Eucharist, at any rate as celebrated in the Corinthian church, included no narration of Jesus' words and actions in connection with the bread and wine. If it had, there would have been no need for Paul to repeat the official summary account in his letter and to remind them that he had taught them this when he came to Corinth (11:23). The words belong to the teaching tradition; they are not part of a liturgical formula.

The Greek word rendered 'memorial' (*anamnesis*) has been of central importance in modern eucharistic studies. Its use in the Greek versions of the Old Testament, and the meanings of the Hebrew terms which it there represents, have been exhaustively examined, as have the occurrences of the idea in Jewish thought of the time of Jesus and after. It was at one time widely accepted that *anamnesis* signified not just the remembering of a past event but the making of it present here and now. This interpretation, however, perhaps owed more to the wishful thinking of scholars who believed they had found a biblical basis for the doctrine that the reality of Christ's sacrifice was made present on the altar at every Eucharist. The majority view would now seem to be that this cannot be legitimately read out of the biblical and Jewish usage.

Perhaps the supreme example of a memorial action in Judaism is the Passover meal, which was either the occasion of the Last Supper or at least its dominating context. *Anamnesis* here is the remembrance with thanksgiving before God of his mighty act of creative deliverance, when Israel was brought safely out of slavery in Egypt and formed into the people of God. It carries with it the prayer that the power of that deliverance should be available still for God's people in the present and bring to consummation the divine plan begun long ago. In commending to his closest followers the ritual of the bread and cup as a memorial of himself, Jesus was identifying his own death on the morrow as something willed by God to be a source of life and blessing for his people and asking them to pray in this way for the consummation of the process which his life and death had begun. This accords closely with the understanding of the bread and cup in biblical terms as a prophetic sign and with Paul's description of them as a proclamation of the Lord's death 'until he comes' (1 Cor. 11:26) – that is, until the time when the kingdom of God would finally be set up.

As a kind of postscript to the observation that the Eucharist at Corinth apparently included no narrative of Jesus' words and actions over the bread and wine, it is worth noting that the same is true of the two eucharistic prayers in a work called *The Didache*, an early Christian treatise dated by scholars either in the first or second century CE. Some have disputed that the prayers are eucharistic, but I myself am firmly in agreement with those experts who maintain that they are.

Notes

Chapter 1

1 *Tantum Deus cognoscitur quam diligitur.*
2 Charlotte Brontë, *Jane Eyre* (London, Heron, n.d.), p. 386.
3 As evidenced by the fact that more than three hundred bodies are now affiliated to the World Council of Churches.
4 John Henry Newman, *Apologia pro Vita Sua* (London, Dent, 1949), pp. 220–21.
5 This trend is noticeable today even within the Roman Catholic Church, to judge from the pastoral provision which has had to be made for members troubled by certain aspects of the Encyclical *Humanae Vitae.*
6 Gen. 1:31.
7 Thomas Hardy, *The Woodlanders* (London, Macmillan, 1974), p. 83.
8 Mark 7:13; cf. Matt. 15:6.
9 Jude 3.

Chapter 2

1 Gen. 1:1–2:4a and 2:4b–9, 18–25 derive from what were originally two separate accounts. Both have long traditions behind them, but the first, in its present form, is the later, being part of the framework of the four books, Genesis to Numbers, as finally edited.
2 In Gen. 1:16 the sun and moon are denied their usual names and are described simply as lamps; while the stars, so important in for example Mesopotamian religion, are dismissed almost as an afterthought.
3 Gen. 1:26–8; 2:19–20. It cannot be too often repeated that, however much Christians may have misused these texts to justify the exploitation of animals, in this biblical picture of life as intended by God before humanity's fall into sin things are very different. Both animals and humans are non-carnivorous (1:29–30) and coexist in peace. Cf. the vision of paradise regained in Isa. 11:6–9.
4 Gen. 10; 11:10–32.

5 One notable example is the way in which the narrative in 2 Sam. and 1–2 Kings has been revised by the writer of 1–2 Chronicles.

6 Cf., e.g., the stories of the Massacre of the Innocents and the Flight into Egypt in Matt. 2:13–18.

7 E.g. the story of Moses in the bulrushes (Exod. 2:1–10), which is similar to one told about Sargon, king of Akkad.

8 Heb. 11:1, 6.

9 John 1:18; 1 John 4:12.

10 Cf. esp. Thomas Kuhn, *The Structure of Scientific Revolutions*, 2nd edn (Chicago, University of Chicago Press, 1970), and the continuing debate arising from this seminal work.

11 Judg. 2:11–23; 4:1–2; 6:1; etc.

12 1 Sam. 8:4–9.

13 1 Sam. 12:14–15; Ps. 89:19–34.

14 Ps. 44:17–22.

15 Jer. 44:15–18.

16 2 Chr. 36:15–19; cf. 2 Kings 17:7–23, applying the same principle to the fall of the northern kingdom.

17 Gen. 18:16–33.

18 Zech. 1:14–17; cf. Isa. 40:2 ('double').

19 Ezek. 36:16–32.

20 2 Kings 21:10–14; 24:3–4.

21 Jer. 44:1–6; Zech. 1:4–6.

22 Jer. 31:27–30; Ezek. 18.

23 Isa. 53:4–12.

24 Judg. 11:24; 2 Kings 3:27 (the king of Moab's sacrifice of his son to Chemosh, the god of Moab, causes that god to intervene and drive out the invading Israelites); Ps. 82:1–2 (the gods of the nations rule their people badly); Mic. 4:5.

25 Exod. 12:12; 15:11; cf. 1 Sam. 5:1–4 (Israel's God, brought into the land of the Philistines in the sacred chest or 'ark', overthrows the Philistine god, Dagon).

26 Isa. 40:19–20; 41:21–4, 29; 42:17; 44:9–20; 46:1–2, 6–7; cf. Ps. 97:7; 115:3–8; 135:15–18.

27 Ps. 96:5; Isa. 43:10–11; 44:6–8; 45:5–7, 14, 18–19, 21, 22.

28 Cf. Ezra 7:1–6, 11–12; 10:16–17; Neh. 8:1–12. The editing of the Law (Genesis to Deuteronomy) in its present form shows massive evidence of priestly influence and codification.

29 E.g. Pss. 34; 37; 73; 92.

30 E.g. Pss. 25; 30; 32; 41.

31 E.g. Pss. 22; 35; 69.

32 Job 11:1–6, 13–20; 22:1–11; 34:1–9, 34–7.

33 Job 33:12–33.

34 Job 38:25–7; 39:5–12; 40:15–24; 41.

35 Job 1:1–2:10.

36 Dan. 12:1–3; 2 Macc. 7:9, 11, 14, 22–3, 28–9; 12:38–45; 2 Esd. 9:9–13.

37 Wisd. 2:21–3:19.

38 2 Esd. 7:1–14.

39 Cf., e.g., 1 Cor. 2:9–10; Eph. 3:5–6.

40 Mark 12:18–27.

41 But see also pp. 85f. and 128f. below for fuller discussion.

42 On this whole subject, see the recent publication by the Church of England's General Synod Commission on Christian Doctrine, *The Mystery of Salvation* (1995), and the excellent short exposition of Catholic teaching in Michael Evans, *Can Only Christians be Saved?*, published by the Catholic Truth Society.

43 In the Church of England in 1967 the newly formed Archbishops' Commission on Christian Doctrine (as it was then called) was asked to make recommendations on the question of assent to the Thirty-Nine Articles of Religion, a fundamental formulary of our Church, dating from 1571. Certain passages in the Articles were giving great difficulties of conscience to clergy, who had to state publicly their general assent to the Articles whenever entering on a new post. They were also causing problems for other Provinces of the Anglican Communion. At its meeting at St Mary's Abbey, West Malling, early in 1968, the Commission found itself deadlocked: even a light revision of the Articles was unacceptable to many members, for a variety of reasons, but all attempts to modify the words of assent failed to produce an agreed formula. But thanks to the prayers of the Sisters in the Community a solution emerged. That evening the thought was given to the present writer that perhaps a Preface to the Declaration of Assent might set out acceptably the wider context of Scripture and Creeds in which assent was to be given, and indicate the relative authority of the Articles within the whole sweep of Anglican belief. During the night he produced a first draft which the Commission then revised and recommended; and this text is substantially the one later adopted by General Synod. The significant point for our present concern is that the Commission's recommended text included in the 'inheritance of faith' which ministers were to take as their 'inspiration and guidance under God' the work of teachers, martyrs and confessors *down to the present day*. This was rejected by Synod, who could not contemplate authority being given even in lesser degree to anything other than the fixed, official formularies of the past.

44 Cf. 'The adventure of faith', the opening chapter of the Report, *Christian Believing* (1976), by the Church of England Doctrine Commission.

45 Ian G. Barbour, *Religion in an Age of Science* (London, SCM Press, 1990), p. 103.

46 T. S. Eliot, 'Fragment of an Agon', *The Complete Poems and Plays* (London, Faber, 1969), p. 125.

47 The ideas at issue here are explored incomparably in that classic work by Thornton Wilder, *The Bridge of San Luis Rey* (London, Penguin, 1954).

48 Deut. 13:1–5; 18:15–22; 1 Kings 22:28; Jer. 28:15–17 etc. The early Christian Church saw delayed fulfilments of many Old Testament prophecies in the story of Jesus.

49 Cf. Alister Hardy, *The Spiritual Nature of Man* (Oxford, Clarendon Press, 1979), and other material from the Religious Experience Research Unit which he founded.

50 Cf. p. 162.

51 For the material underlying this section I am indebted to many works, but particularly to Ian G. Barbour, *Religion in an Age of Science* (London, SCM Press, 1990); Murray Gell-Mann, *The Quark and the Jaguar* (London, Little, Brown, 1994); Stanley L. Jaki, *The Road of Science and the Ways to God* (Edinburgh, Scottish Academic Press, 1978); and A. R. Peacocke, *Creation and the World of Science* (Oxford, Clarendon Press, 1979).

52 It is possible to authenticate this process by studying the life forms in natural 'laboratories' such as isolated Pacific islands where new species have multiplied which are unique to that habitat but related to others found elsewhere.

53 Cf., e.g., Pierre Teilhard de Chardin, *The Phenomenon of Man* (London, Collins, 1975), pp. 181–234.

54 St Thomas Aquinas, *Summa Theologiae* I, q. 2, art. 3. The actual wording varies: e.g., 'this is what everybody understands by "God"' or 'to which everyone gives the name "God"'.

55 E.g. by Bertrand Russell.

56 For a severe criticism of the whole oscillating universe concept, cf. Stanley L. Jaki, *Science and Creation* (Scottish Academic Press, Edinburgh, 1974), pp. 336–57.

57 William of Occam (or Ockham), 1285–1347: *entia non sunt multiplicanda praeter necessitatem.*

58 Col. 1:17.

Chapter 3

1 This aspect of Jesus has been increasingly acknowledged of recent years. Cf. esp. the work of Geza Vermes, *Jesus the Jew* (London, Collins, 1973), and *The Religion of Jesus the Jew* (London, SCM Press, 1993).

2 Cf. Acts 9:2; 19:9, 23; 22:4; 24:14, 22; also 18:25, 26.

3 1 Cor. 2:16; cf. Phil. 2:5.

4 For Paul cf. 1 Cor. 7:10, 12, 25; 11:23; 14:37; 2 Cor. 11:17. In Rev. 1–3 the Holy Spirit inspires John with messages to the churches of Asia Minor from the risen and glorified Jesus.

5 Cf. Matt. 28:18; Gal. 5:1; 1 Pet. 2:16.

6 This use of the passive voice to express the action of God is a reverential idiom taken over from Judaism.

7 A. Roy Eckardt, 'Is there a way out of the Christian crime?', *Holocaust and Genocide Studies* 1.1 (1986), p. 122.

8 Cf. the Qur'an, Sura 4, paras 155–6.

9 1 Cor. 15:13–15.

10 Acts 23:6; Acts 26:8; Acts 17:31.

11 Acts 17:32–3.

12 1 Cor. 15:20.

13 Rev. 1:18.

14 Acts 1:22.

15 Cf. the famous dictum of Leonard Hodgson, *For Faith and Freedom*[2] (London, SCM Press, 1968), p. x: 'What must the truth have been and be if that is how it looked to men who thought and wrote like that?' I criticised this sharply in *The Foolishness of God* (London, Darton, Longman & Todd, 1970), pp. 364–5; but I believe now that I misunderstood his point, which I here gladly restate to fit the present context.

16 Mark 5:22–43 (cf. Matt. 9:18–26; Luke 8:40–56); Luke 7:11–17; John 11:1–44.

17 John 20:15; Luke 24:15, 28; John 21:4; Acts 9:3–5.

18 John 20:16–18; Luke 24:32; John 21:7, 12, 17; Acts 26:15, 19.

19 Cf., e.g., Mark 3:6, 21–2; Luke 13:31; John 7:12; 8:48; 9:24; 11:47–50.

20 Acts 2:32–6; 3:15–16 etc.

21 Acts 4:1–3, 17; 5:40; 8:1–3.

22 Deut. 21:22–3.

23 Acts 2:22; Acts 10:38–9.

24 Cf., e.g., Mark 1:28; 3:7–8; 6:14, 54–6; John 7:31; 11:47–8 etc.

25 Cf., e.g., Luke 7:16–17; John 14:10–11.

26 John 9:30–3.

27 Mark 5:25–6.

28 Mark 5:39: cf. Matt. 9:24; Luke 8:52.

29 Matt. 12:27 and Luke 11:19 (but not in Mark, so possibly Church anti-Jewish polemic); also Mark 9:38–40 and Luke 9:49–50.

30 N.b. the characteristic phrase, 'Your faith has made you well': Mark 5:34; 10:52; Matt. 9:22; Luke 7:50; 8:48; 17:19.

31 Mark 6:5.

32 Mark 4:37–41: cf. Matt. 8:23–7; Luke 8:22–5.

33 Mark 6:45–52: cf. Matt. 14:22–3; John 6:15–21.

34 Matt. 11:2–6; Luke 7:18–23.

35 Matt. 17:24–7.
36 Mark 6:30–44; Matt. 14:13–21; Luke 9:10–17; John 6:1–14.
37 The boy (John 6:9); the grass (6:10); the barley loaves (6:9).
38 John 6:14–15: for the hope behind this cf. Deut. 18:18. Matt. 11:3 and Luke 7:19 have the same reference.
39 Exod. 16: cf. John 6:30–4.
40 1 Kings 17:8–16; 2 Kings 4:1–7, and especially 42–4.
41 Mark 8:14–21. Matthew, in taking over Mark's account, recasts Jesus' words to avoid this particular issue.
42 John 2:1–11.
43 John 2:6–7. This could be taken to imply that only the water drawn out became wine, but the reference to filling the jars 'up to the brim' seems to suggest otherwise.
44 John 2:11.
45 E.g. the Cure d'Ars and St John Bosco.
46 E.g. the Hindu holy man, Sai Baba.
47 Mark 8:2–3: cf. Matt. 15:32. This second feeding is not found in Luke or John.
48 Mark 6:36.
49 John 2:1–3, 9–10.
50 Matt. 14:26; John 6:19.
51 Mark 4:41: cf. Ps. 89:9. In Matthew's account of Jesus walking on the water the disciples make a similar leap of faith explicitly.
52 Matt. 16:1–4: cf. 12:38–39. 'Adultery' is a standard image in the prophets for Israel's unfaithfulness to the covenant relationship with God (cf. Hosea, Jeremiah, Ezekiel).
53 Matt. 4:5–7; Luke 4:9–12.
54 E.g. Mark 5:43; 7:36; 8:26.
55 John 11:47. In 4:48 Jesus himself uses the phrase 'signs and wonders', to describe the demonstration he suspects that the royal official will need before he can find the faith in Jesus necessary for his son's cure.
56 John 6:26; 12:37–40.
57 John 6:30.
58 John 5:17; 9:3–4; 10:37; 14:10.
59 John 4:34; 5:19–20, 26; 10:32, 38; 15:24.
60 John 7:17–18, 28–9; 8:18; 10:34–8.
61 Cf. A. E. Harvey, *Jesus on Trial* (London, SPCK, 1976).
62 John 10:25.
63 John 9:31–3.
64 Cf. Deut. 13:1–5.
65 Mark 3:22: cf. Matt. 12:24; Luke 11:15.
66 John 7:12.
67 Mark 3:28–30: cf. Matt. 12:31–2.
68 Mark 12:10: cf. Matt. 21:42; Luke 20:17; 1 Pet. 2:7–8.
69 Mark 1:9.

70 Cf., e.g., the words Matthew puts into John's mouth at Jesus' baptism (Matt. 3:14).
71 Matt. 11:12–13; Luke 16:16.
72 Matt. 11:11; Luke 7:28.
73 Matt. 11:11; Luke 7:28.
74 Matt. 18:1–4; Mark 9:33–7; 10:31; Luke 9:46–8; 13:30.
75 Matt. 23:11–12; Mark 10:43–4; Luke 22:26–7.
76 Matt. 4:17: cf. Mark 1:14; Matt. 3:2.
77 Matt. 3:7–12; Luke 3:7–17.
78 Mark 4:30.
79 Mark 4:31–2; Luke 13:18–19.
80 Matt. 13:33; Mark 4:26–9; Luke 13:20.
81 Matt. 13:44–6.
82 Matt. 18:3; Mark 10:14–15; Luke 18:17; Matt. 21:31–2.
83 Mark 10:23–5: cf. Matt. 19:23–4; Luke 18:24–5.
84 Matt. 8:10–11.
85 Matt. 5:3–9.
86 Matt. 16:1–3; Luke 12:54–6.
87 Luke 17:20–1.
88 Mark 13:28–9: cf. Matt. 24:32–3; Luke 21:29–31.
89 Mark 4:1–9; Matt. 13:1–9; Luke 8:4–8.
90 Cf. pp. 000 ff.
91 Matt. 13:10, 36; 15:15–16; Mark 4:13; 7:17–18; Luke 8:10.
92 Mark 4:10–12; Matt. 13:14–15; Luke 8:9–10.
93 Cf. Ezek. 17:1–21; 19; Dan. 4:1–27; 8; Rev. 12:1–6; 13; 17:1–6.
94 Mark 12:12; Matt. 21:45; Luke 20:19.
95 Mark 12:37; Matt. 7:28–9; cf. Mark 1:22.
96 Cf., e.g., Mark 1:17–18, 38–9; 6:6b–13; Luke 10:1–2.
97 Isa. 6:9–10: cf. n. 92 above.
98 Cf. J. Bowker, *Jesus and the Pharisees*, 1973.
99 Mark 7:9–13; Matt. 23:16–24.
100 Mark 12:28–33; Luke 10:25–7.
101 Matt. 7:12.
102 Cf., e.g., Mark 4:22–5; 7:15; 9:40, 50; 10:25; Luke 17:37 etc.
103 Luke 14:7–11: cf. Prov. 25:6–7.
104 Cf., e.g., Prov. 25:21–2.
105 Mark 10:1–12; Matt. 19:1–12: cf. 1 Cor. 7:10–11. The absoluteness of this teaching appears to be qualified in Matt. 5:31–2, where divorce is allowed if the wife is shown to have committed adultery. The verse has been regarded by some as lining Jesus up with the strict rabbinic school of Shammai, who allowed divorce only for adultery, as against the lenient school of Hillel, who accepted even quite trivial grounds. It would, however, be unusual for Jesus to engage directly in such controversies; and the combined testimony of Mark and Paul is strong evidence that his stance was in fact stricter than either rabbinic view. A

possible explanation is that because the divorcing husband is said to 'cause' his wife to commit adultery (presumably by driving her to further marriage, cohabitation or prostitution), some literal-minded editor (or Matthew himself) felt that this was impossible if she were already an adulteress, and so inserted a rider excepting divorce on these grounds.

106 Matt. 5:38–48; Luke 6:27–36.
107 Thus, for example, where Luke makes John the Baptist direct his denunciations at the crowds in general, Matthew has him specifically target the Pharisees and Sadducees (Matt. 3:7). Matthew alone has the long catalogue of woes against the scribes and Pharisees (Matt. 23), and attacks on the religious leaders come at regular intervals throughout the gospel: 6:2–6, 16–18; 12:1–14, 22–42; 15:12–14; 16:1–12; 23.
108 Matt. 5:20.
109 Matt. 23:2–3.
110 Matt. 5:17–18.
111 Matt. 18:8: cf. Mark 9:43.
112 Mark 7:20–3; Matt. 15:18–20; cf. 12:34.
113 Matt. 6:12, 14–15; 18:21–35; Mark 11:25; Luke 11:4; 17:3–4.
114 Luke 18:9–14.
115 Cf. pp. 40f.
116 Indicated by the fact that the value of the sacrifice is proportional not to the seriousness of the sin but to the means of the sinner; the poor can atone with a very modest offering: Lev. 5:7–13.
117 Cf., e.g., Dan. 9:3–19; The Prayer of Manasseh.
118 Matt. 7:29.
119 A possible interpretation of Matt. 23:8, depending on one's decision as to whether or not Jesus saw himself as Messiah: cf. pp. 91ff.
120 Matt. 5:21–43; Mark 7:1–23.
121 Cf., e.g., Mark 2:23–8; 12:35–7.
122 John 7:46.
123 The bizarre idea that Jesus never used humour tells us a good deal about the way people read the Bible: cf., e.g., Mark 10:25 (= Matt. 19:24; Luke 18:25); Matt. 11:16–19 (= Luke 7:31–5); 23:24; Luke 16:1–9; 18:1–5, 11.
124 Cf., e.g., Mark 3:23–6; 7:18–19.
125 Widely recognised ever since the publication of the ground-breaking work of C. F. Burney, *The Poetry of Our Lord* (1925): cf. also Matthew Black, *An Aramaic Approach to the Gospels and Acts*[3] (Oxford, Clarendon Press, 1967).
126 Matt. 6:22–3; Luke 11:34–6.
127 Matt. 7:15–18 = Luke 6:43–4; cf. Matt. 12:33, 35.
128 Luke 10:25–9, 36–7.
129 Luke 10:37.

130 Jews or Samaritans: the 'Good Samaritan', also Luke 9:52–5; John 4:7–9. Rulers: Mark 10:42–3: cf. Matt. 20:25–6; Luke 22:25–6.
131 Luke 14:12–14.
132 Matt. 5:39–47: cf. Luke 6:27–35.
133 Mark 1:41; Luke 7:39; 17:16; 19:7; John 8:1–11.
134 Matt. 23:13, 15.
135 Matt. 25:1–13; Luke 13:28.
136 Mark 8:34; Matt. 16:24.
137 Luke 9:23.
138 Mark 8:35–6; Matt. 16:25–6; Luke 9:24–5.
139 Matt. 7:14; Luke 10:2; 12:32; 13:24.
140 Matt. 5:33–7.
141 Matt. 5:38–41, 44; 26:52–3; Luke 6:27–9; 22:49–53. The enigmatic dialogue in Luke 22:35–8 is not enough to outweigh this teaching and example: cf. any good commentary on the passage.
142 E.g. Mark 10:17–25; Luke 9:58; 12:13–21, 22–31.
143 Matt. 5:40; Luke 6:30; Matt. 25:31–40; Luke 10:30–7.
144 1 Cor. 1:25.
145 E.g. Mark 1:10, 12, 18, 20, 21, 28, 29 etc.
146 Mark 6:11.
147 Mark 6:1–5: cf. Luke 4:21–30.
148 Matt. 11:21; Luke 10:13.
149 Luke 19:41–4.
150 The actual Aramaic word is transliterated in the gospels only once (Mark 14:36), but most scholars assume that the vocative form of the Greek 'Father' represents its use.
151 Interestingly another Aramaic idiom of Jesus, the use of the word *amen* in the phrase, '*Amen*, I tell you', meaning 'Truly and solemnly I tell you', is transliterated no fewer than seventy times in the four gospels.
152 Rom. 8:15; Gal. 4:6.
153 Mark 14:36.
154 Cf. Geza Vermes, *Jesus the Jew* (London, Collins, 1973), p. 211.
155 Cf., e.g., Matt. 5:45; 6:6; 7:11; 10:29; Mark 11:25; Luke 6:36; 11:13; 12:30 etc.
156 Matt. 23:9.
157 Mark 3:35: cf. Matt. 12:50; Luke 8:21.
158 Mark 10:29–30: cf. Matt. 19:29; Luke 18:29–30.
159 Witness the *shema* (Deut. 6:4–5), the words which every devout Jew will say each morning.
160 Though we think of Jesus as primarily reaching out to the outcast and poor and the ordinary working folk, the gospels also tell of him as a guest in better off or more prestigious homes: cf. Luke 7:36–50. It should also not be forgotten that senior

religious figures admired him and made contact with him: John 3:1–21; Mark 12:28–34; cf. John 19:38–42.

161 Matt. 10:23b.
162 Matt. 8:11.
163 Mark 1:12.
164 Luke 2:41–52.
165 John 7:10.
166 Matt. 6:9–13; Luke 11:2–4.
167 The version in Matthew is expanded in ways that make it more suitable for liturgical use. Note also the opening 'Our Father in heaven', as contrasted with Luke's simple 'Father'.
168 The Greek word behind the 'daily' in the traditional English version is very rare. The fact that it is common to both Matthew's and Luke's versions of the prayer is strong evidence that each is based on an already existing Greek text. Note that, because the Jewish day runs from sunset to sunset, 'the coming day' actually begins during what we would call 'today'.
169 Literally, 'may your name be sanctified', 'made or held holy'.
170 'Debts' was a common Jewish terms for sins or offences. Luke explains this for his readers by using both words.
171 This final balancing phrase is not in Luke.
172 The real meaning of the first Beatitude as found in Matthew: 'Blessed are the poor in spirit' (Matt. 5:3).
173 Luke 4:16.
174 John 7:15.
175 Luke 4:16–18.
176 John 5:1; 7:10; 10:22; 12:1 etc.
177 Matt. 21:12–13; Mark 11:15–17; Luke 19:45–6; John 2:14–16.
178 Matt. 7:7–11: cf. Luke 11:9–13; Mark 11:24.
179 Mark 11:23; Matt. 17:20.
180 Matt. 18:19–20.
181 John 14:13–14; 15:16; 16:23, 26.
182 Luke 18:1.
183 John 15:7–10.
184 John 11:41–2.
185 John 5:19; 10:30.
186 Mark 14:36.
187 Luke 22:43; John 18:11.
188 Mark 14:21–4; Matt. 26:20–31; Luke 22:14–23; John 13:3, 21–30.
189 Mark 15:34; Matt. 27:46.
190 Mark 1:11; Matt. 3:17; Luke 3:22: cf. Mark 9:7; Matt. 17:5; Luke 9:35.
191 Cf. p. 98.
192 John 1:5; 3:19; 12:35–6, 46.
193 John 8:23–5.

194 Cf. pp. 79, 80.

195 Matt. 27:25.

196 Cf., e.g., Mark 12:13–27; Luke 14:28–32; 15:3–7; 16:10–13; 17:7–10 etc.

197 Mark 1:16–20, cf. 30; 2:14; Luke 8:1–3.

198 Mark 3:31–5; Luke 9:60–2; 14:26.

199 Mark 11:15–17; Matt. 21:12–13; Luke 19:45–6; John 2:13–16.

200 Mark 7:24–30.

201 Mark 5:1–20; Matt. 8:28–34; Luke 8:26–39.

202 Mark 5:10–12.

203 Matt. 12:11; Luke 13:15.

204 Cf., e.g., The Gospel of the Ebionites, cited in Epiphanius, *Panarion*, 30.13.4f.

205 Cf., e.g., Mark 12:2, 4; Matt. 22:3, 4; 24:45; Luke 12:35–48.

206 Philmn. 15–16. Various passages in the gospels reflect a genuinely human relationship between master and slave: e.g. Matt. 10:24–5; 18:27; Luke 7:2–3; John 4:51.

207 Cf. n. 105 above.

208 Luke 7:36–50; John 8:1–11.

209 John 4:7–27.

210 Luke 10:38–42.

211 Luke 8:1–3.

212 Mark 12:13–17; Matt. 17:24–7.

213 John 6:15; Mark 11:11.

214 Luke 22:47–53. Luke has a special concern to prove that neither Jesus nor the early Christians were in any way subversive, but the other accounts of Gethsemane also show that Jesus made no attempt to encourage his followers to resist: Mark 14:48–9; Matt. 26:52–4; John 18:7–11.

215 Mark 2:23–8; Luke 13:10–17; John 5:1–16.

216 Matt. 25:46.

217 Matt. 25:40.

218 Mark 3:33, 35.

219 N.b., e.g., the developed figure of the 'Son of Man', coming as God's judge at the Last Day, surrounded by the angels, to determine the destiny of all nations. On the significance of this, cf. pp. 90f.

220 Matt. 25:41: cf. 13:40–2, 49–50; 18:9.

221 Matt. 8:12. Luke uses the phrase, without the element of outer darkness, to describe the rage and envy of the chosen people when excluded from the kingdom: Luke 13:28.

222 John 3:16; 10:28; 17:12.

223 Mark 10:17–22; Matt. 19:16–22; Luke 18:18–23.

224 Matthew seems to feel the awkwardness of this conclusion, and modifies the exchange between Jesus and the man to soften it;

but the crucial words remain: 'There is only one who is good' (19:16–17).

225 Innumerable saints, both eastern and western, could be cited to illustrate this point: St Francis of Assisi and St Serafim of Sarov are two obvious examples.

226 G. K. Chesterton, *The Everlasting Man* (London, Hodder & Stoughton, 1947), p. 230.

227 John 6:20; 8:24, 28; 13:19: but the same usage is put into the mouth of the man born blind (9:9), so the deeper significance is not automatically present. For the divine name in the Old Testament cf. Exod. 3:14.

228 Mark 9:37; Matt. 15:24; Luke 4:43; John 3:17; 5:36; 10:36; 17:8.

229 Cf. n. 190 above.

230 Pss. 2:7; 89:26–7.

231 John 10:30–9.

232 John 17:5.

233 John 14:8–11.

234 Acts 7:56.

235 Dan. 7:9–10, 13–14.

236 Rev. 1:13: the rendering in some modern versions, 'like *the* Son of Man' is a mistranslation; the Greek has no definite article.

237 For a recent survey of the state of the question, cf. B. Lindars, *Jesus Son of Man* (London, SPCK, 1983).

238 Mark 1:1, 34; 9:41; Matt. 1:16, 18; 2:4; Luke 2:11, 26; 4:41; John 1:17.

239 John 1:41.

240 Mark 8:27–30.

241 Mark 8:31–3.

242 Matt. 16:13–19.

243 Matt. 18:15–17. The injunction, 'let such a one be to you as a Gentile and a tax collector' (v. 17), also reads very improbably as words of Jesus.

244 John 1:41.

245 John 11:27.

246 John 4:26.

247 John 4:29.

248 John 4:40–2.

249 Luke 22:67–8.

250 Mark 14:63–4; Matt. 26:65–6.

251 Luke 22:70.

252 Nicodemus and Joseph of Arimathea may have been the sources.

253 John 19:7: cf. 5:18; 10:33.

254 Mark 12:35–7; Matt. 22:41–5; Luke 20:41–4.

255 Matt. 1:1–17 (esp. vv. 1, 6, 17); Luke 3:23–38 (esp. v. 31).

256 John 7:27, 41–2.

257 Luke 13:28.

258　Eph. 3:1–6.

259　Acts 2:36.

260　2 Cor. 11:22; Phil. 3:4–6.

261　This aspect of Paul has been brought out more strongly of recent years: cf. e.g., E. P. Sanders, *Paul and Palestinian Judaism* (London, SCM Press, 1977); but cf. also H. Maccoby, *Paul and Hellenism* (London, SCM Press, 1991).

262　Cf., e.g., R. P. Martin, *Carmen Christi* (Cambridge, Cambridge University Press, 1967).

263　(1) Heb. 1:1–3: though attributed to Paul in the King James Bible, this Letter has long been recognised not to be his; the real author is unknown. (2) Col. 1:15–23; 2:8–10. Though traditionally included in the list of Paul's writings, there are strong reasons, stylistic and other, for attributing it to another hand, except for some personal sections. Many, even of Paul's authentic letters are almost certainly composite compilations from originally separate documents; and it would be no difficult matter to combine new theological matter with genuine material. (3) John 1:1–18.

264　Isa. 55:9: cf. 40:25; 44:6–7; 46:5.

265　Wisd. 9:17; Ps. 51:10.

266　Cf., e.g., Dan. 3:25; 6:22; 8:16; 9:21–3; 10:5–10; Tobit 5:4–12:22; Matt. 1:20; 2:13, 19; Luke 1:11–20, 26–38; Acts 5:19; 12:7–11; 27:23.

267　Cf., e.g., Ps. 119:47, 54, 72, 93, 103, 130, 165; Sir. 24:23–9.

268　Prov. 8:1–9:6; Wisd. 7:21–9:11; Sir. 24:1–22.

269　A constant theme in the Old Testament: cf., e.g., Exod. 33:21–3; Judg. 13:22; Isa. 6:5: Moses' special status is indicated in one tradition by the unique privilege that he is allowed to see God, Num. 12:8.

270　N.b., e.g., Prov. 8:22, where Wisdom is the first of all created things, i.e. not herself divine.

271　Col. 1:16–17.

272　N.b. especially Wisdom as an emanation from God and radiant with divine light: Wisd. 7:25–6; Heb. 1:3.

273　Phil. 2:7–8.

274　Col. 2:9.

275　Col. 2:11–15.

276　John 1:1–18.

277　Cf., e.g., Isa. 55:11: in Gen. 1 God creates purely by his word, as in v. 3, 'Then God said, "Let there be light"; and there was light' (and so throughout this first creation story). Cf. also Heb. 4:12.

278　The hymn in Philippians is usually dated around 35–40 CE. The fact that Hebrews plainly speaks as though the Jerusalem Temple is still in operation, and that the Letter's whole argument would

certainly have been put differently if it were not, places that
evidence before 70 CE. Colossians and John belong probably to
the period between 70 and 90 CE, but cannot be fixed more
certainly.
279 At the end of this long chapter I must pay tribute to what I
regard as one of the greatest books on Jesus in this century: Jon
Sobrino SJ, *Christology at the Crossroads* (London, SCM Press,
1978). Its influence on the present work at many points has
been immense, even though the disciple can in no way claim to
be 'as his master'.

Chapter 4

1 The 'Nicene Creed': strictly the creed finally formulated at the
Council of Constantinople in 381, and known technically as
the Niceno-Constantinopolitan Creed. This is the one most
widely used in the Eucharist throughout the universal Church.
2 Such as the decrees of the Council of Ephesus (431) and Chalce-
don (451).
3 Heb. 2:9.
4 John 17:5.
5 Col. 1:15; 2 Cor. 4:6.
6 In the gospels according to Luke and John, Jesus' final words
express restored assurance and peace of soul: Luke 23:46; John
19:30. If a choice has to be made, the earlier and harsher tradition
in Mark is historically more probable.
7 As Kierkegaard, Bonhoeffer and Moltmann have all emphasised
from their different standpoints.
8 Cf. the moving passage on the 'child walking alone' in Søren
Kierkegaard, *Gospel of Sufferings* (Cambridge, James Clarke, 1982)
pp. 15–17, 23.
9 Phil. 2:7–8.
10 Heb. 2:9, 10, 14–15, 17–18.
11 Col. 1:19–20.
12 Col. 2:9.
13 Col. 2:13–15.
14 John 10:17–18.
15 John 11:25–6.
16 2 Cor. 5:19.
17 Many of the ideas set out in these sections will be found in two
of my earlier books: *Travels in Oudamovia* (London, Faith Press,
1976), and *The Whole Family of God* (Oxford, Mowbray, 1981).
The present treatment aims to develop these more systematically.
18 Eph. 2:19; 1 Pet. 4:17.

19 John 3:16; 2 Cor. 5:19. It is therefore a distortion when, for instance, the *Contemporary English Version* of the Bible renders 'world' as 'the people of the world'.

20 Cf. p. 73.

21 Matt. 16:18: cf. p. 92. Matt. 18:15–17: the passage seems to presuppose a fairly developed pattern of church life; also the words 'let such a one be to you as a Gentile and a tax collector' do not sound like authentic words of Jesus.

22 John 14:1.

23 Traditionally, unrepented sin subsequent to faith can also exclude one from the number of the saved: but cf. pp. 125ff.

24 John Austin Baker, *Travels in Oudamovia* (London, Faith Press, 1976), p. 29.

25 Cf., e.g., John 12:40; Rom. 11:7; 2 Cor. 3:14; 4:4; 1 John 2:11.

26 John 16:22.

27 2 Cor. 4:4; Gen. 1:26–7.

28 Cf. p. 13.

29 Cf. p. 36.

30 The extent to which social customs in communities of the higher primates share in some degree the nature of human ethics is much debated.

31 Cf. pp. 41, 42.

32 The balance sheet approach is extensively explored in my earlier work, *The Foolishness of God* (London, Darton, Longman and Todd, 1970), pp. 55–69.

33 An entertaining presentation of the ideas mentioned in this paragraph may be found in Peter de Rosa, *The Best of All Possible Worlds* (Niles, Illinois, Argus, 1975).

34 Though, strangely, Homer also was traditionally said to be blind.

35 In scholastic theology sheer existence is held in itself to be a good, and to exist is therefore logically always better than not to exist. It is on this basis that evil is said to be parasitic on good, because it can have no existence of its own, since all existence is a gift of God, and evil to survive must therefore always use something good as a vehicle.

36 Job 41.

37 Sydney Carter, 'Every star shall sing a carol', *Songs of Sydney Carter in the Present Tense*, Book 3.

38 John 16:21–2.

39 John Bunyan, *The Pilgrim's Progress*, Part One.

40 Notably in the teaching of Peter Abelard.

41 The purpose of the so-called *lex talionis* ('an eye for an eye') in the Old Testament, which was designed not to authorise revenge but to control it: cf. Exod. 21:22–7.

42 Mal. 3:6.

43 Matt. 23:23.

44 Cf. the wonderful poem on the true nature of divine judgement, 'Well?', in G. A. Studdert-Kennedy, *The Unutterable Beauty* (London, Hodder & Stoughton, 1947), pp. 135–40.
45 Luke 15:21.
46 Luke 15:19.
47 The idea that at least some animals, especially the higher and companion animals, might have a share in a future life is not encouraged by Christian orthodoxy. But if the whole creation is to be redeemed from suffering and death (cf. Rom. 8:19–23) there should be a place for other creatures; and some of them will find it easier to forgive us in love than do some of our human friends.
48 The whole section on atonement is deeply indebted to a classic modern treatment: Elizabeth R. Moberly, *Suffering, Innocent and Guilty* (London, SPCK, 1978).

Chapter 5

1 Acts 2:44–7; Rom. 12:9–13:4; Eph. 4:17–5:10; Titus 3:1–3; 1 Pet. 2:15; 3:1–2, 16.
2 Col. 2:8.
3 Heb. 2:14–15.
4 Luke 12:4.
5 Rom. 6:1–11; Col. 3:1–4.
6 John 13:15, 34.
7 Cf. pp. 71f., 94f.
8 Matt. 5:45; Luke 6:35–6.
9 Dorothy Daldy, a friend of Michael Ramsey, was the founder of the Ecumenical Teaching Order. The ideas in this paragraph are taken from her unpublished work, *The People of the New Covenant*.
10 The phrase seems to have originated with the Jesuit theologian, Karl Rahner, than whom nobody could have been less arrogant in his attitude to other faiths.
11 Gen. 1:26–7. The variant account (2:18–24) of the creation of man and woman does not use the 'image' terminology, though several features in the story reflect similar ideas of humanity's Godlikeness. At her creation woman is man's equal in this story too. After the 'Fall' she is made subordinate to man as a punishment for her offence (3:16), but it could be argued that the essential equality remains.
12 Roman Catholic teaching holds that Christ is present not only in the eucharistic bread and wine but also, as the true celebrant at every Mass, in the person of the priest. For the reasons given in the text this would not of itself preclude a woman president,

but in modern times the doctrine has been supplemented by the theory that the president must therefore be an icon of Christ. However, the only qualification necessary for being such an icon seems to be that of male gender, and this new departure appears suspiciously like a defensive reaction against secular changes in the status of women.

13 Cf. pp. 146ff. for a fuller reflection on the special ministry of the ordained.

14 In British law until recently abortion was in theory permissible at a stage when the baby would, if born prematurely, have had at least a chance, with specialist care, of survival. In practice the great majority of abortions are carried out at a very early phase.

15 A bizarre example of doublethink came up in the House of Lords during the debate on the Warnock Report on the use of embryos for research. A bishop spoke, quite rightly, in favour of the rule banning experiments after the 14th day of the embryo's life, on the grounds that from then on, though not before, it was demonstrably a potential human being. But how could that position be reconciled with the stance of his Church (and mine) that it is permissible to abort a child, for legally recognised reasons, between the fifth and sixth month of pregnancy?

16 This is obviously one argument against capital punishment. But opposition also rests on other powerful considerations, most notably the proven risk of convicting the innocent.

17 Gen. 2:15.

18 Gen. 1:28.

19 'Vegan': or at any rate 'fruitarian' (!): Gen. 1:29. 'Tyranny': Gen. 9:1–3.

20 Isa. 11:1–9.

21 E.g. the ravaging of the rain forests, to meet the demands of the affluent nations, is paralleled by 'slash and burn' cultivation and deforestation for fuel, to supply the basic needs of the poorest of the poor. The denial of justice by the rich is exemplified by the global debt structure within which the poor pay the rich in interest more than they receive from the rich in aid.

22 Rev. 18:11–24, strikingly apposite today.

23 Matt. 5:7: cf. 9:13; 12:7; 18:21–35.

24 Cf., e.g., Jane Lawick-Goodall, *In the Shadow of Man* (London. Collins, 1971), and many other studies.

25 Job 38:29–39:18; 39:26–30; 40:15–41:34: cf. Ps. 104: 10–23.

26 Progress is made both nationally and internationally, e.g. by education, legislation, replacement of animals by *in vitro* experiments and the like, but it is painfully slow; and as soon as one small victory is gained, a whole range of new abuses spring up, e.g. the recent farming of ostrich in utterly inappropriate conditions to provide a new kind of meat for pampered western tastes.

27 Cf. p. 139.
28 Gal. 5:22–3.
29 The traditional so-called 'cardinal' virtues.
30 This, despite the efforts of James Boswell, William Countryman and others to find a different conclusion in Scripture, is the way most scholars correctly read the evidence.
31 In the UK today what used to be Christian principles of sexual conduct are often more notably upheld by members of other faiths.
32 There is disagreement over the percentage of homosexuals in the world population. Psychologically some people are hard to classify, and may at some stage change. Cultural factors suppress numbers in some societies, and heighten them in others. But the once popular figure of 10% is widely agreed to be too high. Those who are stable in their homosexuality and happier with themselves to be so are perhaps between 3.5% and 5.0% of humankind.
33 In Romans 1 St Paul seems to regard homosexual desire as a kind of moral plague sent by God to punish the Gentiles for the sin of idolatry.
34 It is sadly a well attested clinical fact that the lovemaking of gay men has often resulted in serious physical trauma and infection, quite apart from the scourge of AIDS.
35 Genetic, psychological, educational and cultural theories have all been put forward. It may well be that some or all of these factors can be involved in any particular case.
36 Matt. 7:16–18.
37 Matt. 5:37; Mark 10:2–12.
38 Matt. 5:38–41; Luke 6:27–31.
39 This was also prohibited because soldiers were required to pay homage to the emperor as to a god. On this whole subject cf. C. J. Cadoux, *The Early Christian Attitude to War* (New York, Seabury, 1982).
40 St Francis of Assisi, Tolstoy, Pope Benedict XV, Gandhi.
41 E.g. the Religious Society of Friends (Quakers) and the Hutterites.
42 Hence the impasse where generations of grievance and mutual injury have made love, humanly speaking, well nigh impossible, as in Northern Ireland. We have to face, however, the truth in the lapidary words of Franziskus Stratmann OP: 'Through the sword, things remain as they were' (*The Church and War*, London, Sheed & Ward, 1928, p. 91). Cf. also Jean Lasserre, *War and the Gospel* (London, James Clarke, 1962).
43 The argument for this position was one of the main themes of my own book, *The Foolishness of God* (London, Darton, Longman & Todd, 1970).
44 1 Pet. 2:25; 5:4.

45 John 10:1–6, 11–16.
46 Heb. 7:11–28; 9:6–14.
47 Heb. 10:5–10.
48 1 Pet. 2:5, 9; Rev. 1:6.
49 Luke 22:27.
50 Mark 10:45.
51 It is thus particularly unjust when Churches which have the threefold structure of the ordained ministry refuse to acknowledge the ministries of other Churches which combine the three roles in a single order.
52 Matt. 5:13; 13:33; Luke 13:21.
53 Quakers have no sacraments; the Salvation Army has evolved its own rite for admission to membership.
54 Cf. p. 109.
55 Cf. Acts 8:26–38; 16:31–3; but contrast Acts 9:17–18; 19:1–7.
56 St Paul seems to have taken an even more inclusive attitude, at least on one interpretation of 1 Cor. 7:12–14. It is clear also that Paul did not condemn the Corinthian practice by which Christians were baptised as proxies for deceased relatives and friends (1 Cor. 15:29), though scandalised commentators have tried hundreds of ways to prove that his words do not mean what they plainly do!
57 The probable sense of 'as often as you drink it'; but these words are found in Paul alone (1 Cor. 11:25).
58 Cf. Appendix B, pp. 203f.
59 One possible implication of the Emmaus story: Luke 24:28–35.
60 Philosophical explanations of how this could be come much later.
61 Ignatius of Antioch, *Ephesians*, 20:2. The sense is of an antidote against physical death: cf. already 1 Cor. 11:30.
62 It is noticeable that even in the rightly praised report of the Anglican–Roman Catholic International Commission on the Eucharist the difficulty for Anglicans posed by the statement that the bread and wine 'become' the body and blood of Christ could not really be resolved.
63 As shown, e.g., by the problems at Corinth (1 Cor. 11:20–2): cf. Appendix B, pp. 208ff.
64 A friend from Lichfield, John Salford, a layman, relates in a privately circulated autobiography how, during the invasion of Normandy in 1944, he once celebrated Holy Communion for himself and two comrades with army biscuit and cold tea at a time of intense danger. They cannot have been alone in such an action. Are we to say that these were not authentic Eucharists?
65 John 16:13.
66 A possible example is the phrase, 'The holy seed is its stump' in Isa. 6:13.

67 Luke 1:46–55: a hymn that is a standard element in many forms of Christian evening prayer.

68 John 4:22.

Chapter 6

1 Sometimes, sadly, what we ask is an indicator merely of our selfish desire to be spared trouble or delivered from anxiety.

2 Mark 9:28–9.

3 Matt. 6:2.

4 Cf. p. 47. The raising of Lazarus, if historical, would, for this reason, certainly be a true miracle; but for reservations cf. p. 53.

5 There is no reason at all why God should not from time to time make lighthearted interventions in the world as a kind of calling card, but the majority of trivial so-called miracles should be treated with some scepticism!

6 Athanasius says that the divine Word took human nature 'as an instrument of suffering'.

7 1 John 4:8, 16.

8 Perhaps we may think of the relation between divine and human suffering in this way: what was in the Father's heart when Jesus on the Cross uttered the human cry, 'Why have you abandoned me?'

9 The Son as the Father's agent in the cosmic work of creation is also the Crucified: cf. pp. 97f., 107.

10 Cf., e.g., the traditional Eastern Orthodox representation of the Trinity as the three heavenly visitants who came to Abraham (Gen. 18), well known through the many reproductions of the icon by Andrei Rublev.

11 Col. 1:19; 2:9.

12 One of the unresolved problems of trinitarian doctrine is to say how this can be true when, traditionally, the Father is the Source of the being of the other two Persons.

13 All accounts of the future life which take seriously the imperfection of humanity and God's loving desire for our perfecting find themselves forced to incorporate into their scheme something corresponding to Purgatory, however averse they may be to that on sectarian grounds. I myself have always found the idea of Purgatory not only essential but also one of the most encouraging parts of the theological synthesis.

14 From Alice Meynell, 'Christ in the Universe', in *The Faber Book of Religious Verse* (London, Faber, 1972), p. 292.

15 2 Cor. 5:1–5.

16 2 Cor. 3:18.

17 This lovely phrase, originated, I believe, with Charles Williams.
18 Rom. 8:19–23.
19 Cf. p. 141.
20 Cf. esp. the highly influential work by John Zizioulas, *Being as Communion* (London, Darton, Longman & Todd, 1985).
21 Cf. p. 136.
22 Cf. the 'Prayer to St Paul' in *The Prayers and Meditations of St Anselm*, translated by Sister Benedicta Ward SLG (London, Penguin, 1973); also Julian of Norwich, *The Revelations of Divine Love*, ed. James Walsh SJ (Wheathampstead, Anthony Clarke, 1973).
23 1 John 4:18.
24 1 Cor. 13:12.
25 1 John 3:2.
26 Cf., e.g., the Intercession in Eucharistic Rites A and B in the Church of England *Alternative Service Book 1980*.
27 Wisd. 11:24–6.
28 Heb. 11:16.
29 Anselm of Canterbury, *Proslogion*, chh. 25–6, ed. J. Hopkins and H. W. Richardson (London, SCM Press, 1974), p. 111–2.

Index